CRIME ECONOMICS

Presenting an original institutional approach, this book makes the case for an empirically based crime economics that aims to guide the fight against crime within a logic of reasonable capitalism and the common good.

Historically, it was not until a seminal article by Gary Becker that mainstream economists showed any interest in the criminal economy. The new field of crime economics was, in reality, little more than an extension of rational choice theory and cost-benefit analysis to a new subject. However, reducing crime to a single profit perspective has proven reductive: it ignores, for example, crime that affects public order (e.g., vandalism), and the individualistic approach does not seem to be very relevant when dealing with criminal organizations. Criminal phenomena therefore call for a renewal of the analysis. Inspired, in particular, by the work of Veblen and Commons, this book calls for a renewal of the analysis. It argues for an institutional focus on the integration of individuals into organizational and institutional contexts which provides a richer analysis of criminal choices and reintroduces collective and power-seeking motivations. The study of illegal markets uses an evolutionary approach to highlight their dynamic, cooperative, and interconnected dimensions. The question of criminal infiltration of the legal economy is assessed beyond the issue of money laundering to include territorial control strategies. Finally, a review of the liberal economic discourse and the values it embodies raises questions about the responsibility of the legal economy and its players in the expansion of the criminal economy, as well as the risk of a blurring of the boundary between legality and illegality.

This renewed global vision is useful both for those who study criminal issues (students and researchers in economics, criminology, law, sociology, and political science) and for practitioners.

Clotilde Champeyrache (economist and criminologist) is an associate professor at the Conservatoire National des Arts et Métiers, attached to the Security – Defense – Intelligence Department. She lectures on topics related to criminology, criminal economy, and crime control. Her research focuses on organized crime, with a particular interest in mafia-type organizations and criminal infiltration of the legal economy.

CRIME ECONOMICS

An Original Institutional Approach

Clotilde Champeyrache

LONDON AND NEW YORK

Designed cover image: EtiAmmos Getty Images

First published 2025
by Routledge
4 Park Square, Milton Park, Abingdon, Oxon OX14 4RN

and by Routledge
605 Third Avenue, New York, NY 10158

Routledge is an imprint of the Taylor & Francis Group, an informa business

British Library Cataloguing-in-Publication Data
A catalogue record for this book is available from the British Library

ISBN: 978-1-032-39699-6 (hbk)
ISBN: 978-1-032-39698-9 (pbk)
ISBN: 978-1-003-35095-8 (ebk)

DOI: 10.4324/9781003350958

Typeset in Times New Roman
by Apex CoVantage, LLC

To those who keep watch while we sleep.

CONTENTS

ABOUT THE AUTHOR

Clotilde Champeyrache (economist and criminologist) is an associate professor at the Conservatoire National des Arts et Métiers, attached to the Security – Defense – Intelligence Department. She lectures on topics related to criminology, criminal economy, and crime control.

Her research focuses on organized crime, with a particular interest in mafia-type organizations and criminal infiltration of the legal economy. She has published *Quand la mafia se légalise. Pour une approche économique institutionnaliste* (CNRS Editions, 2016), *La face cachée de l'économie. Néolibéralisme et criminalités* (Presses Universitaires de France, 2019), and *Géopolitique des mafias* (Le Cavalier bleu, 2022).

INTRODUCTION

When someone thinks of the criminal economy, the first thing he's likely to think of is drug trafficking and/or the mafia. However, this is only one aspect of the issue, though not an insignificant one. In reality, activities as varied as illicit trafficking (drug trafficking, human trafficking, migrant smuggling, etc.), financial crime (money laundering, financial fraud, corruption), cybercrime (ransomware, phishing, online scams), and even terrorism are involved. In addition, new illegal activities may emerge following the adoption of new legislation. The field of the illegal economy is therefore vast and evolving. The criminal economy also refers to what criminal organizations – of which mafias are just one form – do. In very practical terms, even if this often goes unnoticed, it means that the criminal economy is broader than the strictly illegal economy. Indeed, when criminals infiltrate the legal economy and own businesses that appear to be "in order", they are in effect bringing part of the legal economy within the scope of the criminal economy in its true and complete meaning: the activity may well be legal, but the motives of the business are determined by the criminals and, as such, pursue criminal objectives, which are not limited to money laundering alone. This initial delimitation of the field reveals a phenomenon that is by no means anecdotal, a criminal economy that is anything but marginal despite its inherently hidden nature and the resulting difficulties, particularly in quantifying it. What is more, economists of all stripes have not really taken up the subject, or have done so in a way that seems inappropriate because it does not allow us to understand the empirical reality. The main aim of this book is therefore to fill a gap by proposing a crime economics inspired by the original institutional approach.

DOI: 10.4324/9781003350958-1

A criminal economy far from marginal

The criminal economy is a reality that cannot be ignored, even if quantifying its extent requires to be cautious, since data on the subject is, by its very nature, patchy and subject to the vagaries of estimates. If we focus on the figures, however, some are circulating about illegal profits. In reality, there are very few of them; many are old but circulate in a loop, gradually becoming facts by repetition, even though they no longer reflect the reality of an ever-changing illegal world. These figures, all too often unsatisfactory, nevertheless have one thing in common: they are impressive. One of them is the one drawn up in 1998 by the IMF, afterward labeled a "consensus range": money laundering would represent 2–5% of global GDP. In 2011, a research report published by the UNODC on the estimation of "illicit financial flows resulting from drug trafficking and other transnational organized crimes"[1] explicitly refers to the IMF estimate and puts forward the following results:

> A study-of-studies, or meta-analysis, conducted for this report, suggests that all criminal proceeds are likely to have amounted to some 3.6 per cent of GDP (2.3–5.5 per cent) or around US$2.1 trillion in 2009. The resulting best estimate of the amounts available for money-laundering would be within the IMF's original "consensus range", equivalent to some 2.7 per cent of global GDP (2.1–4 per cent) or US$1.6 trillion in 2009. From this figure, money flows related to transnational organized crime activities represent the equivalent of some 1.5 per cent of global GDP, 70 per cent of which would have been available for laundering through the financial system.
>
> *(5)*

More recently, in 2017, the US think tank Global Financial Integrity announced that the global business of transnational crime was worth between $1.6 and $2.2 trillion a year.[2] In 2023, the Interpol website remains rather vague when it promotes its cooperation with the FATF to identify flows of illegal wealth worth USD trillions every year.[3]

While more recent and accurate figures do exist, they are often specific to a particular illegal activity and/or country. And it is naturally the narcotics market that gets most of the attention. In France, for example, the director of OFAST, the French anti-narcotics office, stated at a hearing before a Senate committee of inquiry into drug trafficking that it is the world's biggest criminal market, and that "in France, it represents an estimated turnover of three billion euros and [that] an estimated 240,000 people make their living directly or indirectly from this traffic".[4] Once again, these figures must be treated with extreme caution. They can be derived by cross-checking different types of data. In addition to illicit gains, the weight of the criminal economy can also be assessed in terms of the estimated number of consumers, the quantities of goods produced, and even losses (e.g., in human lives or damage to consumer health). For example, drug consumption is also estimated based on sewage analysis in some urban centers, traces of cocaine left on banknotes, and the number of syringes sold compared with the estimated consumption for legal use. In terms of production capacity, aerial images allow us to estimate some of the agricultural areas dedicated to raw materials (coca, poppy, and cannabis plantations) for plant-based drugs. Seizures also provide information. Seizures of narcotic substances have often been in the news in recent years, particularly in Europe, where records have been set. In 2023, for example, 116 tons of cocaine were seized in the Belgian port of Antwerp. However, as always, this figure says only what it is, that is, the identified share of the traffic. The seizure is the result of both an intensification of the fight against drugs (with the not insignificant impact of decrypting messages exchanged by criminals on the Sky ECC application), and an increase in trafficking. Seizure numbers do not say how much is actually circulating, although legal authorities tend to consider that for every ton intercepted, ten pass through. The only certainty is that these major seizures have not affected the market: cocaine remains available, at a stable or even falling price. The number of consumers has also increased, on a global scale. In its 2023 annual World Drug Report,[5] the UNODC estimates the number of people injecting drugs worldwide at 13.2 million. Worldwide, more than 296 million people (one in every 17 people) are estimated to have used drugs in 2021, representing a 23% increase over the previous decade. This also translates into an increase in the number of people affected by drug-induced disorders: 39.5 million individuals, representing a surge in cases (+45% in ten years). The number of narcotics available for consumption is also increasing, with the development of new synthetic products: over the last 15 years, the number of new psychoactive substances (NPS) identified has reached 1,165, and could reach 1,184 by 2022.

These – fragmentary – figures paint a worrying picture, both in absolute terms and in terms of dynamics, not only because both supply and demand are increasing but also because the anticipated trend is neither downward nor even stabilizing: the African continent is particularly targeted for cocaine, and NPS can be produced anywhere, with mainly Asian criminal networks ready to supply the chemical precursors needed to synthesize them. In its 2021 report, the UNODC forecasts growth in the narcotics market of 40% in Africa and 11% worldwide by 2030. The problem is therefore global.

Drug trafficking attracts a great deal of attention and is generally considered the world's largest illegal market. However, this should not obscure the fact that the illegal economy covers a very wide range of activities, some of them long-established, such as counterfeiting and arms trafficking, and others new, such as cybercrime (linked to technological developments) or waste trafficking (linked to the development of environmental law). Some activities reemerge sporadically (piracy for instance), and others change scale (counterfeiting has industrialized). It is hard to get an overall picture, which reflects both the difficulty of understanding activities that by their very nature are designed to remain hidden and also a lack of interest – beyond the sensationalism of the criminal cases that make the headlines from time to time – on the part of economists in particular, as I will come back to later. Yet here too, the trends are significant. A recent report by United Nations researchers focused on the issue of forced labor, highlighting its international spread and rapid development: criminal networks exploiting it could earn $236 billion a year, an increase of $64 billion in just one decade.[6] On its website, Interpol lists seven areas of crime that are set to increase sharply by 2022: drug trafficking, serious organized crime, cybercrime, child sexual abuse and exploitation on the Internet, financial fraud, human trafficking and migrant smuggling, and environmental crime. These headings are further broken down into various categories: for example, environmental crime includes waste trafficking, trafficking in species of fauna and flora protected by the Washington Convention, smuggling of natural resources (particularly timber, oil, and rare resources), and improper construction. Some types of trafficking receive less attention, but remain problematic: this is the case for art trafficking; arms trafficking is probably not receiving the attention it should either, at a time when armed and civil conflicts are multiplying. Disturbances to public order often receive little attention, even though their cost to society is increasing, and major criminal riots lead to material destruction as well as destruction in terms of economic and social development potential. Just think of the situation in Haiti or Ecuador. Less visibly, outlaw motorcycle gangs are also expanding.

Many different actors are at work. Some are local, and others have an international presence. Some are short-lived, responding more to a logic of economic opportunity than to a genuine desire to structure themselves for the long term, as is the case, in an extreme form, with mafia organizations characterized by transgenerational duration. These criminal organizations can be found all over the world, even if they obviously do not all have the same capabilities or radius of action. This is not an epiphenomenon, but a generality. A list – by no means exhaustive – of criminal organizations around the world illustrates this fact: Cosa nostra, camorra, 'ndrangheta, stidda, sacra corona unita, banda della Magliana, Casamonica family in Italy, mocro-mafia in the Netherlands and Belgium, Albanian-speaking clans, Balkan criminal networks, Turkish organized crime, vory v zakone (literally "thieves with a law") from former USSR countries, Israeli underworld, Nigerian cult groups, Hell's angels worldwide, prison gangs, Mexican drug cartels (Juarez, Sinaloa, Gulf cartels, los Zetas, etc.), Brazilian gangs such as the Primeiro Comando da Capital, the Terceiro Comando Puro, the Comando Vermelho, and many others, maras from Latin and Central America, street gangs under various names in North America, D-Company in India, Japanese yakuzas, and Chinese Triads are just a few examples of this criminal swarming. A 2024 Europol report counted no fewer than 821 criminal networks operating in Europe.[7]

In short, the criminal economy is varied in its activities and actors and is evolving to such an extent that organized crime is widely identified as a major threat. This is the case for Interpol and Europol (2024), which is not surprising given their remit. However, the same is true of the US intelligence community. In its February 2024

Annual Threat Assessment of the US Intelligence Community,[8] transnational criminal organizations feature prominently, with an emphasis on narcotics, money laundering and financial crimes, cybercrime, human trafficking, and, very interestingly, the ability to "undermine the rule of law". This last point reconnects the question of criminal economic activities with the political and social functioning of our countries. This is in line with the problems raised in Belgium and the Netherlands by drug trafficking: the rise of organized crime in these territories, linked to the low level of control over port activity, was confined to a commercial logic, where the flow of illegal goods was in a way reduced to an undesirable but unavoidable consequence of globalization. The financial power acquired by the drug traffickers, the rise in violence linked to settling accounts but also affecting innocent victims, and the threats made against members of the institutions underlined the threat posed by these criminal organizations to the functioning of democracy. This threat to the legal economy and politics is corroborated by Europol's finding that corruption and infiltration of the legal economy are prominent features of criminal organizations in Europe, with two-thirds of them regularly using bribery and over 80% of criminal networks using legal business structures (Europol, 2024).

All this information, among others, underlines a number of points:

- The illegal economy accounts for a significant share of the economy.
- The criminal economy does not live in a vacuum and includes a dimension of infiltration of the legal economy through corruption, money laundering, and the ownership of legal productive enterprises.
- The consequences of these economic activities in the hands of criminals go beyond the economy in the strict sense of the term, and impact on the economic, social, political, and democratic functioning of countries, while threatening their security.

Economists have invested surprisingly little in the subject

Despite these disturbing findings, economists remain largely silent on the subject. Crime remains an insufficiently explored field in economics, both in absolute terms and in relation to its importance in terms of markets and illegal profits. This silence is all the more surprising given that a number of disciplines (including sociology, political science, anthropology, and history) have taken up the subject, and that a discipline was even formed in the 19th century to deal with the theme of crime. Criminology[9] is essentially multidisciplinary as it aims to understand crime through the varied contributions of medicine, psychology, law, sociology, statistics, geopolitics, and so on. Economists could make a contribution but ultimately remain absent. This silence raises questions and deserves to be challenged. All the more so as it contributes to making the criminal dimension of the economy even more obscure than its illegal nature already makes it. Just look at the very term "criminal economy". On the face of it, anyone would think they could give content to the term. However, beyond the usual considerations of illegal markets, particularly the narcotics market, there is no guarantee that the descriptions overlap and/or are complete. The criminal economy – and its main, but not exclusive, actors, as I will come back to, criminal organizations – is a field that is far more often fantasized than analyzed. The result is an all-too-often truncated vision of the scope and dynamics of the subject, as well as an overemphasis – largely fed by the media – on certain aspects (first and foremost drug trafficking) to the detriment of other realities (such as infiltration into the legal economy) that are just as worrying, if not more so, for their medium- and long-term consequences. This lack of interest in the issue is also all too often reflected in university curricula. It is not uncommon for a student in economics to complete a full course (bachelor's and master's degrees) without the issue of the criminal economy ever being mentioned, even incidentally. Illegality seems to be relegated to the margins of economic thought. The dominance of liberal economic thought also tends to promote a pacified, irenic vision of the economic world, which is not necessarily conducive to understanding the illegal economy.

It would be unfair, however, to consider that economists' silence on crime is total. There is a branch of the discipline known as crime economics. It is a recent and marginal branch: recent, since its birth is traditionally associated with the publication in 1968 of an article by Gary Becker; marginal because, although Becker has had successors, few economists have devoted all or most of their work to the economics of crime, and most of the time it is the method – rational choice theory – that motivates this work, rather than a genuine interest in the specific theme of crime. A look back at the context in which traditional crime economics was born helps to understand the framework in which studies on criminal economic issues emerge, as well as the dissatisfaction it can arouse. In broad outline (the model will be presented in greater depth later), Becker's seminal article (1968) extends cost–benefit analysis and rational choice theory to a new field of application: crime. He proposed a model of rational criminal behavior, rejecting not only psychological or psychiatric explanations in terms of insanity but also sociological and cultural explanations in terms of deviance. From there, a theoretical literature based on mathematical modeling developed. In parallel, more empirical literature emerged to test certain hypotheses, notably through the use of econometrics. Embedded in a specific body of thought, however, traditional crime economics tends to remain locked in a Beckerian logic, never questioning the individualistic and strictly rational dimension of criminal behavior upon which it is grounded. Thus, the models are based on microeconomic reasoning based on the calculations of a reference individual supposed to be representative of *homo economicus*, that is, in essence, a profit maximizer under constraint.

From dissatisfaction to the prospect of an institutional renewal of crime economics

The Beckerian-inspired model may seduce by its mathematical rigor and also, let's face it, by the flattering character of a human being driven not by (inglorious) egoism, as in Smith (1776), but by rationality. It leaves the reader, motivated by a desire to understand the reality of the criminal economy, more dissatisfied. Explaining crime solely in terms of profit may indeed seem reductive to the observer in the field: it ignores, for example, crimes against public order (notably vandalism) as well as the non-profitable activities carried out by certain criminals with a view to building a social consensus (distribution of income, food aid, quasi "social benefits", etc.). What is more, methodological individualism (that famous reference individual whose behavior we study in order to extrapolate the behavior of all) does not seem very relevant when the major actors in the criminal economy are criminal organizations and not isolated or simply aggregated individuals.

In view of these initial sources of dissatisfaction, it seems to me that criminal phenomena – if they are to be understood in their reality and combated effectively – call not only for a greater effort in economic studies but even more so for a renewal of the analytical grids too often employed. This is the aim of this book: to propose a crime economics inspired by the original institutional approach. The aim is to break away from the Beckerian logic and the dominant economic vision that places the market at the heart of all thinking. The mobilization of the original institutional economists, in particular among its founders Thorstein Veblen and John R. Commons, aims at revitalizing crime economics, anchoring it in the study of criminal reality and not in the promotion of a scheme of analysis. The approach is not to apply an existing theory to a new field, but to study criminal organizations on the basis of observations made by those working in the field (law enforcement and specialized agencies, investigative units, members of criminal organizations, etc.). It is only by starting from empirical reality that it will be possible to offer a global vision of the criminal economy and to suggest ways of combating organized crime. The original institutional approach developed here is therefore also intended to be an operational crime economics. In this sense, the book is not just for economists. It is also aimed at anyone studying criminal issues (students and researchers in economics, criminology, law, sociology, political science, etc.), as well as practitioners (law enforcement agencies, judges and magistrates, intelligence units, customs officers, etc.).

This new approach is still largely exploratory. One of its aims is to mobilize methods and concepts specific to the original[10] institutionalism in order to broaden and strengthen our understanding of the criminal economy. In particular, the interest of original institutionalism lies in its emphasis on the collective dimension of human behavior, and on the norms and rules, including tacit ones, of groups of people. Original institutionalism – and Commons (1924) in particular – also places a fundamental emphasis on the connection between law and economics, which is relevant to the understanding of activities defined as forbidden by law. Reconnecting the individual to the group, and the economy to the legal framework, changes the way we look at the functioning and impact of criminal organizations: the criminal economy in all its variety is viewed not in a fragmentary way (the individual criminal and/or the illegal market), but in a systemic logic (with imbrications, evolutions, and interactions). This overcomes some limitations of traditional crime economics. In particular, alongside the objective of profit maximization, original institutionalism allows us to reintroduce the quest for power by criminal organizations. Likewise, original institutionalism reintroduces to the analysis parts of the criminal economy that are generally forgotten or even denied: the infiltration of the legal economy in ways that go beyond the mere laundering of dirty money, the modalities of territorial control and economic conditioning, and the role of a gray zone between legality and illegality in the expansion of crime. The criminal economy thus extends beyond the strict confines of illegal markets and does not operate in isolation from the legal economy. This has implications for the assessment of the dangerousness of criminal phenomena and therefore for the determination of objectives and means in the fight against organized crime.

The aim of this book is to provide answers to specific questions about the criminal economy. It also opens up avenues for further reflection, as an original institutional crime economics has yet to be fully developed. This also explains why authors who may have different positions on certain issues are included. The question of developing a purely Commonsian crime economics did indeed arise. In the end, we opted to maintain references to Veblen in order not to limit our thinking and in line with our desire to contribute to the development of a new field of analysis. In this respect, I consider, in connection with the arguments developed by Miller (1998), that what unites Veblen and Commons is more significant than what distinguishes them,[11] particularly with regard to what remains a crucial element for an operational crime economics: the conviction that individuals are architects of the societies in which they evolve. Nor does the book claim to embrace all criminal phenomena. A global vision of the criminal economy does not mean an exhaustive one. There are at least two main reasons for this. The first is technical: in essence, sources on crime can only be partial, and when they do exist, they are not necessarily (easily) accessible, not least because of the confidentiality of sources but also because some countries disclose more information than others. The second reason is the sheer breadth of the subject: the variety of activities and actors involved makes the subject extremely rich and complex to handle. This means that the researcher has to give priority to certain aspects of the field, to the detriment of others. Readers of this book will undoubtedly note a "bias" in favor of references to so-called mafia criminal organizations, particularly Italian ones. This is due as much to my specific field of expertise as to the ease of access to varied and dense sources on the subject. However, this should not be seen as a limitation on reflection. On the contrary, it is part of the process of participating in the future construction of an original institutional crime economics. My hope is that the reader will appropriate the proposed reading grid, open avenues for reflection, and develop them in line with the criminal reality he or she may observe.

Steps in the process

This book is divided into two parts. The first part, as its title "Traditional crime economics versus original institutionalism insights" indicates, is dedicated to the contribution of an approach inspired in particular by Veblen and Commons to crime economics as it is currently conceived. This theoretical section is complemented by a second more applicative section, dedicated to "original institutional economic variations around criminal realities".

In short, the first part sets out the theoretical issues involved in building a new framework for crime economics. Although it refers to debates and oppositions between schools of economic thought, it is intended to be accessible to a non-economist and is divided into three chapters aimed at establishing the interest and originality of a new approach to the economic study of crime. Logically, the starting point is an introduction to traditional crime economics, its birth, its main characteristics, and its shortcomings (Chapter 1). In response to the criticisms leveled at this dominant corpus, an alternative is presented for its ability to improve economists' understanding of crime. Emphasis is placed on the need to reconnect economics with law, in order to understand activities whose main characteristic is that they do not respect the law. Yet the notion of "legal-economic nexus" – in short, this profound interweaving of law and economics – is central to original institutionalism and reveals all its relevance in the exploration of crime (Chapter 2). More broadly, original institutionalism mobilizes concepts – such as collective action, going concerns, working rules, and power – that are particularly relevant to understanding crime (Chapter 3).

Armed with these tools, the second part mobilizes the concepts of original institutionalism to analyze different aspects of the criminal economy and to shed new light on criminal issues that are not theoretical but empirical. The aim is not to present a normative model of what the criminal economy and crime deterrence should be, but to understand the criminal economy as it is, so as to better confront it. The question of entry into the criminal sphere cannot be neglected, especially as it links the individual and collective dimensions, and allows us to relativize the share of rationality in the decision to break the law (Chapter 4). The most obvious dimension of the criminal economy, illegal markets, is also studied, revealing an evolutionary and cooperative logic far removed from traditional representations in terms of monopoly and violence (Chapter 5). Finally, two issues underline even more specifically the added value of an original institutional crime economics in revealing issues that are ignored yet crucial to the functioning of our societies. The first concerns the infiltration of legitimate businesses by criminal organizations: beyond the existing objectives of money laundering, it is the capacity to build criminal power via the legal economy that is exposed (Chapter 6). The final issue is a kind of zoom-out, widening the field of reflection and returning to the theoretical issues highlighted in the first part. The recurrence of a gray zone in the functioning of the illegal economy, the forms of tolerance or even complicity observed in the legal economy toward illegal activities, and the trivialization of offenses and corruption among agents not affiliated with criminal organizations highlight a process of blurring the boundary between the legal and the illegal (Chapter 7). The last three chapters, in keeping with the aim of building an operational crime economics useful to practitioners, each dedicate a final subsection to possible policy implications in the fight against organized crime.

Notes

1 BOOK_Illicit financial flows.indb (unodc.org).
2 Transnational Crime is a $1.6 trillion to $2.2 trillion Annual "Business", Finds New GFI Report – Global Financial Integrity (gfintegrity.org).
3 FATF-INTERPOL partnership: putting trillions in illicit profits back into legitimate economies.
4 Audition on November 27, 2023: https://videos.senat.fr/video.4185321_6564ec0c06951.narcotrafic – audition-de-stephanie-cherbonnier-cheffe-de-loffice-anti-stupefiants
5 World Drug Report 2023 (unodc.org)
6 March 19, 224: World News in Brief: $236 billion a year profit from forced labor, Senegal election update, peacekeepers in Lebanon | UN News.
7 www.europol.europa.eu/publication-events/main-reports/decoding-eus-most-threatening-criminal-networks
8 See p. 36–38: ATA-2024-Unclassified-Report.pdf (odni.gov).
9 The definition of which may be that proposed by Emile Durkheim: "We call crime any act that is punished, and we make crime thus defined the object of a special science, criminology" (Durkheim, 1895, p. 35).
10 The specifics of this approach will be presented in greater detail in Chapters 2 and 3.
11 Miller (1998) seeks to respond to those who may have considered that the difference between Veblen and his notion of instrumental value and Commons (and his theory of reasonable value) is strong enough to be considered antagonistic paradigms (see Ramstad, 1989). His conclusion is that "both [Veblen and Commons] are strong adherents of the concept of community when it comes to matters of primary relevance: that is, that individuals are social beings, that they are bound together by a sense of mutual obligation, that there is such an attribute as the public interest, and that policies should be pursued to achieve it. In light of these areas of agreement, it is difficult to accept the view that the ideas of Commons and Veblen are representative of competing paradigms" (Miller, 1998, p. 26).

References

Becker, Gary, "Crime and Punishment: An Economic Approach", *Journal of Political Economy*, 76(2), 1968, 169–217.
Commons, John R., *Legal Foundations of Capitalism*, New York: Macmillan, 1924.
Commons, John R., *Institutional Economics*, New York: MacMillan, 1934.
Durkheim, Emile, *Les règles de la méthode sociologique*, Paris: Félix Alcan, 1895.
Europol, *Decoding the EU's Most Threatening Criminal Networks*, Luxembourg: Publications Office of the European Union, 2024. www.europol.europa.eu/cms/sites/default/files/documents/Europol%20report%20on%20Decoding%20the%20EU-s%20most%20threatening%20criminal%20networks.pdf
Miller, Edythe S., "Veblen and Commons and the Concept of Community", in Warren J. Samuels (ed.), *The Founding of Institutional Economics. The Leisure Class and Sovereignty*, London and New York: Routledge, 1998, 14–29.
Ramstad, Yngve, "'Reasonable Value' Versus 'Instrumental Value': Competing Paradigms in Institutional Economics", *Journal of Economic Issues*, 23(3), 1989, 761–777.
Smith, Adam, *Investigations into the Nature and Causes of the Wealth of Nations*, Paris: Flammarion, 1776 (1991).

PART 1

Traditional crime economics versus original institutionalism insights

1

TRADITIONAL CRIME ECONOMICS

Birth and shortcomings

Economists, by and large, do not talk much about crime and only start to do so at a late time. If there is now a branch of analysis called crime economics – which we will call traditional crime economics – its birth certificate only dates back to 1968 with a founding article by Gary Becker. It must be said that economic theory, from its inception – and the phenomenon has become more pronounced with the domination of orthodox liberal thought – has tended to reason within a framework that presents a peaceful market world, one could even say a world that is pacified by competitive market mechanisms. This has left little room for reflection on deviance, offense, and crime. Despite this global indifference, some authors have taken this path, following in the footsteps of Cesare Beccaria (1764) and Jeremy Bentham (1811). Two economists, in particular, deserve attention for their initiating role and for the impact they will have on the further work carried out in crime economics.

The first is the aforementioned Gary Becker who will mathematically model the rational behavior of the criminal and the no less rational policy of fighting crime. His 1968 article will be at the origin of developments modeling the crime market. The second economist did not enjoy the same fame as Gary Becker, but his impact on the way economists generally think about crime is notable. Thomas Schelling wrote in 1967 and 1971 two articles on illegal markets and organized crime.

While these works have the merit of raising important issues about the links between crime and the economy, they also tend to confine economic thinking to a limiting framework. This restrictive framework will then be found in all the literature inspired by these early works. This leads to the traditional crime economics being an often biased whole which, when confronted with the observable criminal reality, suffers from a certain number of shortcomings. The aim, here, is not to present traditional crime economics in its entirety, but to highlight its limitations and

DOI: 10.4324/9781003350958-3

the impact it has on a biased view of crime (biased at least because it is incomplete, and sometimes even because it is wrong) of crime.

Economic theory, a peaceful world

If economists have said little about crime, it is probably simply because many of them, from the very origins of the discipline, have adopted a very peaceful and pacified vision of the world. In the 19th century, the Classics emphasized the positive aspects of the market and industrial economy: productivity gains through the division of labor, growth through international trade, and the enrichment of the nation as a result of the quest for individual profit are examples. This "optimistic bias" – contested by a Marxist theory that is now marginalized – was reinforced by the deployment of liberal thought at the end of the 19th century around the neoclassicals and by the preponderance of this thought today. The use of the concepts of market, scarcity, and economic free will of agents is linked to the description of a world pacified by economic transactions. This leads, moreover, to a process – not necessarily explicitly assumed by the various authors – of somehow erasing law in favor of economic criteria and values alone. This erasure, as I shall return to in Chapter 2, is not without effect on the problem of crime, which is obviously intrinsically linked to the issue of law. But before that, let us return to the construction of a pacified world around key concepts of economic theory.

The market itself is presented as a factor of harmony in human relationships insofar as it is thought to be a natural order and therefore unquestionable and uncontested. The classical economists – first and foremost Adam Smith – set themselves the goal of identifying economic laws based on the observation of the market and its functioning. From the outset, they considered these laws to be natural laws marked by universality: as such they are supposed to be valid at all times and in all places. The prevailing law, for example, is the law of supply and demand, which governs the meeting in a competitive market of the wills expressed by buyers and sellers. This meeting makes it possible to discover the market price – fluctuating around the equilibrium price – of the various goods. Reacting to this observable price, buyers and sellers will choose whether or not to, respectively, consume and produce. The personal characteristics of individuals are not taken into account. Human action has no influence on the determination of prices. It is indeed the competitive market that, by allowing the meeting of supply and demand, causes the price to emerge spontaneously. It is in this sense that the market imposes itself as a natural order and not as the largely political product of human decisions. It follows that the equilibrium reached by the market – in terms of the price set and the transactions actually carried out for that price – is also a natural equilibrium. This is so even if the end result in access to goods can be considered unequal, even unjust. To oppose the law of the market would therefore be equivalent to adopting a literally "unnatural" vision.[1] To say that economic laws are natural implies that one can only accept them and submit to them.

After the Classics, mainstream economics developed in the wake of economic science and mathematical modeling, which began at the end of the 19th century. Clearly liberal in inspiration, this current of thought reinforced the logic of the founding fathers of economics. If the market produces inequalities, they are natural and even just insofar as they only reflect a fair reward for the efforts of each individual. The market can be modeled in a normative and ideal (not to say idealized) form: that is to say, the advent of the model of pure and perfect competition. Totally and overtly disconnected from empirical reality, this ideal market serves to illustrate the superiority of the market economy over any other economic system in terms of optimal allocation of resources. On this market, a (natural) equilibrium is determined, allowing for a maximum number of transactions between buyers and sellers who are free to choose. Optimality derives from the satisfaction of a maximum number of participants in the exchanges, even if some are excluded from the transactions when the equilibrium price is too high for the buyer and too low for the seller. Here again, this presentation of the natural and spontaneous functioning of the market of pure and perfect competition feeds the irenicism of the dominant thinking in economics. It dismisses, without even considering it, the question of conflict, power, and violence. Moreover, it presupposes a freedom of economic agents which, in the absence of tangible content, is potentially illusory, and I will come back to this.

If the issue of conflict, power, and violence is dismissed, it is also largely through the manipulation of another concept: scarcity. Inherently a source of conflict through the question of resource appropriation, scarcity is paradoxically rather presented as a source of harmony through the institution of the market.

Already present in the Classics as one of the explanatory elements of value, scarcity acquires a major status in 20th-century economic thought. For Lionel Robbins, it is even at the core of the definition of the discipline. According to him, economics is none other than "the science which studies human behavior as a relationship between ends and scarce means which have alternative uses" (Robbins, 1935, p. 16). An economist is, then, someone who studies the optimal allocation of scarce resources. Yet, this study fits in well with the adoption by supporters of "economic science" of methodological individualism, that is to say, a method based on the analysis of a reference individual – sometimes referred to as *homo oeconomicus* – who is supposedly rational, calculating, and maximizing. Constrained by scarcity, the individual makes trade-offs and rational choices. This includes, as we shall see, the case of offenses.

But this vision, focusing on individual choices assessed through the rationality hypothesis, also contributes to orienting mainstream economic reasoning toward an exaggeratedly peaceful and pacified vision of the world. The postulate of scarcity should rather lead to a picture of the world as one of competition between individuals who want to monopolize resources; such competition can occur with peaceful methods but may naturally also include the use of violence, intimidation, manipulation, conditioning, and so on. On the contrary, mainstream economists choose to transform scarcity into a factor at the origin of harmonious human relationships. The market becomes the instrument of pacification of the economy, replacing the law of the strongest. The argument is based on the idea that the market makes it possible to impose a peaceful solution to the problems raised by exogenous scarcity. The market then presents itself as the central institution of our societies. It becomes so not only because it maximizes the number of transactions. It becomes so above all because it is pictured as creating harmony between divergent interests. Adam Smith's selfish individual interest is transformed into a shared interest in the name of rationality. Thus scarcity leads to the institution of the market, thanks to which it creates order by avoiding the use of violence. The whole system is guaranteed by the existence of property rights that are clearly defined, enforced, and enforceable in case of dispute. The meeting and matching of individual private interests is carried out in a non-conflictual manner as each agent exercises his free will in deciding to buy (or not) or sell (or not). No constraint other than the budgetary one for the consumer or the production costs for the producer weighs on economic agents. Reduced to a strictly market dimension, the economy is then limited to exchanges that take place only when they are perceived as mutually advantageous by rational market participants. Mainstream liberal thought thus succeeds in not associating scarcity with conflicts over the appropriation of resources and in making scarcity the source of a peace-producing institution. Obviously, this is done at the cost of a heavy silence on questions relating to violence, crime, and power in economics.

In reality, the behavioral assumptions associated with *homo oeconomicus* (rationality, calculative, and utility-maximizing capacities) lead mainstream liberal economists to enhance the idea that economic agents are free and equal. However, this is more of an illusion than a reality. Agents are ultimately rather inerrant and subject to the natural laws of the market, supposedly implementing a rationality whose foundations are not justified (is the maximization of profit/utility the only form of rationality? What about the internalization by the individual of this strictly economic imperative, excluding the social, political or other spheres?), and which is only a rationality of immediacy (the transaction here and now). Here again, the assumptions underlying mainstream reasoning naturally lead to the conclusion that the market is basically a peacemaker. The shift to methodological individualism has also made it possible to move away from previous reasoning in terms of social classes. But, precisely, reasoning in terms of social groups allowed us to take into account conflicts resulting from social groups with divergent (in the case of the Classics) or even contradictory (in the case of the Marxists) interests. Methodological individualism takes the problem of power and power asymmetry out of the field of economics. Yet this dimension is fundamental to understanding criminal phenomena, whether or not these power stakes are materialized by recourse to effective violence, as I shall return to.

If exchanges are mutually agreed upon in a competitive market, it is because the agents participating in the transactions are free and equal. They are free because they can choose at any time to produce or not, to sell or not, to consume or not. The choices made by other economic agents have no influence on the individual freedoms thus exercised: only the price observed on the market determines the decision. And this price cannot be manipulated by one or more agents precisely because they are equal as well as free. They are not equal in terms of their initial endowments (budgetary capacity, productive resources, etc.) but in relation to the mechanisms and laws of the market. This results from the assumption of market atomicity: the multiplicity of agents on both the supply and demand sides means that no agent is likely to exercise power over the market and influence the price level. Agents are therefore said to be not price makers but price takers. They cannot therefore manipulate markets through corruption or cartels; they cannot adopt methods such as deception (the assumption of homogeneity of the product on the market excludes this), blackmail, or threats. If market power arises – typically, in the literature, monopoly power – it is studied as a deviation from the reference model of pure and perfect competition. Here again, a theoretical process of pacification *via* the market is at work. The mathematical modeling of the reference model of the competitive market basically enshrines the thesis, already present among the philosophers of the Enlightenment, and taken up by Adam Smith (1776) in Books 2 and 5 of *The Wealth of Nations*, of "doux commerce" (Montesquieu). Trade – including international trade – is supposed to bring a surplus of wealth to all the participants; it is also supposed to regulate the behavior of the contracting parties by rewarding honesty and loyalty, which creates the trust that is necessary for the pursuit of trade. Trade is therefore virtuous and softens the mores.[2]

In short, classical thought, and then, in an even more marked way, the dominant liberal thought of today have built a theory that promotes the market economy, but they have done so by introducing a non-negligible bias of perception. No doubt in a largely unconscious way, the idealization of the market is supported by a totally irenic representation of economic relationships. The much-repeated image of the "invisible hand" of the market leads to the assertion that the harmony of interests systematically results from the free functioning of the market. It is not absurd to consider that this is a rather naive and illusory vision of the economic world. Above all, this framework of thought leaves little, if any, room for taking into account the potentially criminal dimension of trade and the economy. Recognizing that economics textbooks basically describe a pacified world may contribute to understanding the lack of interest in crime shown by economists.

The beginnings of economic thinking on crime

Despite this irenic theoretical framework, which is not very conducive to thinking about crime, Gary Becker provided an economic analysis of criminal behavior in 1968. However, the model he proposed – if it may seem innovative, especially compared with the works on crime proposed by other disciplines such as sociology, anthropology, and criminology – is largely based on reflections initiated in the 18th century.

In particular, Cesare Beccaria and Jeremy Bentham – with Montesquieu in the background – appear as the precursors of economic thinking on crime. The first is an Italian nobleman, jurist, and philosopher, author in 1764 of *Des délits et des peines*, a work representative of the philosophical ideas of the Enlightenment, but applied to criminal policy. The second is a British philosopher who is interested in issues linked to legislation, crimes, and punishment and who develops a doctrine that he qualifies as "utilitarian" from 1781. According to this doctrine, individuals make hedonistic calculations based on the pleasures and pains they can derive from each action. They will then practice activities for which the pleasures exceed the pains. This principle, which is applicable to all human activities, is also applicable, according to him, to offenses and to the understanding of the effectiveness of sanctions. The two authors had in common their concern for the errors of criminal justice in their time, as well as for the infringement of liberties resulting from an absolutist exercise of royal power. Inspired by the dynamic context of the Enlightenment – marked by increasing urbanization, the beginnings of industrialization in Europe and then in the rest of the world, and by the increase in life expectancy – they wished to free themselves from the ways of thinking of the old world. This justifies their recourse to the notion of utility as a gauge to define an act. At the same time, they rejected as obsolete the qualifiers – prevailing in the Middle Ages – of "good" and "just". Montesquieu, the French philosopher of the Enlightenment, elaborated on the principle of the separation of powers, the foundation of our democracies, and questioned the legislative system in *De l'esprit des lois* (1748).

However, if the 18th and 19th centuries are characterized by positive elements such as economic development and growth, criminality shows no sign of abating. The economic and social changes of the period are reflected in the evolution of crime, with a decrease in homicidal violence but also an increase in property crimes (increase in thefts). In addition, and this partly explains the previous point, urbanization leads to a decrease in social control, which encourages crime in a context where the police and the justice system remain generally ineffective (in the sense that few culprits are apprehended and convicted). The need for security expressed by the population raises questions as to the improvement of the efficiency of the repressive and legal system as well as the possibility of making sanctions dissuasive. This calls into question the medieval principle of the exemplary nature of punishment: punishment, because it was infrequent, had to be conspicuous (mainly public execution with a search for stigmatization) and even excessive. The excessive nature of the punishment compensated for the inadequacy of its application. Utilitarian thinking was to replace the logic of exemplarity with that of efficiency: the aim was to strike less severely but more systematically. In this, they simply took up the thesis of Montesquieu (1748) according to which a moderate but certain punishment is more effective than a terrible punishment in a global context of impunity.

Furthermore, both Beccaria and Bentham go back over the usefulness of proscribing certain acts. This is in line with the desire to stop reasoning in moral terms of "good" and "just", a position that will be found again in Gary Becker. Thus, according to Beccaria, the measure of crime and its gravity is strictly a function of the "harm done to the nation" (p. 17). For Bentham, the penal system should only punish acts that produce "disutility". He therefore militates for the right to divorce, the decriminalization of homosexuality, and the suppression of slavery. Only acts that produce more pain than pleasure for society should be prohibited by law. In terms of punishment, he advocates the abolition of death penalty. In general, punishment is also thought of in utilitarian terms. In order to be dissuasive, it must make the offender fear a punishment at least equal to the pleasure caused by the illegal act. In this sense, the minimal punishment cancels out the pleasure derived from breaking the law; eventually, it creates a disutility to the offender.

What Cesare Beccaria and even more Jeremy Bentham manage to elaborate on is a real theory of deterrence against the possible perpetrator of an offense after having redefined the field of what it was useful to punish. The aim is to interfere as little as possible with individual liberties, hence the plea already mentioned in favor of abandoning some incriminations. Bentham considers that legislating must be an activity kept at the lowest possible level because "every law is an evil, for every law is an infraction of liberty" (1764, p. 24). He considers that criminal sanctions must have an incentive – and not merely a repressive – value to lead citizens to choose to respect the law. This leads him to favor moderate rather than severe penalties as long as the functioning of the police and the justice system allows for a sufficiently high level of certainty in the application of thc penalty for the guilty. What is interesting – though it will be lost in Gary Becker – is that, as Montesquieu had done before, Jeremy Bentham does not consider criminal punishment as the only way to punish – and thus deter – crime. Montesquieu is the first to indicate that "love of one's country" and "shame or fear of blame" are factors pushing to law-abiding behaviors. Jeremy Bentham also looks at the non-criminal sanctions associated with wrongdoing. He also identifies what he referred to as "natural sanctions" (e.g., pathologies affecting the alcoholic), "popular sanctions" (in the form of the blame that the family or relatives may address to the offender), and "religious sanctions" (the belief in the existence of hell for sinners). The legislator must also integrate these elements in the elaboration of dissuasive sentences. Moreover, the penal sanction, again for strictly utilitarian reasons, must be proportional to the seriousness of the crime, a seriousness itself defined by its level of disutility. The aim of this scale of penalties is to make the offender choose the offenses that are the least harmful to society, as these are the ones that will also bring him relatively the least displeasure.

Utilitarianism and the trade-off between punishment and pleasure were already present in 19th-century thought; they were even present in connection with the question of law enforcement. They will be the basis – even if some elements will be truncated, such as the one concerning non-strictly penal sanctions – of the 1968 article by Gary Becker. But only Jeremy Bentham is mentioned in the bibliography.

Becker's seminal article and the birth of crime economics

Gary Becker's 1968 article entitled "Crime and punishment: an economic approach" is considered the founding article for crime economics. However, its conception and its place in the work of its author paradoxically illustrate the still marginal dimension of the crime issue for economists. Indeed, far from being the result of an enduring concern with the criminal economy, the Beckerian model of criminal behavior is both the product of chance and a mere illustration of a general method of analysis.

In his speech for the Nobel Prize in Economics awarded in 1992, Gary Becker explains the anecdote that led him to discuss crime. Here it is:

> I began to think about crime in the 1960s after driving to Columbia University for an oral examination of a student in economic theory. I was late and had to decide quickly whether to put the car in a parking lot or risk getting a ticket for parking illegally on the street. I calculated the likelihood of getting a ticket, the size of the penalty, and the cost of putting the car in a lot. I decided it paid to take the risk and park on the street. (I did not get a ticket.)
>
> *(Becker, 1992, p. 41)*

The basis of the cost–benefit calculation applied to the law-abiding versus law-breaking trade-off is in place. Becker also narrates in this speech what forms the basis of his crime deterrence policy:

> As I walked the few blocks to the examination room, it occurred to me that the city authorities had probably gone through a similar analysis. The frequency of their inspection of parked vehicles and the size of the penalty imposed on violators should depend on their estimates of the type of calculations potential violators like me would make. Of course, the first question I put to the hapless student was to work out the optimal behavior of both the offenders and the police, something I had not yet done.
>
> *(Becker, 1992, p. 41)*

Even if the article is born *a priori* from a personal experience, Gary Becker writes in the context characterizing the United States in the late 60s. After the 1930s and the end of Prohibition, the 1950s and 1960s were not quiet decades in the United States. In 1950, the US Senate established a Special Committee on Organized Crime in Interstate Commerce under the leadership of Senator Estes Kefauver. The focus was on criminal organizations operating in major American cities. Organized crime is extensively analyzed in the light of the American Cosa nostra. This was reinforced when the Special Committee, renewed in 1951, visited New York City. Later, the obsession with a specific form of criminal organization, mainly foreign in origin, was reinforced by Joe Valachi's collaboration with the justice system. When questioned by the Senate McClellan Committee of Inquiry, Joe Valachi gave extensive details about the internal composition of the criminal organization to which he belonged and about the illegal activities carried out. Gary Becker, however, does not refer to these events. Instead, he mentions in his bibliography the President's Commission on Law Enforcement and the Administration of Justice. This Commission, which was in operation in 1967, did not take the same approach. President Johnson's objective was to wage "a war on crime" by relying on massive data collection and by studying more specifically the response of the repressive, judicial, and penitentiary systems. The focus is no longer on organized crime in the strict sense, but rather on delinquency and micro-crime. This prism (the system's response and isolated criminality) can be found in Becker's treatment of the criminal question.

Moreover, Becker's treatment of crime reveals other forms of bias in his perception of criminal events. I will not dwell on the form that his initial anecdote at the origin of the article takes: unauthorized parking remains an offense of little consequence, including in terms of costs and benefits. What is more problematic and reflects – I will come back to this in Chapter 2 – a major misunderstanding of the nature and place of law in a society, is the way Gary Becker addresses the question of one of the most frequent offenses: theft. Abandoning any questioning of the *ratio* of the law, Gary Becker chooses to turn any law-breaking activity into an activity like any other, involving costs and benefits. In this, he does not differ from some of his colleagues who remove the moral stakes or the question of values in order to bring some activities within the scope of economic rationality: Coase (1960) thus transformed the problem of pollution into a simple question of negative externality devoid of any reference to a victim (the polluted) and a culprit (the polluter). This theoretical stall allows Gary Becker to make no real difference between the buyer and the thief of a vehicle. Thus, he writes that "punishment in any economic system based on voluntary market transactions inevitably must distinguish between such 'debtors' [offenders] and others". But he adds:

> If a rich man purchases a car and a poor man steals one, the former is congratulated, while the latter is often sent to prison when apprehended. Yet the rich man's purchase is equivalent to a "theft" subsequently compensated by a "fine" equal to the price of the car, while the poor man, in effect, goes to prison because he cannot pay this "fine".
>
> *(Becker, 1968, p. 31)*

The excerpt remains in the field of morality insofar as Gary Becker specifies that the buyer is rich and the thief is poor (which may in fact constitute a negation of white-collar crime by associating crime and poverty). Again, the 1992 speech is enlightening on the relationship to institutions, as Gary Becker re-expresses his neutrality toward theft:

> In the early stages of my work on crime, I was puzzled by why theft is socially harmful since it appears merely to redistribute resources, usually from wealthier to poorer individuals. I resolved the puzzle (Becker [1968, fn. 3] by recognizing that criminals spend on weapons and on the value of the time in planning and carrying out their crimes, and that such spending is socially unproductive – it is what is now called "rent-seeking" – because it does not create wealth, only forcibly redistributes it. The social cost of theft was approximated by the number of dollars stolen since rational criminals would be willing to spend up to that amount on their crimes. (I should have added the resources spent by potential victims protecting themselves against crime.)
>
> *(Becker, 1992, p. 42)*

According to these lines, theft is a problem for society only because it involves unproductive protection expenses on the part of the owners and of the offenders (alarms, shielding, fencing, safes, tools, weapons, etc.).

Gary Becker builds a model of criminal behavior based on the tools offered by the theory of rational choice. Thus, there is no elaboration of a model based on in-depth empirical studies, but rather an extension of an existing model to a new application. Crime is not a meaningful subject in itself; it serves to illustrate the ability of mainstream economics to model all human behavior in the social field. The contribution of other disciplines, especially those that have been dealing with crime for decades already, is dismissed:

> a useful theory of criminal behavior can dispense with special theories of anomie, psychological inadequacies, or inheritance of special traits and simply extend the economist's usual analysis of choice.
>
> *(Becker, 1968, p. 2)*

The model is based on methodological individualism: an individual, assumed to be rational, calculating, and maximizing, serves as a reference for understanding the behavior of all agents. This individual makes choices, independently of any interaction with society and other individuals, according to his preferences and in order to maximize his utility. These choices can be summarized as rational arbitrations between one option and its opposite in the do/not-do mode. This binarity of choices can be developed *ad infinitum*: not only to consume/not to consume, to work/not to work, to save/not to save, but also, as Gary Becker explains, to marry/not to marry or, for our purposes here, to respect the law/to break the law. In the latter case, the individual must estimate the costs and benefits of the two paths open to him. If the utility of not respecting the law is greater than the utility of respecting the law, then it is rational to opt for law infringement. This allows Gary Becker to say that "some persons become 'criminals', . . . not because their basic motivation differs from that of other persons, but because their benefits and costs differ" (Becker, 1968, p. 9). Anyone is potentially – and rationally – a criminal.

It should be pointed out that the gain from committing an offense is subject to uncertainty: unlike the utility associated with the legal option, the utility associated with the illegal option can only be an expected utility. It is a function of two elements that may fluctuate:

- The cost of the penalty in case of incrimination
- The subjective probability of being caught and convicted: this probability is estimated by the individual as a function of his/her risk aversion (i.e., his/her greater or lesser fear of being punished) and therefore varies from one person to another.

It is on these two elements that a crime deterrence policy can be elaborated. But before coming to that, it is important to note that the configuration thus presented is one of a doubly isolated criminal behavior: the individual acts alone (the "crime" has no collective dimension) and without influence (this refers to the image of Robinson Crusoe often used by critics of methodological individualism: the formation of the agents' preferences is not considered to be the result of social interactions between the said individuals). These preferences are not studied as such: the Beckerian model is not interested in the ultimate causes of crime; it focuses on the elements that determine the costs and gains associated with illegal activities. The choice of the rational individual is also a trade-off that takes place in a time and place without any contextual depth, just like the transactions featured in the ideal market of pure and perfect competition. This raises a problem whenever understanding the organized dimension of both the activity and the criminal association is at stake.

In the end, Gary Becker's article dwells relatively little on the modeling of criminal behavior. What interests him most is developing a theory of crime deterrence, a deterrence that is evaluated in terms of economic optimality and not in terms of adherence to the social pact. In this sense, too, Gary Becker stands out from other disciplines. The latter have focused on punishment and rehabilitation. Gary Becker's objective is to reduce the incidence of crime, as crime costs society more than it brings in. It should be remembered that theft is considered merely as a displacement of property without loss of wealth and that it is a problem only inasmuch as it leads to unproductive protection expenses. The idea is then to play on the cost–benefit calculation of individuals to make the law-breaking option relatively less attractive than the law-abiding option. To do this, two instruments are available, which may be combined:

- One is to increase the severity of the sanction (e.g., by increasing the fine to be paid or by lengthening the duration of the prison sentence incurred).

- The other is to try to increase the probability of being caught and convicted (e.g., by increasing police patrols).

In both cases, the expected utility of law-infringement decreases, making compliance relatively more valuable, to the extent that for some individuals the calculus reverts in favor of the second option.

However, the costs incurred by the enforcement of a deterrence policy must also be taken into account. The debate around the Johnson Commission clearly influenced thinking at the time: the penal response had to be made more effective. This leads Gary Becker and his successors to evaluate the optimal level of response to the criminal issue and to favor the instrument of fines over other types of sanctions.

Increasing police patrols to raise the likelihood of being caught and thus to deter potential criminals comes at a cost to society: it is necessary to pay salaries to the police and possibly to provide them with vehicles and other security equipment; in addition, an increased number of arrests also leads to more recourse to the courts and thus to a further increase in costs. It is therefore essential to ensure that these costs do not outweigh the gains obtained from a reduction in crime. Optimality in crime control policy is about reaching the point where gains and costs balance. This requires an accurate estimate of all such gains and costs. Moreover, it means that crime control is not a total commitment, nor is it determined by the level of crime observed at a given moment, or even by a specific objective such as a level of crime that would be considered socially tolerable. The determination of the optimal level of means to be engaged in the fight against crime is made in strictly monetary and economic terms, knowing that – in this framework – the economy has abstracted itself from any moral framework or even disembedded itself from the law (see Chapter 2). One may then wonder whether this does not explain part of the logic behind the implementation of the fight against drugs and its overall failure: by targeting small-scale dealers, one targets criminal actors who allow a ratio that focuses on the means employed (e.g., law enforcement forces deployed and therefore paid) and the results obtained (number of arrests), even though trafficking itself has not been interrupted in any real way, as operators on the wholesale markets are not affected and continue to supply new, easily recruited dealers. In other words, retail transactions are momentarily impeded while stocks continue to flow. There is then a gap between the weak forms of crime (local dealers) and the criminal organizations *stricto sensu* (international wholesale producers). The question of the optimal level of deterrence already seems to be unable to grasp the associative dimension taken on by many criminal activities. This underlines the necessity to focus not on individuals but rather on groups.

Still, in a logic of economic efficiency and cost–benefit calculation, Gary Becker also argues in favor of the widest possible use of fines among the range of possible sanctions. His argument is that fines, unlike prison sentences, do not generate costs for society: they are simply a "transfer payment", whereas prison requires infrastructure, paid staff, and a loss of resources due to the prisoner's forced inactivity.

Fines are adorned with all the virtues: "Fines provide compensation to victims, and optimal fines at the margin fully compensate victims and restore the status quo ante so that they are no worse off than if offenses were not committed" (Becker, 1968, pp. 28–29). However, to result in an optimal fine, the calculation at the margin must be done on a case-by-case basis.

Crime, a market like any other

Gary Becker's idea of integrating crime into the theory of rational choice subsequently gained ground. However, this did not lead to a major line of thought: crime economics remains to this day a little-explored branch of economic theory. However, various works have been derived from Becker's initial model of rational criminal behavior. This is not the place nor the scope to present them exhaustively. Rather, the aim is to highlight the general common features of these works in order to stress their shortcomings and failings in relation to what would be an original institutional approach.

According to Levitt and Miles (2006), the economic analysis of crime in the tradition of Becker (1968) is characterized by four salient features that distinguish it from work in other social sciences, namely:

- An approach that focuses on the role of incentives in guiding the behavior of individuals,
- The frequent use of econometric models,[3]
- Emphasis on public policy implications,
- The use of cost–benefit analysis to evaluate these policies.

The study of criminal behavior in itself is therefore not fundamental except in terms of an adaptive response to anti-crime policy; the latter is judged purely in terms of cost–benefit. There is no consideration of, for example, the social norms of the environment in which the potential criminal operates. The focus on the question of incentives and on preferences – whose construction process is totally left aside – makes it possible to integrate the criminal question into the more general framework of market and equilibrium theory. Ehrlich thus appears as the main successor of Becker in the construction of a true "market, or equilibrium, model of crime".

Initially, Ehrlich's work, from 1973 onward, dealt with crime from the point of view of the labor market and the allocation of time. In the rational arbitrage of the individual, Ehrlich (1973) gives particular importance to the alternatives to crime and, more particularly, to the opportunities offered by a job in the legal sphere. It is the first occupational choice model dedicated to crime. Individuals are faced with the possibility of allocating their available time between legal and illegal activities according to the expected costs and benefits of each option. We can then consider several configurations with not only some individuals opting entirely for one or the other sphere but also others opting for mixes of legal and illegal activities. The legal sphere then plays a role in deterring crime: the level of wages paid, the availability of legal jobs, and economic growth are elements of rational choice.

Subsequently, Ehrlich builds a market model of crime based on the standard market model with, this time, a supply and a demand for crime. The supply of crime can be considered already dealt with by the Beckerian model of criminal behavior. The "demand for crime" remains to be modeled. Then, in order to remain in the logic of a crime deterrence policy, it has to be linked to the law enforcement system. The overall project aims to address the interactions between criminals (who generate the supply of crime) and potential consumers and victims (who express themselves through the demand for crime), as well as the impact of State intervention. To this end, Ehrlich (in particular 1981 and 1996) models a virtual crime market. This market, like any other market in the theory, allows us to determine an equilibrium quantity of crime corresponding to the optimality of the market. From this "natural" level of crime, in a mainstream economic logic, one can also determine the optimal level of resources that a society should devote to crime control. Once again, this optimal amount is determined by economic efficiency criteria in resource allocation and not by legal, social, moral, or ethical considerations. In addition to the volume of crime and the optimal level of protection, the equilibrium on the crime market is also used to establish the net return per offense.

The difficulty in developing this type of model arises from the identification of the demand for crime whenever one wishes to aggregate different kinds of offenses on a global crime market. The question is simple if we consider illegal activities consisting in supplying prohibited goods or services: there is indeed an identified demand on the part of consumers. At the forefront of these activities is drug trafficking, which can be modeled as a market in which transactions in a particular drug take place. However, the question is more complex when one turns to predatory activities (e.g., theft or fraud) or activities that undermine public order (such as vandalism, murder, etc.). Ehrlich circumvents the difficulty by deriving the demand for crime from the demand for safety expressed by individuals. This demand for security is expressed negatively by valuing the resources diverted from their productive use in order to protect property and to try to avoid the losses associated with committed offenses. It includes, for instance, the sums spent on the purchase of alarms, door armor, fences, safes, defensive weapons, and so on. The demand for security therefore corresponds to a negative demand for crime.

This modeling of a crime market encounters the same limitations as those identifiable for more traditional markets. While Ehrlich shows that the demand for crime is not evaluated in the same way according to the nature of the crime (productive or predatory, destructive), the generalization of the model abolishes this distinction: "for simplicity we . . . assume that offenses are of a uniform type (there is a single virtual market), and that all agents are risk-neutral" (Ehrlich, 2010, p. 5). In order to obtain general results, it is necessary to assume a homogeneity of the "crime" product, which obviously does not correspond to empirical reality and therefore does not allow the response to crime to be adapted to the different illegalities observable. Moreover, the demand for protection does not allow us to distinguish between what is private (self-protection) and what is the responsibility of the State (police and justice system). Finally, as Ehrlich (2010) himself acknowledges, the model presented is a partial equilibrium in which "the criminal sector of the economy has been analyzed separately from the general economy" (p. 19). However, the interactions between the illegal and legal spheres are numerous and indispensable to the understanding of the criminal issue. In this sense, this crime market model is unsatisfactory.

What about organized crime? Schelling's contribution

The market model of crime assumes a standardization of illegal activities. One might add that it also assumes – as does any mainstream market model – a standardization of actors: the supposed atomicity of agents in the model allows to set aside the problem of the nature of the actors involved. However, an illegal activity can be carried out by an isolated individual or by a group of individuals. The law differentiates between these two modalities: it considers the possibility of incriminating criminal conspiracy and/or of adding the aggravating circumstance of commission in an organized gang. The reasoning based on methodological individualism erases this legal distinction because it cannot fully integrate the collective dimension of human actions.

However, some (rare) economists will try to deal more specifically with organized crime while remaining constrained by the dominant way of thinking. Once again, the intention here is not to be exhaustive, but to identify key contributions and authors that shaped mainstream crime economics. One name stands out because it embodies this focus on organized crime and because it has a notable impact on the way most economists consider crime even nowadays. Thomas Schelling's first article on the subject in fact even precedes Becker's. Failing to address the issue of criminal organization directly, Schelling bypasses the problem by focusing on illegal markets. Schelling thus uses the concepts of mainstream industrial economics to try to spot the specificities of illegal markets. His thinking is based on two main notions: the constitution of monopolies and the use of violence. Thereafter, the association between illegal markets and the duo of monopoly plus violence will regularly become the rule in the minds of most economists. This association will even go beyond the field of economic reflection and will be considered always valid, especially in the media sphere. The empirical reality, as I shall return to, imposes a relativization of these characteristics. To be honest, it should be noted that the work of Schelling (1967, 1971) is more nuanced in its formulation than what has generally been retained.

Schelling (1967) broadly anticipates Becker (1968) in the goals he sets to his research: "identifying the incentives and disincentives to organize crime", "evaluating costs and losses due to criminal entrepreneurs", and "restructuring laws and programs to minimize the costs, wastes, and injustices that crime entails" (Schelling, 1967, p. 62). While he explains that not all illegal activities are necessarily associated with some form of monopolistic market, Schelling (1967, pp. 65–66) outlines four major reasons for monopoly to form in the underworld:

- "High overhead costs or some other element of technology that makes small-scale operation more costly than large-scale";
- "Prospect of monopolistic prices", an element that he connects to the intimidation capacity of organized crime;
- Obtaining a monopoly reduces certain costs, such as those associated with violence ("a large organization can afford to impose discipline, holding down violence if the business is crime") or those induced by the corruption of law enforcement agencies;
- The attraction of not only being able to dominate a market but also to exercise a dominant position in the underworld and thus contribute to its governance.

Schelling points out that the degree of monopolization of illegal markets is also a function of the institutional response. He notes that prohibition without real enforcement leads to competitive black markets, whereas prohibition guaranteed by real enforcement will result in an organized monopoly. He also associates benefits with the monopolization of illegal markets: according to him, the monopoly, in order to defend its goodwill, will tend to offer better quality services. This being the case, if the consumer of illegal goods and services can derive satisfaction from it, the monopoly in the hands of organized crime remains globally problematic. The source of this monopoly is to be found in the legislation: by prohibiting certain goods/activities, the State creates simultaneously though involuntarily black markets sheltered from competition from law-abiding people and thus favors those with skills in law-breaking. Prohibition also encourages corruption, which in turn helps to build and protect the monopoly situation. Finally, the monopoly generated by prohibition makes the criminal organization ever more powerful thanks to the profits it generates. To legislate, to prohibit is therefore to favor the development of a criminality that is ever more centralized, organized, and capable of corrupting on a large scale. Schelling thus advocates legalization while making a distinction (not always easy to grasp) between black markets created by prohibition and what he calls "an inherently criminal activity" (1967, p. 62). It is in his 1971 article that Schelling more directly associates organized crime and monopoly by specifying: "from all accounts, organized crime does not merely extend itself broadly, but brooks no competition. It seeks not merely influence, but exclusive influence . . . . Organized crime is usually monopolized crime" (1971, p. 645). But the discourse appears a bit tautological as it also explains that many black markets – such as those related to currency and gold trafficking, arms, and tobacco smuggling – are immune to organized crime. Finally, the idea emerges that one enters into organized crime when there is a monopoly and that, conversely, the fragmentation of the market is the responsibility of petty crime or disorganized crime (Schelling gives the specific example of gangs of burglars).

In parallel, Schelling links the issue of organized crime to the use of violence through two channels. The first is related to the constitution of the criminal monopoly, which is achieved using criminal means to destroy competition, namely, violence and intimidation. The second channel is specifically linked to the practice of extortion, which he defines as "living off somebody else's business by the threat of violence or of criminal competition" (Schelling, 1967, p. 63). He then joins the reflection carried out by Demsetz (1967) who considers that illegal markets are fundamentally markets with a criminal authority and that this authority cannot be based on the legitimacy of the law and of institutions, so it relies on violence or on the credible threat of recourse to violence in the event of non-compliance. Violence, then, seems likely to become a major indicator of criminal presence in an economy.

Mainstream crime economics or the reasoning bias

Mainstream crime economics derived from the work mainly of Becker, Ehrlich, and, more marginally, Schelling, suffers from a number of limitations that stem both from the methodological choices on which they are based and from notable discrepancies with the empirical reality of the criminal economy (that is to say, the criminal economy as it is and not as it should be according to the model).

What law enforcement agencies point to in their experience with crime on the field regularly contradicts the findings that mainstream economists associate with criminal economies. For example, the association between illegal markets and monopoly structures does not hold, including for drug-related markets. Even the practice of racketeering challenges economic rational thinking. Certainly, the strong territorialization of this predatory activity implies that one single criminal organization does unduly levy a tax on merchants and/or entrepreneurs. A multiplicity of extortions would make each request not very credible (especially since racketeers regularly justify racketeering as the price to pay for criminal protection) and, above all, it would lead to a denunciation of the facts and a reaction from the public authority. On the contrary, the territory thus ransomed cannot be very large. Even for powerful criminal organizations capable of systematic racketeering (i.e., regular and repeated racketeering) such as the mafias, it is not a unitary practice over large territories: each mafia family practices extortion according to its own modalities in the territory it controls. There is thus a multiplicity of racketeers in the Sicilian territory, with implementation methods that vary from one area to another.

The fact that there are very few monopolies in the real illegal economy means that other economic relations than those of eliminating competition within the criminal world must be considered. It is thus necessary to open the reflection to the issue of cooperation between criminal organizations. Consequently, the equation between violence and illegality must also be rethought. Without denying that the underworld knows less restraint in the use of violence, it would be wrong and naïve to reduce crime to the use of violent methods. The objective of maintaining the continuity of trafficking requires actors to reflect on whether or not to resort to violence. Collaboration, subcontracting, and specialization by segments of the production chain shed a different light on criminal *modus operandi*. They also make many illegal activities less easily detectable.

The interrelations between the legal and illegal economies are also generally absent from the reflection (Ehrlich acknowledges this, as we have seen earlier), even though they are fundamental to understanding not only the overall functioning of the economy as a whole but also the real impact of crime: impact not only on the economy, of course, but also on civil society, on politics, and on institutions. Mainstream crime economics tends to maintain – unintentionally and, it seems, mainly out of naivety – the illusion of a separation, a form of watertightness between legality and illegality. The reasoning is done by modeling exclusively one or more illegal markets. Or, in the tradition of Becker, both spheres are taken into account, but either in a tipping logic (cost–benefit analysis applied to the law-abiding/law-breaking trade-off) or in a splitting logic (models of time allocation between two activities, one legal, the other illegal, the two not being in a complementary or joint relationship).

Finally, the dependence of mainstream crime economics on Becker's original model (1968) is problematic in that it models the behavior of an isolated, unsocialized individual, unshaped by a socio-economic environment. This raises at least two questions about the relevance of such a methodological choice. On the one hand, does modeling individual behavior of this type allow us to understand the criminal logic of groups, whether they are highly structured criminal organizations or much looser organizations? In other words, does the Beckerian model allow us to understand the criminal economy in the extreme diversity of its actors and activities? On the other hand, does not excluding the question of the environment in which each individual formulates his or her choices and expresses his or her preferences constitute a retreat from criminological thinking? Crime varies in time and space. This is, of course, due to changes in legislation – such as when what was a crime or an offense ceases to be a crime or an offense (such as homosexuality in many countries) or *vice versa* – and possibly with technical developments (such as the development of cybercrime enabled by the web). But national statistics on crime regularly show geographical disparities that may be stable over time.[4] How, then, can we understand these disparities without taking our thinking out of the confines of pure rational calculation?

Mainstream crime economics, driven by the logic of economic hegemony claimed by Becker (see Lazear, 2000), has finally put blinders on the eyes of the few economists who have studied and study this field. This has led to a very fragmented study of the crime issue. In this respect, it is interesting to recall the fact mentioned in the introduction: while illegal and, in a broader sense, criminal activities occupy a non-negligible place in our economies, even if only financially, the topic is of little concern to economists and rarely – often never – appears on the curriculum of university economics courses (bachelor's and master's level). This has also led to a skewed view of criminal issues beyond the academic sphere. The approach based on a supposed rationality of criminal behavior has locked the definition of both organized and isolated crime into the sole logic of opportunity and profit maximization. This prevents the complexity of the criminal sphere from being taken into account. The economic irrationality of some criminal activities is dismissed because it does not correspond to the mainstream *doxa*. The fact that a systematic racketeering operation that lasts for a long time and affects almost all the economic actors in a territory can generate major logistical costs in relation to the sums collected is an example. The same is true when criminal organizations engage in activities that could be described as welfare: distribution of food aid baskets during the health crisis of 2020 as with El Chapo, aid to the victims of the earthquake and tsunami of 2011 by the yakuzas in Japan. These actions make no sense in terms of a strictly economic rationality. In order to be analyzed and understood, they require the reintroduction of the concepts of institution and power.

Such a reintroduction is all the more urgent as mainstream economic thinking has helped shape the legal definition of organized crime. By reducing it to the sole logic of the pursuit of profit, it contributes to a misunderstanding of the diversity of objectives pursued by criminals. It reduces the prism with which we apprehend the activities and actors of crime, leaving in the shadow power issues that are nevertheless fundamental for the future of our societies. As a consequence, it also biases anti-crime policies by too often favoring a vision in silos, that is to say, a vision that focuses on this or that market in isolation and which avoids considering the overlaps with other sectors of activity and the poly-activity of many criminals and of many criminal organizations. It may also underestimate the criminal presence in the legal sphere by presupposing a natural capacity of the legal economy to expel these undesirable actors when our economies are in fact increasingly fragile without the protection of the law.

Notes

1 See Dugger (1989) on the construction of the market myth or Nooteboom (2014).
2 Adam Smith's thinking is actually more subtle even though he remains very pro-trade. Smith, indeed, also considers the possibility that merchant nations enriched by trade might use some of the gains to finance wars to conquer new markets (see Paganelli and Schumacher, 2019). Peace is not necessarily systematically acquired thanks to trade in Smith. But following theorists will largely forget this nuance.
3 which presupposes abundant and reliable quantitative data.
4 The Frenchman André-Michel Guerry and the Belgian Adolphe Quételet are two precursors of the study of criminal statistics. They reasoned in terms of social trends rather than individual inclinations, and identified so-called "laws of constancy", i.e., statistical regularities of crime from one year to the next. For instance, Quételet (1869) identifies a "thermal law of crime" which underlines the influence of seasons and climate on crime:

the south is more affected by crimes against persons, especially during the hot season; crimes against property are more frequent in the north and during the cold season. Guerry (1833) shows that, over time, there are recurrent disparities in the distribution of criminal acts according to region, sex, and season. These statistical laws are hardly compatible with the assumptions underlying the rational behavior of the criminal.

References

Beccaria, Cesare, *Dei delitti e delle pene*, Livourne, 1764.

Becker, Gary, "Crime and Punishment: An Economic Approach", *Journal of Political Economy*, 76(2), 1968, 169–217.

Becker, Gary, "The Economic Way of Looking at Life", *Economic Sciences*, 1992, 38–58.

Bentham, Jeremy, *Theory of Legislation*, London: Trübner & Co, 1764.

Coase, Ronald H., "The Problem of Social Cost", *Journal of Law and Economics*, 3(4), 1960, 1–44.

Demsetz, Harold, "Towards a Theory of Property Rights", *American Economic Review*, 57, 1967, 347–359.

Dugger, William M., "Instituted Process and Enabling Myth: The Two Faces of the Market", *Journal of Economic Issues*, 23(2), 1989, 607–615.

Ehrlich, Isaac, "On the Usefulness of Controlling Individuals: An Economic Analysis of Rehabilitation, Incapacitation and Deterrence", *American Economic Review*, 71(3), 1981, 307–322.

Ehrlich, Isaac, "Crime, Punishment and the Market for Offenses", *Journal of Economic Perspectives*, 10(1), 1996, 43–67.

Ehrlich, Isaac, "Participation in Illegitimate Activities: A Theoretical and Empirical Investigation", *Journal of Political Economy*, 81(3), 1973, 521–565.

Ehrlich, Isaac, "The Market Model of Crime: A Short Review and New Directions", in B. L. Benson and P. R. Zimmerman (eds.), *Handbook on the Economics of Crime*, Cheltenham: Edward Elgar Publishing, 2010, 3–23.

Guerry, André-Michel, *Essai sur la statistique morale de la France*, Paris: Crochard, 1833.

Lazear, Edward P., "Economic Imperialism", *The Quarterly Journal of Economics*, 115(1), 2000, 99–146.

Levitt, Steven D., and Thomas J. Miles, "Economic Contributions to the Understanding of Crime", *Annual Review of Law and Social Science*, 2, 2006, 147–164.

Montesquieu, *De l'esprit des lois*, Genève: Barrillot et Fils, 1748.

Nooteboom, Bart, *How Markets Work and Fail, and What to Make of Them*, Cheltenham: Edward Elgar, 2014.

Paganelli, Maria Pia, and Reinhard Schumacher, "Do Not Take Peace for Granted: Adam Smith's Warning on the Relation Between Commerce and War", *Cambridge Journal of Economics*, 43(3), 2019, 785–797.

Quételet, Adolphe, *Physique sociale ou essai sur le développement des facultés de l'homme*, Bruxelles: C. Muquardt; Paris: J.-B. Baillière et fils, 1869.

Robbins, Lionel, *The Nature and Significance of Economic Science*, London: Macmillan, 1932 (2nd ed. 1935).

Schelling, Thomas C., "Economics and Criminal Enterprise", *The Public Interest*, 7, 1967, 61–78.

Schelling, Thomas C., "What Is the Business of Organized Crime?", *Journal of Public Law*, 20, 1971, 71–84.

Smith, Adam, *Recherches sur la nature et les causes de la richesse des nations*, Paris: Flammarion, 1776 (1991).

2

UNDERSTANDING CRIME

The necessary revival of the legal-economic nexus

From an analytical point of view, crime economics should be at the confluence of law and economics. Yet mainstream crime economics seems far removed from this positioning. Detached from any moral or ethical judgment, it is often tinged with ambiguity toward illegality. This can be explained by a tendency to see the law as separate from, or even subordinate to, the economy. The result is an unraveling of the legal-economic nexus of original institutionalism. However, the disentanglement of law and economics leads to a biased, one-sided, and partial vision of the criminal economy. Indeed, dealing with crime requires taking into account the definition of what is legal and what is illegal. Reference to the law is therefore a necessary step. It is through the law that human societies draw the line between what is permitted and what is forbidden. The legitimacy of these prohibitions rests on arguments that are not only economic in nature. Questioning the *ratio* of the law helps to understand the workings of society and of the economy; it also enables us to consider the different types of illegality with their different implications in the economic field. The aim, here, is therefore to argue for a revival of the legal-economic nexus as a first step in the process of building a crime economics inspired by original institutionalism. Returning to this essential interweaving of law and economics opens up new perspectives for understanding criminal phenomena. It also allows us to reintroduce crucial notions such as power and security. The question of criminal economies is no longer confined to market definition and profit maximization but reintroduces issues with deeper implications, notably those relating to the protection of democracies and the pursuit of a reasonable capitalism that promotes the common good. However, the elaboration (or attempted elaboration) of a definition of organized crime tends to neglect this more global dimension by focusing solely on the economic dimension of illegal financial gain. Here again, we need to return to the legal-economic nexus to better define criminal phenomena and combat them effectively.

DOI: 10.4324/9781003350958-4

The ambiguity of economists with regard to illegality

The intent is not to assert that all economists deny the illegal dimension. However, on a number of occasions, an ambiguity or a kind of detachment from legal logic on the part of some economists can be observed. This detachment leads to reasoning outside the legal framework. These economists then propose a purely economic treatment of a question that is nonetheless linked to the definition of what is authorized and what is not. In concrete terms, some works or positions by economists free economics from legal, ethical, and moral issues.

The issue of money laundering and the recycling of dirty money into the legal sphere is a case in point. In *Economic Analysis of Law*, Posner openly poses the question "should the entry [of criminals] into legal markets be encouraged or discouraged?" (1986, p. 224). The underlying question is that of the personal characteristics of investors (in this case, their membership in criminal organizations) and the boundary between the legal and the illegal. When Posner's book was published in 1986, the United States had, for the first time, criminalized money laundering with the Money Laundering Control Act (Public Law 99–570). This Act should, in itself, provide an answer to the question. However, Posner prefers not to draw any conclusions and considers that cost–benefit analysis can provide an answer based on the various possible configurations. Criminal infiltration is even presented as a possible trajectory toward the legalization of criminals: they would eventually abandon illegal activities characterized by aleatory property rights (Demsetz, 1967) and move toward legality. This hypothesis of the "redemption" of criminals through legal activities – to which I will return later – proves fragile when confronted with reality. It holds up even less well when the criminals in question are affiliated with strong criminal organizations, that is, those best placed to invest illegal gains in the legal sphere. Not only does this line of reasoning tend to equate illegal and legal gains, but it also reduces criminal infiltration of the legal sphere to a logic of neutral financial flows (according to the famous Latin expression *pecunia non olet*, money has no smell). In this case, the fact that financial flows leave the illegal sphere to return to the legal sphere is perceived as an entry into the legal economic circuit, and therefore as a positive element for the economy. This is what enables MacMichael (1971) to present any repressive policy against legal businesses in the hands of criminals as detrimental to the economy's profitability. For him, this is an argument against the prevention of recycling. This article predates the criminalization of money laundering, at a time when the notion of narco-State is not yet used to designate States where drug trafficking has reached such a level that official institutions are subject to the power and wealth of criminal organizations. This did not prevent similar works from appearing later. Fiorentini and Peltzman (1995) use cost–benefit analysis to answer Posner's question. The alternative is reduced to a trade-off between legal and illegal activities, in a very Beckerian way. If a criminal organization generates substantial profits, the authors argue that it is better to reinvest them in the domestic legal economy rather than in the illegal economy, or even abroad. This is a purely mechanical argument, which reduces the criminal economy to financial flows with no long-term impact. The patrimonial dimension that arises from the accumulation of such initially dirty financial flows is denied (Champeyrache, 2016, pp. 137–142), which allows us to remain within the fiction of an economic world without conflict or power.

Posner also raises the question of the relationship between economics and ethics. This time, the example of corporate behavior leads him to settle the debate. He does so in favor of disconnecting from ethical rules. Ethical rules are not seen as habits of thought and ways of doing things that structure entrepreneurial behavior. They are subject to a purely economic evaluation. If they do not pass the efficiency test, then they do not have to be respected. Posner justifies this subordination of ethics to economic values as follows:

> An important question about the social responsibility of corporations is whether the corporation should always obey the law or just do so when the expected punishment costs outweigh the expected benefits of violation. If expected punishment costs are set at the efficient level, the question answers itself; the corporation will violate the law only when it is efficient to do so. If those costs are set at a too low a level, the corporation has an ethical dilemma. One resolution is for the corporation to proceed on the assumption that it is not its business to correct the shortcomings of the politico-legal system; its business is to maximize profits. Notice that if instead it takes the ethical approach, this will have the perverse result of concentrating corporate resources in the hands of the least ethical businessmen.
>
> *(Posner, 1986, p. 397)*

In this logic, ethics is not one of the moral barriers that, in criminology, may deter some people from committing a crime, alongside punishment.[1] Ethical behavior is subject to the logic of rational choice: the alternative between respecting and ignoring ethics is evaluated by cost–benefit calculations. Infringement and non-compliance with corporate social responsibility occur whenever it is efficient to do so. In a way, if the rule is broken, it is because the political and legal system does not punish the offense in a sufficiently dissuasive way. Another striking feature of Posner's proposal is that the recognition of ethics as a value that does not need to be evaluated according to an economic efficiency criterion leads to sanction, this time by the market. Indeed, those who choose to respect the rules of social responsibility would incur higher costs than others and would end up exiting the market. According to Posner, this would have the unfortunate consequence of concentrating "corporate resources in the hands of the least ethical businessmen"! In short, it is the virtuous company that becomes guilty of favoring the non-virtuous. This argument is all the more paradoxical in that, if the company that wanted to be ethical aligns itself with the others, then only the least virtuous businessmen remain anyway.

This positioning is intended to be a rational one, unbiased by ethical considerations perceived as intrinsically subjective and fluctuating in time and space, whereas economic efficiency as output maximization is intended to be an objective, neutral measure. In reality, however, this leads to a hierarchy of values such that the values promoted by the economy (those of efficiency and rationality) are *de facto* considered superior to the others. Ethics and law are implicitly subordinated to economics. This leads to illegalities being treated on the same level as law-abiding behavior.

Gary Becker himself adopted a particularly ambiguous attitude in his Nobel Prize for Economics acceptance speech in 1992. As he returned to the applications of rational choice theory to the question of crime, he expressed his perplexity about theft, as already mentioned in the previous chapter. He explains how, initially, the question of theft did not appear to him to be economically problematic: "In the early stages of my work on crime, I was puzzled by why theft is socially harmful since it appears merely to redistribute resources" (Becker, 1992, p. 42). Setting aside all moral considerations, he evaluates theft in terms of output maximization: insofar as no wealth is destroyed, the operation is economically neutral and reduced to its redistributive dimension. Becker even adds, as if to justify the theft, that the transfer is "usually from wealthier to poorer individuals" (idem). This conciliatory remark shows, above all, that Becker subscribes to the sequence that would have us believe that crime – including theft – is the fruit of poverty. This relationship is not statistically validated; it is largely contradicted by the work of criminologist Edwin Sutherland (1939) on white-collar crime. But it is true that, in his 1968 article, Becker claims to abstract from work on crime carried out in disciplines other than his own . . . He completes this logic of trivializing theft by explaining how he reintroduces theft into his theory using the convenient category of "unproductive expenditure":

> I resolved the puzzle (Becker [1968, fn. 3] by recognizing that criminals spend on weapons and on the value of the time in planning and carrying out their crimes, and that such spending is socially unproductive – it is what is now called "rent-seeking" – because it does not create wealth, only forcibly redistributes it. The social cost of theft was approximated by the number of dollars stolen since rational criminals would be willing to spend up to that amount on their crimes. (I should have added the resources spent by potential victims protecting themselves against crimes.).
>
> *(Becker, 1992, p. 42)*

We note in passing that these poor thieves have the time and money to equip themselves with weapons, which hardly corresponds to necessity theft. Above all, this way of reducing the problem caused by theft to a dimension of private costs (unproductive expenditure by the thief and investments in security devices) ignores the institutional dimension of the issue: theft – especially if it is frequent in a society – calls into question the way property rights function. If property rights exist but are not enforced, then the institution of property collapses. And with it, the market economy collapses too, as only trust in the guarantees accompanying the transfer of property in a transaction can make it happen.

These examples of economists' ambiguity when faced with issues involving the legal question of the boundary between legality and illegality raise questions about the relationship to the law that mainstream economists have in fact adopted. It would appear that – although not necessarily the result of an approach assumed by all – the currently dominant liberal thinking tends to erase the law either by marginalizing it (through the indifferent treatment of legal and illegal options) or by subordinating it to strictly economic evaluation criteria. In the latter case, the ratio of the law loses substance, becomes one-dimensional, and the law is limited to becoming a tool unilaterally at the service of the economy. This concept is the antithesis of the legal-economic nexus dear to original institutionalism.

A problematic tendency to economic hegemony

Mainstream economics, of which traditional crime economics is a part, seems to have progressively erased law from economics, even among proponents of law and economics. This is a process not claimed by liberal economists, but implicit in the irenic view of the economic world. Even when economists – sometimes referred to as neo-institutionalists – try to reintroduce the question of the institutional framework – notably via the question of property rights and the firm as a "nexus of contracts" (Jensen and Meckling, 1976) – they do so by granting law an often ancillary place: law is evaluated in terms of its capacity to promote efficiency, or as an initial framework that can be rearranged via transactions geared toward greater efficiency in resource allocation. The law is necessary for the market to function properly in the first place, insofar as it guarantees the completeness and enforcement of full property rights (i.e., rights of use, exclusivity, and alienability), and brings the market closer to the normative model of pure and perfect competition through anti-trust legislation. In such cases, the law becomes an instrument of the market and is not intended to establish rules that transform the market from a natural order into a human construct.

If we consider that market transactions enable the establishment of peaceful economic relations,[2] then the law tends to lose its importance in framing economic life. Private negotiation, in which individual interests are brought together peacefully in accordance with Smith's "invisible hand" principle, justifies a kind of split between economics and law. The absence of conflict renders the latter *de facto* secondary. This is all the more the case given that the functioning of the market is presented as obeying a natural order, which is difficult to reconcile with a legal framework that is essentially shaped by collective human choices and therefore valid only within a circumscribed spatial and temporal space.

The dissociation between law and economics is implicit and gradual. Its beginnings can be traced back to Léon Walras. Ronald Coase's famous article on the "social cost problem" (1960) can be seen as a further step in the process. Gary Becker completes the erasure of law by explicitly claiming to be a supporter of "economic hegemony": these economists are asserting their desire to appropriate all areas of thought and to have economic tools adopted by the other social sciences (Lazear, 2000). These three authors have an impact – indirect for Walras and Coase, direct for Becker – on the way crime economics approaches the relationship with the law. Let us see how.

Léon Walras initiated the disentanglement of the legal-economic nexus when he defined the scope of economics. In *Eléments d'économie politique pure* (1874), he illustrates how the economist can abstract from law and morality. He takes the example of a substance producing two different effects depending on who consumes it: it can cure a patient suffering from a certain pathology; it can kill when administered to a healthy person. There are two potential buyers: a doctor and a murderer. According to Walras, the characteristics of the agents – and therefore the use each intends to make of the substance – are not important to the economist. On the market, what matters is the willingness of each to pay. If the murderer offers the highest price, it is because the utility he derives from the substance is higher than that which the doctor would derive from it. As for the seller, he also maximizes his utility by selling to the highest bidder, even if that bidder is an assassin. The identity of the buyer is therefore irrelevant. Economically, the question is only interesting from the point of view of the existence of the market (there is indeed a supply and a demand) and the maximization of the agents' utility. It is up to the law to punish the murderous use of the substance, but it is not the economist's job to comment on the legitimacy of the transaction. In this sense, the logic of competitive exchange takes precedence over the legal and moral qualifications associated with the two possible uses of the substance.

Coase's 1960 article on the "problem of social cost" occupies a major place in economic literature. It has been the subject of numerous interpretations, notably in terms of the "Coase theorem". The aim here is not to review the various readings of this seminal article, but rather to re-read the text with the question of the relationship between economics and law in mind. In particular, it is the nature of this relationship that is at the heart of the interrogations, in order to show how far the reference to the legal framework in Coase (1960) is from the original institutional approach. Overall, Coase's thinking is in line with the irenicism of liberal thought: to resolve a negative externality, Coase rejects recourse to arbitration through law and State intervention in favor of a privately negotiated solution. This private negotiation is, by assumption, peaceful and leads to a satisfactory solution for both parties – the perpetrator of the externality and the agent suffering its external cost – because neither has power over the other. One of the most common configurations of negative externalities is pollution: a producer pollutes in the course of his activity, and another agent incurs clean-up costs in order to continue his own activity. Before Coase (1960), this situation was dealt with, even by economists, using the legal notions of victim (the polluted party) and perpetrator (the polluter). The traditional economic treatment of the problem was to prohibit or limit (by establishing production quotas) the activity causing the pollution or to tax the polluting activity according to the Pigouvian tax principle (Pigou, 1920).

Coase's (1960) originality lies in the fact that he frees himself from the victim/offender typology to make negative externality "a problem of a reciprocal nature" (2). In the logic of the competitive market where free, equal, and powerless agents operate, Coase assumes a symmetry between polluter and polluted that excludes any judgment on the act of polluting. Pollution is merely a consequence of production. The economist's role is then reduced to determining how to reach the optimal level of pollution. It turns out that this is not defined by the environmental standards to be respected, but by a criterion of economic efficiency: maximizing the total gain of the agents involved. We are not talking about an agent's right to pollute, or how this right should be regulated. What we are really looking for is an optimal level of production in the presence of pollution-related costs. The economically acceptable level of pollution follows directly from the determination of the optimal level of production. The private negotiation solution can thus give rise to a configuration in which the polluted pays the polluter to pollute less, compensating him for the drop in production that it implies.[3] The rejection of the offender/guilty distinction is part of the process of erasing the law. The predilection for private negotiation denies any dimension of conflict between the interests of the polluter and the interests of the polluted, even if Coase later relativized this point by reintroducing the possibility of blackmail into negotiation (Coase, 1988). Negotiation can be manipulated by an agent in a position of power: the polluter may, for example, threaten to pollute more in order to force the polluted to pay him more to reduce his production. Recourse to negotiation also negates the ability of the law to resolve the conflict linked to negative externalities, to arbitrate in favor of an interest deemed legitimate, and thus to choose to protect the victim from the guilty party.

Coase (1960) also dissociates economics and law by highlighting their potentially divergent objectives. He notes: "The reasoning employed by the courts in determining legal rights will often seem strange to an economist because many of the factors on which the decision turns are, to an economist, irrelevant" (Coase, 1960, p. 15). But this time, differently from what supposedly happens in the market, there will be no spontaneous, free, and peaceful convergence of divergent interests. On the contrary, there will be a first step toward asserting the primacy of economics over law, as Coase makes the following recommendations to the courts:

> It would therefore seem desirable that the courts should understand the economic consequences of their decisions and should, insofar as this is possible without creating too much uncertainty about the legal position itself, take these consequences into account when making their decisions. Even when it is possible to change the legal delimitation of rights through market transactions, it is

> obviously desirable to reduce the need for such transactions and thus reduce the employment of resources in carrying them out.
>
> *(Coase, 1960, p. 18)*

Courts would thus have to rule solely on the basis of economic considerations, leaving aside the legal, moral, or ethical criteria of the society. This is tantamount to subordinating the legal to the economic, a conception totally opposed to that put forward by the original institutionalists with the legal-economic nexus.

In the end, Gary Becker's work, and in particular his 1968 article on the modeling of criminal behavior, simply confirms the erasure of law through an open claim to economic hegemony. We saw in Chapter 1 that the application of rational choice to crime made no difference between strictly legal alternatives (consume/not consume, produce/not produce, etc.) and an alternative including illegality (break the law/respect the law). The fact that breaking the law means evading the rules governing economic activity is not subject to any moral judgment. The distinction between legal and illegal activity is an exogenous fact whose *ratio* is not discussed; the only specificity it brings is that of the uncertainty weighing on the income from illegal activity (uncertainty integrated via expected utility). It follows that, for Becker, anyone who derives greater utility from an illegal activity than from a legal activity will switch to illegality. The switch is a fairly automatic and ultimately passive one: the individual gives in to a supposedly rational calculation, possibly unfettered by internalized moral and ethical barriers. In this sense, *homo economicus* is not really subject to the law; indeed, the law no longer has any real legitimacy if it can be discredited by a simple cost–benefit calculation. This allows Becker to ignore the contributions of other disciplines and established notions of criminology. The rejection of the notion of differential association[4] makes the individual a being without social interaction, who does not learn from his environment (family, friends, professionals, etc.). The rejection of the anomie[5] explanation means the negation of any reference to norms and values common to a social group, including those formalized by law. This a-moral stance – in the sense that it refuses to integrate ethical, moral, and legal considerations that differ from economic rationality – provides a better understanding of Becker's aforementioned ambiguity on the question of theft. This potentially paves the way – I will come back to this in Chapter 7 – for the acceptance and even *de facto* institutionalization of certain behaviors that are illegal but conform to economic rationality. This is particularly true of crimes and misdemeanors considered – rightly or wrongly – to be "victimless": money laundering, certain forms of white-collar crime, corruption, and so on. This approach is deployed by Becker and his supporters in the name of a claimed "economic hegemony". This hegemonic project can only lead to a deconstruction of the legal-economic nexus of original institutionalism. Yet reconstituting the legal-economic nexus is a fundamental step toward building a renewed crime economics capable of understanding the scale of the challenge posed by organized crime not only to our economies but also to our societies and democracies. All the more so since, if there is one issue that cannot be divorced from the legal dimension, it is that of crime.

The law: the absolute reference for the boundary between legal and illegal

To talk about crime is to talk about the boundary between legal and illegal. Legislative prohibitions determine what is and is not permitted. When an activity is not explicitly prohibited by law, it is *de facto* legal. This does not mean, however, that the boundary is immutable: prohibitions evolve over time and space, and there is nothing universal about them. Original institutionalism is precisely capable of integrating the evolutionary nature of the law, whereas market models are limited to a static framework in which legislation is all too often an exogenous given. The notion of legal-economic nexus – the antithesis of the disconnection between law and economics – is, moreover, able to provide keys to understanding the evolution of laws. Indeed, the decision by many mainstream economists to disconnect law and economics may stem from the difficulty of reconciling models in which economic laws are thought of as natural (valid at all times and in all places) with the reality of the relativity of legal laws.

The relativity of laws and prohibitions raises the question of the interests underlying the writing of legal texts. Commons (notably 1950) analyzed the co-production of law by different groups of actors with different, even divergent, interests. Law is thus the fruit of collective action. Commons himself was directly involved in this law-making process, as part of the progressive reforms led by Governor Robert La Follette in the state of Wisconsin in the early 20th century.[6] More pessimistic about the law-making process, Katherina Pistor (2020) shows that the interests of capital owners have shaped law-making to their benefit. In Pistor's analysis, legal instruments are created to protect the interests of the owners of capital (notably in property and contract law). But conflicts also preside over the drafting of laws establishing prohibitive measures, since the latter have economic effects. These conflicts are reflected in the wording of laws, in the determination of the severity of penalties, and even in the implementation of effective enforcement measures. Thus, the fight against drugs in the United States does not affect whites and blacks in the same way, with repression hitting heroin users (who tend to be black Americans) harder and cocaine users (who tend to be white) relatively less (Laurent, 2016).

So there really is no universal prohibition. Even murder can, under certain conditions, be legally accepted. For example, the Kanun, a text of medieval Albanian customary law, authorizes murder as long as the purpose is to avenge another murder. In this case, the practice of "taking blood" is legal. The same applies to narcotic substances, despite attempts to harmonize legislation since the second half of the 20th century. A psychotropic substance is characterized by two elements: on the one hand, its consumption has an immediate effect on the user's perceptions, mood, and behavior; on the other hand, it creates a dependency or addiction that translates into sensations of physical and/or psychic withdrawal. However, not all substances with these two characteristics are illegal. If only because some drugs (e.g., anxiolytics, certain hypnotics, and anti-inflammatories) are used as medicines. The illegal nature of what is often referred to as drugs can fluctuate over time: opium, heroin, and even cocaine entered the market legally as products of the pharmaceutical industry.[7] Prohibition also fluctuates spatially: some drugs are legal or decriminalized in certain countries. The boundary between the legal and illegal worlds is therefore not strictly and universally established.

Understanding why prohibitions exist is therefore of great value, as these prohibitions determine the nature (illegal or not) of markets and actors. They also tell us a great deal about institutions, and more specifically about the values that drive them. Indeed, there are a variety of principles – ethical, moral, economic, social, or political – that can guide legislative choices. But these principles do not necessarily converge. They will therefore be articulated, opposed, combined, and adjusted according to the general context in which laws are passed. From this point of view, when a prohibition is legally adopted, it reflects this process of confrontation between principles and can be used to distinguish between political institutions dominated by economic principles (broadly speaking, we will find countries that tend to limit prohibition measures as soon as supply and demand exist) and institutions that give priority to ethical principles (those, e.g., that value principles such as the non-commodification of the human body in order to prohibit the trade in blood, organs, and prostitution). Taking into account the possible conflict between the different principles justifying or not a prohibition measure also enables one to understand any discrepancies between international norms and local practices. For instance, many environmental standards for the protection of species of flora and fauna have been adopted at an international level (notably via the 1975 Washington Convention on International Trade in Endangered Species of Wild Fauna and Flora (CITES)). But their implementation can be complicated locally by the non-adherence of local populations who do not perceive their principles and legitimacy (see, e.g., Shelley, 2018). For example, a local community may see tiger poaching as both a means of protecting the village from deadly feline attacks and a source of income. This relativizes the legitimacy of measures to protect the species in the eyes of those who should be implementing them. Thus, the drafting of laws is the result of arbitration between different conflicting interests. But law enforcement is also a source of potential conflict, as the legitimacy of prohibitions is not accepted by individuals or groups of people.

If we return to the question of the boundary between legality and illegality and its link with the economic dimension, we can take up Rey's typology (1993). He establishes a triptych – which I summarize as agent – method – activity – which has the merit of going beyond the framework of illegal markets alone, and captures the diversity of the criminal field. There are three categories of illegality:

- The first type of illegality concerns *agents* and arises when agents who are not authorized by the standards in force nevertheless carry out a regulated activity: this is the case for smuggling, counterfeiting, usury, illegal gambling, arms trafficking, and so on.
- Another category of illegality concerns *methods* where the exchange of goods and services or the provision of monetary benefits are accompanied by acts of violence, deception, or abuse of power against others: these include theft, robbery, receiving, extortion, and sequestration, as well as fraud and breach of trust.
- The third and final type of illegality relates to *activities* in which the production, transport, and marketing of goods and services are explicitly prohibited by law, such as certain narcotics, pimping, human trafficking, and so on.

The consequences of these different illegalities are varied. In this respect, the illegal economy is far from being a homogeneous whole and reducible to a profit logic transplanted into the illegal sphere. Although the typology below does not precisely correspond to the one above, illegal activities can be categorized according to their logic and consequences:

- Criminality that aims at undermining public order, which generally involves the destruction of wealth. This is the case of vandalism and deliberate damage to common or public structures.
- Crime of an appropriative nature, which can be read in terms of the improper transfer of wealth and property. It includes activities such as theft and extortion, as well as those carried out by unauthorized agents (smuggling, counterfeiting, etc.).
- Productive crime refers to the ability to create value in the illegal sphere through the production and exchange of goods and services prohibited by law. This type of crime comes closest to the logic of the legal productive sphere, as it brings into play mechanisms for creating value and passing through the market.

This third category – the productive one, which joins the category relating to the prohibition of certain goods in the previous typology – is the best known, and the one around which most of the debate on prohibition, depenalization, legalization, and liberalization revolves. Legal debates – but with a scope that goes beyond the strictly legal – on the desirability of prohibiting some activities revolve around different options, the meaning of which is not always clear, even among economists, particularly with regard to the difference between legalizing and liberalizing. Depenalization does not mean the lifting of all prohibitions (i.e., prohibitions on production, transport, and marketing). Production and marketing remain illegal. On the contrary, consumption may be totally authorized or remain prohibited but be reclassified from a misdemeanor (with criminal penalties) to a simple infraction (possibly punishable by a fine). Legalization goes further than depenalization, as it makes it possible to produce and market the good or service, albeit under State control. Control of the activity may be restrictive: for example, limiting sales to people of legal age or restricting use to therapeutic rather than recreational purposes. This implies that an illegal parallel market may still develop in the event of legalization. Replacing prohibition with legalization is therefore not enough to put an end to the illegal economy. Moreover, legalization is a far cry from the liberalization of the activity: the latter grants total freedom of production, marketing, and consumption of the good or service; it allows the constitution of a legal private market as exists for standard goods.

The decision to make certain activities illegal is made on the basis of arguments belonging to different registers: one is economic, but it is not the only one. Ethical, moral, environmental, political arguments, public health, and other considerations also come into play. In the case of drugs, the primary argument is public health, for a number of reasons. The deterioration in the health of consumers imposes costs on society as a whole, costs which are compounded by the addictive nature of the products. To this, we can add the problem of deviant behavior (violence, theft, vandalism, etc.) that withdrawal crises can engender. Ultimately, these arguments can be incorporated into economic analysis, through monetary evaluation of the costs associated with these various problems. However, there are other arguments in favor of prohibition that are not economic, or even conflict with the logic of profit, the market, or cost–benefit analysis. Such is the case of the principle of "non-patrimoniality of the human body" enunciated by the World Health Organization in 1991. For essentially ethical reasons, the commodification of the human body – in its entirety (forced prostitution) or in part (blood, organs) – is prohibited. To compensate for the negative effects of this "non-commercialization", the market is replaced by donation. Donation makes blood transfusions and organ transplants possible. The fact that it is not remunerated guarantees that the act is totally voluntary for the donor. For many liberal economists, the existence of supply and demand could suffice to justify the existence of a market for blood and organs. This is what Becker and Elias do in a 2007 article when they model a kidney market that establishes an equilibrium price for the kidney that is sufficiently attractive to maximize the number of transplants. Disregarding the ethical arguments underpinning the non-patrimoniality of the human body, Becker and Elias represent a market typical of the irenic worldview pictured in Chapter 1. They dismiss the ethical argument of the non-patrimoniality of the human body by relying on the theory of "natural rights": as everyone is the owner of his or her own body, everyone is entitled to do with it as he or she pleases. This exclusive right of use means that anyone can freely choose to prostitute himself or sell his blood and organs. This right is achieved through private negotiation between those who wish to sell and those who wish to buy, a negotiation that leads to a transaction if the parties agree that it is mutually beneficial. The real argument is the shortage of organs and its medical consequences. The introduction of a market should, according to the model of pure and perfect competition, make it possible to achieve an equilibrium between supply and demand for organs. In reality, equilibrium would not mean the end of the shortage. It would probably lead to an increase in the number of transplants, but also to rationing, as not all demands could be met. This rationing would be in favor of those with sufficient ability to pay to meet the market price.

Furthermore, Becker and Elias fail to take into account the fact that the commodification of organs (or blood) could encourage people in extreme need to sell to anyone willing to pay a relatively high price for vital reasons. Seemingly legal and free of any constraint, the transaction would in fact be carried out under duress, with the seller forced by poverty to accept an exchange that he would have declined had he enjoyed a decent income. This dimension of asymmetry in the bargaining transaction is quite absent from mainstream theory, but it lies at the heart of Commons' institutional thinking. The irenicism of private bargaining typical of Coasian thought (one need only think of Coase's (1960) peaceful negotiation between polluter and polluted) clashes with the reality of a more conflictual world. In this real world, the balance of power, including economic power, modifies the choices made by some; it limits the effective free will of agents. Moreover, the concrete experience in Iran confirms the limits of establishing a market for organs. In the 1980s, Iran decided to legalize the sale of organs.[8] Even though the number of transplants has increased and the market is highly regulated, observers from the World Health Organization point out that the market relies on the strong inequalities that run through Iranian society: it is the poorest who sell their organs to the richest. According to Organs Watch, a class of intermediaries has even emerged to canvass the most destitute populations and encourage them to sell a liver or kidney.

There is nothing stabilized or natural about the boundary separating the upper world from the underworld. It is a human tracing that follows an evolutionary logic and cannot be pertinently considered an immutable and exogenous datum. The evolution of laws and prohibition measures partly reflects the criteria that underlie the drafting of laws: for example, do the laws of the market weigh more heavily than ethics when it comes to authorizing the creation of an organ market to replace donation by sale and provide at least a partial response to the shortage of transplants? Beyond criteria and values, the legal framework also reflects an institutional balance of power between supporters and opponents of prohibition. It also embodies some interests that prevail over others and is the fruit of the resolution of a conflict of arguments. The law crystallizes this conflict by putting an end to it at a given moment. But this result can later be called into question, leading to a transformation of the law. When liberal economic discourse is dominant, liberal interests will have a larger audience, and arguments in favor of the market are more likely to prevail: advocates of legalization, or even liberalization, will develop an argument revolving around maximizing the number of transactions, in the case of the commodification of organs, regardless of the nature of the "good" and the characteristics of suppliers and demanders. The emergence of a class of intermediaries exploiting the economic constraints weighing on the poorest can in contrast be taken into account if we return to the legal-economic nexus.

The importance of reconstituting the legal-economic nexus: a security issue

One of the characteristics shared by the various original institutional economists is their holistic approach: the economy is embedded in other dimensions and cannot itself be reduced to a set of markets. The interweaving of the economy with other dimensions is particularly evident in its relationship with the law. This relationship is central to Commons' thinking, as reflected in the title of one of his major works: *The Legal Foundations of Capitalism* (1924). However, the beginnings of this multidimensional conception can be found in Veblen's thinking on institutions as "habits of thought" that structure the behavior of individuals. The economy is thus fed and shaped by evolving cultural elements, beliefs, and values that do not refer exclusively to economic motivations.

Samuels (1989) uses the term legal-economic nexus to designate the interrelation established between law and economics in original institutional thought. It is not just a question of interweaving, but of dynamic co-production. Samuels describes it as follows:

> In the legal-economic nexus, the law is a function of the economy, and the economy (especially its structure) is a function of law. The economy is a function of law in that law either facilitates or determines what takes place in the economy, for example through government spending or definition and assignment of rights. The law is a function of the economy at least in that the problems confronting law and the materials available to law are economic in origin. Further, it is clear that the fundamental development of law is in some sense derived from the systemic transformation of the economic system. In both regards, the arena of the economy and the law – the economy and the polity – are jointly produced, not independently given and not merely interacting.
>
> *(Samuels, 2007, p. 27)*

For Commons, the existence of the legal-economic nexus has a double signification: it is both a statement of fact and a valuable tool. It is an observation in the sense that Commons does not wish to elaborate an abstract, normative model toward which we should strive. His method consists in starting from empirical observation of reality, from which to identify problems (already manifest or yet to come) to which we can look for practicable solutions, that is, toward which we could strive. That law and economics are intertwined is an observation that Commons can make, not only by virtue of his intellectual training but also because his professional experience in the field has brought him into close contact with the law, its workings, and its role in the economic system. His expertise in government commissions and his participation in the drafting of legislation in the field of labor law have taught him to integrate this co-production of the law and the economy. Laws create the framework within which economic activities take place; in return, economic actors put pressure on the political and legal systems to evolve in a way that reflects their interests. This process is not harmonious or unanimous; on the contrary, it is conflictual, reflecting power relations and bargaining powers, insofar as individuals may be equal in law, but unequal in economic terms. This double movement, in which law and economics influence each other, is the opposite of the logic of the economicization of law professed by Posner and his successors, in which laws are evaluated according to the yardstick of economic efficiency. We are also at odds with the dominant view that agents are merely atoms, isolated, unsocialized, and devoid of any bargaining power. Affirming the existence of the legal-economic nexus is also a way for Commons and the institutional economists who follow in his footsteps to claim a reformist intent. Where laissez-faire doctrine emphasizes an ultimately passive submission to market rules, original institutionalism offers a tool for collective action. Taking the legal-economic nexus into account enables us to work toward what Commons called a "reasonable capitalism", or what more recently Whalen (2022) calls a capitalism for "the common good".

Dominant economic theory denies conflict; it therefore denies the need to regulate the economic sphere in order to resolve the conflicts generated by scarcity, or at least to control the effects of these conflicts in terms of inequality. Original institutionalism reintroduces conflict by considering it for what it is: a normal manifestation of both individual and collective human relations. This conflictual dimension calls for the creation of institutions. These institutions propose common rules, or working rules, as well as mechanisms to ensure that these rules are respected. These mechanisms can be positive: the perceived legitimacy of these rules induces spontaneous compliance; or negative: sanctions punish the offender or threaten to punish the offender-to-be. The institution is not seen as an obstacle – even if it constrains people's actions – but as a factor of emancipation. The law is a major tool for this emancipation, not only because it determines what is and is not allowed but also because it must help determine access to economic opportunities for the various actors, by possibly choosing specific interests to protect. This is a departure from the irenic vision of a world naturally pacified by the market. The reconnection between law and economics enables therefore to reformulate conflict-related issues and move beyond the individual/society dualism to reconnect the two dimensions.

By its very nature, law is capable of acknowledging the conflictual nature of some individual and even collective interests. It is also capable of resolving these conflicts by making value judgments – that is, judgments shaped by time, history, and culture – about the interests at stake. And these values – in keeping with the holistic vision espoused by the original institutional economists – go beyond economic efficiency alone and may even include moral or ethical criteria, or even customs and traditions. In such cases, a whole range of criteria come into play, prohibiting the commodification of certain goods and services, for example. The

World Health Organization's already-mentioned principle of "non-patrimoniality of the human body" is not based on economic arguments. Yet it is widely implemented throughout the world and accepted as legitimate by a large majority of people. Opponents of this position – including, as we have seen, Gary Becker – rely on the theory of "natural rights" and consider that, as each person is the owner of his or her own body, they are free, if they so wish, to sell all (prostitution) or part of their body (organs, blood) if the price they get for it on the market suits them. However, the proposal put forward by the advocates of natural rights only holds if there are very strong guarantees that the transaction is free and unrestricted. By unconstrained, we mean that the sale must take place without violence, but also without constraint of necessity (such as that weighing on the destitute, who may see the sacrifice of an organ as an indispensable source of income for subsistence purposes). In reality, this is based on a dual vision of the individual and society. And it is extremely complex to detect coercion when it is not accompanied by conspicuous violence, let alone denunciation. In order to protect the weakest, it may be preferable to prohibit the sale of all or part of the human body, even if this means fewer transplants. In this way, the law guarantees the protection of the interests of the weakest, in a logic of reasonable capitalism.

Methodological individualism studies the behavior of a reference individual abstracted from his or her socio-cultural context. The market as modeled has no historical or territorial specificity. There is no society in the real sense of the term: human groups are not studied as groups, but as a collection of atoms with no real interactions. Even the preferences expressed by agents in markets are not shaped – even if only marginally – by the effects of fashion, imitation, or culture. Yet this thesis is particularly well deconstructed by Veblen (1899) when he expounds on the notion of conspicuous consumption: the consumption of certain goods is not merely aimed at satisfying a need but expresses the display of a certain social status (as with luxury goods). Ostentatious consumption is then the prerogative of the upper or leisure classes but is imitated by those in the lower classes who aspire to a higher status.

Unlike theories based on methodological individualism, original institutionalism reconnects the individual and society, without over-institutionalizing the individual. In the spirit of Commons (1934), individual action remains important, but it is partly controlled by collective action, insofar as each individual is a member of several institutions in the broadest sense of the term (family, school, professional environment, associations, trade unions, State, etc.). These institutions draw up and implement working rules that guide individual decisions. Obviously, there is a hierarchy between these institutions, which subordinates certain rules to the respect of other superior rules. This collective dimension is apparent right from the essential economic activity of the transaction. Where mainstream economists study the decision of an individual to acquire a good or not, the original institutional economists emphasize that the transaction necessarily brings two or more individuals into contact, and this encounter is a genuine and dynamic process, rather than the determination of a static point of equilibrium. Commons defines the transaction as follows: "The transaction is two or more wills giving, taking, persuading, coercing, defrauding, commanding, obeying, competing, governing, in a world of scarcity, mechanisms and rules of conduct" (1924, p. 7). There is nothing mechanical about a transaction. On the contrary, transactions involve major stakes. This is all the more true for goods and commodities whose use extends over time and which are likely to generate non-immediate income. This is what Commons calls futurity. A transaction is therefore much more than a simple transfer of a commodity from one individual to another. By this term, Commons refers to the "present importance of things and persons and classes of persons in view of their expected uses and behavior in the immediate or remote future" (Commons, 1925, p. 377). The price paid to obtain the good or service is also the price paid to obtain legal control over it. The legal dimension of the transaction is therefore just as important as the economic one. As for legal control over commodities and services, this is guaranteed by the legal framework that guides and constrains individuals, providing a compass that specifies the rights, duties, liberties, and exposures of individuals at both individual and collective levels. Commons refers to the "legal foundations of capitalism" because the law sets:

- What the individuals must or must not do (compulsion or duty);
- What they may do without interference from other individuals (permission or liberty);
- What they can do with the aid of the collective power (capacity or right);
- What they cannot expect the collective power to do on their behalf (incapacity or exposure).

In relation to this compass, which confers on the individual a margin for individual and collective action in interaction with the margin for action of the individuals with whom he is confronted, every transaction takes on a far more complex and richer dimension than in the mainstream corpus. Above all, this gives the law a fundamental dimension in the real functioning of the economy.

By reconnecting law and economics, original institutionalism restores the legitimacy, utility, and force of collective action. Original institutionalism – far beyond Commons' thinking alone – is a reformist and voluntarist way of thinking oriented – as I will come back to – toward problem-solving and the quest for progress. The progressive vision naturally does not sit well with the normative, static equilibrium-dominated representation of mainstream economics. The latter corresponds to a logic in which the market is adorned with all values, and in which regulation – insofar as it does not explicitly seek to bring the market closer to the hypotheses of pure and perfect competition, notably through anti-trust legislation – is perceived as a hindrance to free market forces. In this respect, the definition of legality and illegality is not seen as essential, as engaging in illegal activity might be economically efficient. Conversely, the notion of legal-economic nexus opens the way to a new reading of the need to prohibit or not certain activities, goods, or services. It also opens up the possibility of understanding the stakes involved in criminal infiltration of the legal economy. Even if the original institutional economists – Commons included – do not really address the question of crime, the aims of building a reasonable capitalism and a "workable mutuality" can – and must! – perfectly well include a reflection on crime.

As Rutherford points out,

> Commons does not regard voluntary exchange as a sufficient basis for the creation of a workable mutuality and he approaches questions of efficiency only within a broader context that emphasizes power relationships, distribution, and the need for a 'reasonable' framework of rules.
>
> *(1983, p. 736)*

The need to move away from a vision dominated by the sole criterion of the quest for profit, and the urgency of taking into account the dimensions of power and coercion (in the sense of conditioning power, not exclusively the use of visible and conspicuous violence), are particularly prevalent in organized crime. The road is a long one because economic discourse has largely permeated the other spheres of society. This process of impregnation is further confirmation of the relevance of the legal-economic nexus: the interaction between law and economics is reciprocal, and the economy also helps to shape the law. The influence of mainstream economics is reflected in the very definition given to transnational organized crime in the 2000 United Nations Convention against Transnational Organized Crime, known as the Palermo Convention.[9] Article 2 of the Convention defines key terms, foremost among them that of organized criminal group:

> "Organized criminal group" shall mean a structured group of three or more persons, existing for a period of time and acting in concert with the aim of committing one or more serious crimes or offences established in accordance with this Convention, in order to obtain, directly or indirectly, a financial or other material benefit.[10]

This definition is very economically oriented, insofar as criminal organizations are generally assimilated to entrepreneurial structures aiming for "a financial or other material benefit". Profit maximization seems to be the exclusive raison d'être of organized crime. But what then of organized gangs whose primary activity is vandalism and disruption of public order? Do they fall outside the scope of organized crime? Can productive criminal organizations even be reduced to the quest for material enrichment? Recent criminal events in Belgium and the Netherlands, with the rise of new criminal organizations linked to drug trafficking, the explosion of violence, and the attempt to establish a balance of power with the institutions (via the assassination of a journalist, a lawyer, a member of the judiciary, and threats to the life of the Belgian Minister of Justice) show that there is also a power dimension to the criminal phenomenon. Here again, the legal-economic nexus and the original institutional vision make it possible to understand both the logic of profit and that of power and thus apprehend the criminal issue in all its richness, versatility, and dangerousness. It is interesting to note that, in 2008, the Council of the European Union adopted a definition extremely close to that of the Palermo Convention (Council of the European Union 2008, Article 1.1). However, in April 1997, the European Union had listed various criteria for identifying acts of organized crime. The list includes 11 criteria:

1. Collaboration of more than two people,
2. Each with their own appointed tasks,
3. For a prolonged or indefinite period of time,
4. Using some form of discipline and control,
5. Suspected of the commission of serious criminal offenses,
6. Operating on an international level,
7. Using violence or other means suitable for intimidation,
8. Using commercial or businesslike structures,
9. Engaged in money laundering,
10. Exerting influence on politics, the media, public administration, judicial authorities, or the economy,
11. Motivated by the pursuit of profit and/or power.

According to this list, you have organized crime when at least six criteria are met, including mandatory criteria 1, 3, 5, and 11. The last criterion on the list is the one that attracts the most attention: it rightly includes the quest for power as an alternative or complement to the quest for profit. It could be argued that the European Union had then adopted an institutional vision of organized crime, more relevant than the narrowly economic one of the Palermo Convention.

Naturally, economic activity and economic enrichment are a source of power, but conversely, economic power makes it possible to condition other economic actors and to influence politics, justice, or, as criterion 10 indicates, the media. This raises questions about what defines a narco-State or about the possibility of some territories developing logics of "criminal dissidence"[11] (Thomas, 2017). Making capitalism reasonable can also be seen as addressing the question of how much (economic) power we are prepared to concede to criminal actors. Again, original institutional thinking is illuminating in this respect, as Commons associates the quest for reasonable capitalism with the courts' search for reasonable value. By this, he means "that degree of economic power through control of relative scarcities, which individuals may be permitted to exercise conformably to the habits, common practices, common law and common policies of the time and place" (Commons, 1925, p. 382). It opens up a new perspective for crime economics: thinking of the criminal economy not (only) in terms of efficiency but (also) in terms of security. Concerned about the plight of workers and the underprivileged, Commons makes law the instrument through which capitalism can be improved, by guaranteeing better access to economic opportunities. Security is a priority at the heart of his concerns. As a labor economist (see Chasse, 2017), he focused on workers' rights as a means of increasing people's freedoms and offering them the security and stability necessary for progress. For him, this meant recognizing workers' right to unionize and prohibiting employers from making hiring conditional on a commitment not to unionize. By restricting the rights of some (employers in a position of power), this gave others access to a job and an income. One of the aims of this book is to extend the Commonsian concern for security to the issue of crime. Fighting the criminal economy means securing the economy, protecting our societies, and preserving democracy. One of the major lessons to be learned is that security – particularly when it is opposed to efficiency and when it is inspired by the principles of workable mutuality and reasonable value – is not the enemy of capitalism and democracy, on the contrary. Rather than witnessing a deterioration in the relationship with legality and a shift in the economy in favor of increasingly powerful criminal groups, we would then have at our disposal the tools to rebuild a healthier economy, embedded in the legal sphere for the common good. In this project, original institutional economics offers relevant approaches, concepts, and tools for understanding the criminal economy.

Notes

1 Bentham (1811) emphasizes that penal sanctions are not the only deterrent factor in the calculation of pleasures and punishments for the potential criminal. He mentions natural sanctions (cirrhosis for alcoholics), religious sanctions (fear of hell), and, above all, popular sanctions (mainly rejection by family and friends for breaking the rules). Integrating the risk of this stigma may be enough to prevent any further action. Later, criminologist Walter Reckless developed a containment theory based on the notion of barriers to criminal action. He distinguishes between inner self-controls (internal barriers forged by the individual to resist the temptation of crime) and outer social controls (external barriers forged by the social structure, reflecting the individual's integration into the group through assimilation and respect for rules) (see for instance Reckless, Dinitz and Kay, 1957).

2 See Chapter 1.

3 According to Coasian logic, if we take two agents both using the same river, which agent A pollutes by producing and which agent B uses, paying depollution costs for its own production, everything will depend on who owns the property rights to the river. If agent A is the owner, then it is up to agent B, who suffers the external costs, to propose a negotiation. It is he who, although polluted, will pay for A to produce less and therefore pollute less. He will do so as long as the cost is less than or equal to the gain obtained in terms of lower pollution abatement costs. This reasoning formed the basis of the pollution rights market formalized by Dales (1968), but only the polluter-pays principle has been validated for its implementation. For readers interested in the more technical question of the importance of transaction costs in Coasian reasoning, please refer to Champeyrache (2013, 2024).

4 The term was coined by Edwin Sutherland (1939). The criminologist emphasized that crime is learned (values, methods, and objectives) through interpersonal interactions. It is the association with people who promote illegal behavior that explains the transition to deviance.

5 Emile Durkheim (1895, 1897) uses the term anomie to explain behaviors such as delinquency and suicide. This term refers to the disintegration or loss of values and norms specific to a society.

6 Commons was instrumental in transforming Wisconsin's legislation on public administration (Civil Service Law, 1905), public utilities (Public Utilities Law, 1907), minimum wage (1911), workers' compensation (Workmen's Compensation, 1911), and unemployment insurance (1932). The latter inspired the New Deal legislation introduced under Roosevelt.

7 Heroin was marketed at the end of the 19th century by Bayer to treat respiratory ailments and morphine addiction, particularly among soldiers (in fact, it replaced one addiction with another). Heroin was even used as a sleeping pill for children. Cocaine, for its part, was used as an anesthetic, and its use was recommended by Sigmund Freud.

8 This market is highly regulated and theoretically reserved for Iranians only, in order to avoid medical tourism. The seller benefits from double financing: the transplant recipient pays part of the price, and the State also grants a gratification for altruism, as well as one year's free health insurance.

9 www.unodc.org/unodc/en/organized-crime/intro/UNTOC.html

10 www.unodc.org/documents/treaties/UNTOC/Publications/TOC%20Convention/TOCebook-e.pdf

11 In the words of the author, who discusses the security situation in the French suburbs in the article, criminal dissidence "translates into a particularly violent form of oppressive delinquency, which has substituted its own model of society and culture – a veritable syncretism of Third World cultures and anarcho-capitalism – for the values of the Republic".

References

Becker, Gary, "Crime and Punishment: An Economic Approach", *Journal of Political Economy*, 76(2), 1968, 169–217.

Becker, Gary, "The Economic Way of Looking at Life", *Economic Sciences*, 1992, 38–58.

Becker, Gary, and Julio J. Elias, "Introducing Incentives in the Market for Live and Cadaveric Organ Donations", *Journal of Economic Perspectives*, 21(3), 2007, 3–24.

Bentham, Jeremy, *Théorie des peines et des récompenses*, Paris: Bossange, 1811.

Champeyrache, Clotilde, "The Assumption of Law Neutrality: Property Rights Theory *versus* Legal-Economic Nexus", *Oeconomia*, 3(3), 2013, 391–419.

Champeyrache, Clotilde, *Quand la mafia se légalise. Pour une approche économique institutionnaliste*, Paris: CNRS Editions, 2016.

Champeyrache, Clotilde, "Economic Hegemony and the Institutionalization of Law Infringement", *Journal of Economic Issues*, 2024 (to be published).

Chasse, John D., *A Worker's Economist. John R. Commons and His Legacy from Progressivism to the War on Poverty*, New York: Routledge, 2017.

Coase, Ronald H., "The Problem of Social Cost", *Journal of Law and Economics*, 3(4), 1960, 1–44.

Coase, Ronald H., "Blackmail", *University of Chicago Law Occasional Paper*, 24, 1988, 1–22.

Coase, Ronald H., "The Institutional Structure of Production", *American Economic Review*, 82(4), 1992, 713–719.

Commons, John R., *Legal Foundations of Capitalism*, New York: Macmillan, 1924.

Commons, John R., "Law and Economics", *The Yale Law Journal Company*, 34(4), 1925, 371–382.

Commons, John R., *Institutional Economics*, New York: MacMillan, 1934.

Commons, John R., *The Economics of Collective Action*, New York: MacMillan, 1950.

Dales, John H., *Pollution, Property and Prices*, Toronto: University Press, 1968.

Demsetz, Harold, "Towards a Theory of Property Rights", *American Economic Review*, 57, 1967, 347–359.
Durkheim, Emile, *Les règles de la méthode sociologique*, Paris: Félix Alcan, 1895.
Durkheim, Emile, "La Prohibition de l'inceste et ses origines", *L'Année Sociologique*, 1, 1897, 1–70.
Fiorentini, Gianluca, and Sam Peltzman (Eds), *The Economics of Organized Crime*, Cambridge: Cambridge University Press, 1995.
Jensen, M.-C., and W.-H. Meckling, "Theories of the Firm: Managerial Behaviour, Agency Costs, and Ownership Structure", *Journal of Financial Economics*, 3(4), 1976 October.
Laurent, Sylvie, *La couleur du marché – Racisme et néolibéralisme aux Etats-Unis*, Paris: Seuil, 2016.
Lazear, Edward P., "Economic Imperialism", *The Quarterly Journal of Economics*, 115(1), 2000, 99–146.
MacMichael, David C., "The Criminals as Businessmen: A Discussion of the Legitimate Business Operation of Organized Crime Figures", *Mimeo*, Stanford: Stanford Research Institute, 1971.
Pigou, Arthur C., *The Economics of Welfare*, London: Macmillan, 1920.
Pistor, Katharina, *The Code of Capital: How the Law Creates Wealth and Inequality*, Oxford: Princeton University Press, 2020.
Posner, Richard A., *Economic Analysis of Law*, Boston: Brown, 1986.
Reckless, Walter C., Simon Dinitz, and Barbara Kay, "The Self-Component in Potential Delinquency and Potential Non-Delinquency", *American Sociological Review*, 22(5), 1957, 566–570.
Rey, Guido M., "Relazione Introduttiva", in *Economia e criminalità*, Rome: Camera dei Deputati, 1993, 3–50.
Rutherford, Malcolm, "J. R. Commons's Institutional Economics", *Journal of Economic Issues*, XVII(3), 1983, 721–744.
Samuels, Warren J., "The Legal-Economic Nexus", *George Washington Law Review*, 57, 1989, 1556–1578.
Samuels, Warren J., *The Legal-Economic Nexus*, London and New York: Routledge, 2007.
Shelley, Louise, *Dark Commerce. How a New Illicit Economy Is Threatening Our Future*, Oxford: Princeton University Press, 2018.
Sutherland, Edwin H., "White-Collar Criminality", *American Sociological Review*, 5, 1939, 1–12.
Thomas, Charles-Antoine, "Les banlieues ou la dissidence criminelle – Approches comparées et solutions de sortie de crise", *Revue Politique et Parlementaire*, 1082, 2017. www.revuepolitique.fr/les-banlieues-ou-la-dissidence-criminelle-approches-comparees-et-solutions-de-sortie-de-crise/.
Veblen, Thorstein, *Theory of the Leisure Class: An Economic Study of Institutions*, New York: MacMillan, 1899.
Walras, Léon, *Elements of Pure Political Economy or Theory of Social Wealth*, Whitefish: Kessinger Publishing, 1874 (2010).
Whalen, Charles J., *Reforming Capitalism for the Common Good*, Cheltenham: Edward Elgar Publishing, 2022.

3

UNDERSTANDING CRIME

The relevance of original institutionalism

Mainstream crime economics struggles to account for the reality and diversity of crime; in a way, it contributes to denying certain fundamental characteristics by disconnecting economic reflection from the legal and ethical dimensions. And yet, the criminal economy in its broadest sense – illegal activities but also the criminal presence in legal activities – is not marginal and anecdotal. It is therefore essential for economists to take up the issue, not in order to crush other disciplines in a logic of economic hegemony, but to contribute to understanding the problem. The importance of the legal-economic nexus highlighted in the previous chapter draws attention to the original institutionalism. The relevance of this school of thought to the renewal of the economics of crime can be seen at three levels: that of the method, that of the concepts that can be mobilized, and that of the usefulness of the results obtained.

A method that takes criminal complexity into account

Mainstream crime economics tends to commodify the world, reducing human activity to binary trade-offs (do/not-do) decided by cost–benefit analysis. The emphasis is on the market, with the supply and demand for crime modeled in the work following Becker. This produces a commodity-focused analysis, devoid of any connection with human motivations and their possible group structuring. It also produces a stationary analysis, with reasoning focused on achieving an equilibrium equivalent, in this case, to an economically acceptable level of crime. These features of mainstream economic normativism fail to take into account the complexity of crime: its diversity, its malleability, and its globality. On the contrary, original institutionalism is based on a method that puts forward a theory of human behavior, integrating the question of how choices and decisions are formed (instead

DOI: 10.4324/9781003350958-5

of making them exogenous and immutable data), taking into account the temporal dynamics of behavior and the contribution of other disciplines to the understanding of phenomena that go beyond the economic sphere alone.

Becker (1968) proposes a model of criminal behavior based on methodological individualism and the assumption of the agent's rationality (a rationality defined in terms of utility maximization). It is therefore a model in which the agent's preferences are exogenous and not influenced by the socio-economic context in which the individual makes his or her choice. Original institutionalism proposes a completely different vision of human behavior: the agent makes individual decisions, but these are shaped by his or her environment. *Homo economicus* does not exist; he is replaced by *homo institutionalis* in the sense that

> human conduct and motivation have their genesis in the culture and social milieu into which the individual is born. Human conduct and economic behavior, then, are institutional, in the sense that they are conditioned by the totality of elements which characterize a culture, in the comprehensive sense in which this term is used by cultural anthropologists.
>
> *(Kapp, 2011, p. 65)*

So there is a social and subjective dimension to human actions. This dimension influences our perceptions and habits and takes root over time through the transmission of culturally determined behavioral patterns. This concept of the individual as an institutionalized being is the result of empirical observation of people and societies. If we consider that the majority of members of a society choose to respect the law and its prohibitions not out of individualistic calculation, but through acceptance of common rules transmitted socially and culturally, it also becomes possible to integrate deviant behavior into our thinking, as well as the processes leading to the inflexion of certain prohibitions (e.g., the abolition of the ban on homosexuality in many countries).

In this logic, which incorporates the institutionalized dimension of human behavior, the individual ceases to be reduced to a vector mobilizing means to achieve a goal (maximizing utility/profit) previously defined independently of his or her own will. The original institutionalism describes individuals as driven by needs and desires – needs and desires that evolve over time, depending on the social environment and the degree to which they are satisfied. Satisfying a need or desire at a given moment is not an end in itself. Rather, it is a stage in an evolutionary process. This satisfaction may call for a renewal of the said need or desire and may also create new needs or desires. This is a far cry from the representation of the economy as a market tending toward equilibrium. Veblen was particularly instrumental in explaining human behavior in terms of needs and wants. In *The Theory of the Leisure Class* (1899), he distinguishes two main categories:

- The first category corresponds to what we might call the means of subsistence, those that enable us to satisfy basic physical needs.

- The second category refers to what he calls "higher wants", which he describes as habits gradually acquired by individuals or society. This category has a strong psychological and "aspirational" dimension, insofar as these needs are not aimed at satisfying essential needs, but rather aspirations to a certain level of self-esteem and reputation in the eyes of others (which may explain why, in all irrationality, some may seek to satisfy part of the higher wants by sacrificing the satisfaction of elementary needs).

Applied to the question of the choice of illegality, this categorization of needs and desires can help us understand criminal acts where the notion of belonging to a criminal group is important. It also provides a link with criminological theories and concepts such as Sutherland's differential association (1939). Here, the criminologist describes criminal behavior as the result of learning through interactions with the environment (family, friends, community, school, neighborhood, etc.). Learning covers techniques for committing offenses, attitudes, motives, and the rationalization of the act through self-justification. Criminal identity is thus fundamentally acquired, with contact with delinquent peers or future delinquents themselves playing an essential role. The concept of differential association has points of contact with the theory of human behavior and with the emulation processes put forward by Veblen. This aspect will be developed in greater detail in Chapter 4 on criminal choice beyond instrumental rationality.

In this sense, the original institutional theory of human behavior offers much more open-ended possibilities for understanding entry into the criminal field than the strict criterion of monetary rationality. Without totally rejecting the question of the rationalization of the act, it reintroduces the question of the influence of the external environment on individual choices. The notion of rationality is itself defined more extensively than the ultimately very formal, accounting-based notion of cost–benefit analysis: the rationality of choices cannot be reduced to a calculation of profitability based on an objective defined in monetary terms (maximization of utility/profit) and imposed on all; rationality in the original institutional theory allows the quest for other objectives to be included, taking into account man's biological needs as well as his social needs (self-esteem, recognition, power, respect, etc.). By broadening the range of objectives (and combinations of objectives) pursued, the individual regains a freedom of choice that he or she has actually lost in mainstream theory and can envisage alternatives by anticipating – without certainty – the consequences beyond the precise moment of decision-making. This last point underlines another major contribution of the original institutional method: historicism and the evolutionary vision of economics.

The pursuit of satisfying their needs is part of a dynamic logic where the achievement of a result opens up new perspectives and where choices are made in the absence of certainty about what the future will be. Once again, this institutional vision of things puts the relevance of cost–benefit calculations into perspective. As Dewey (1922, p. 190) points out:

> future pleasures and pains are influenced by two factors which are independent of present choice and effort. They depend upon our own state at some future moment and upon the surrounding circumstances of that moment. Both of these are variables which change independently of present resolve and action.

To build a theory of economic equilibrium on this calculus of pleasures and pains seems hardly credible unless one considers only economic relations characterized by immediacy and unlikely to influence successive scenarios. This makes the economic system a fundamentally closed one, independent of the society and culture in which it exists, and obeying immutable, predetermined mechanics. In this supposedly natural order, the supposedly free individual is, in reality, subject to economic laws – also supposedly natural – that deny the interactions, interdependencies, and dynamics continually at work in the strictly economic sphere, as well as in the societal and political spheres. The result is an economic model that is purely normative and disconnected from reality, as it aims to be universal in the sense of atemporal and a-geographical. On the other hand, original institutionalism asserts historicism and empiricism. Economic analysis is rooted in the observation of real facts, not in the construction of abstract models representing idealized worlds. Observing reality helps to counter certain cognitive biases, notably those known as the "illusion of knowledge"[1] and the "anchoring bias".[2] For example, to automatically assume, without taking into account the reality on the ground as revealed by law enforcement investigations and court cases, that illegal markets are necessarily oligopolistic because Schelling (1967) says so leads to a dead end. In the same context, the continued use of the term "drug cartels" to designate South American narcotraffickers leads to an overestimation of the level of concentration in cocaine production, where the situation is far more fragmented than the term implies. Many preconceived ideas circulate about the criminal economy, leading to erroneous interpretations of the subject. Another example is the question of criminal infiltration of the legal economy (a subject that will be dealt with in greater detail in Chapter 6) when it takes the form of productive investment in businesses. The illusion that the legal and illegal spheres are watertight is sufficiently widespread that the question of the impact of these criminally-owned businesses on the rest of the economy is very often dismissed: if the activity is legal and declared, the market – as idealized and not as it actually functions – is seen as capable of excluding from itself agents who do not respect the laws of the market and are not particularly competent from an entrepreneurial point of view. The mainstream model of the competitive market fails to identify the problem of criminal infiltration into the legal productive sphere, whereas the complaints that may be lodged by entrepreneurs operating in high-crime areas, the work of police investigators, and the sentences handed down in anti-crime trials make this a matter of concern for the real-life economist.

The historicism of original institutionalism also refers to the study of the economy and society from a dynamic, evolutionary angle. Factors of evolution and economic trajectories are at the heart of our thinking. This is the antithesis of mainstream logic, which is confined to the static dimension of achieving equilibrium. Thanks to this emphasis on the possibility of evolution and change, it is methodologically possible to reintroduce into crime economics thinking questions that are generally forgotten or marginalized: for example, the evolution of the structuring of criminal organizations as a function of both economic opportunities and legislative developments; the acquisition of a form of reputation or even social legitimacy by criminal organizations when they persist in time and space; the slow transformation of economic players' relationship with respect for the law when the offense is perceived as economically efficient (an aspect to be developed in connection with white-collar crime in Chapter 7); and so on. This also helps us to understand not only the mutations of criminal phenomena but also their permanence. Moving away from the atomistic framework of agents assumed to be free and equal also enables us to re-establish the notion of power, noting that power relations are also built up over time within a logic of stock accumulation (financial, material, and immaterial), which contrasts with a vision reduced to a logic of financial flows.

A return to an evolutionary vision of economic phenomena, and the reintroduction of biological and psychological dimensions in the expression of human needs and thus in the formulation of human choices, requires the articulation of economics with other disciplines. The relationship between economics and law in original institutional thought was discussed at length in Chapter 2, and I will not dwell on it here, other than to reiterate the primordial role of law in the formulation of prohibitions in a society. Other disciplines contribute to the analysis of economic reality, if we wish to enter into the complexity of the facts:

> Rather than trying to "decompose" the complex pattern of the mutual interaction of a multiplicity of factors into more or less isolated relationships between individual sets of variables, original institutionalists have favored an "integrative" approach – particularly in the study of such cumulative processes as environmental disruption, socio-economic stagnation, and socio-cultural change and development.
>
> *(Kapp, 2011, p. 15)*

The same applies to the study of crime by economists. To deny multidisciplinarity is to engage in a work of "dès-encastrement", to use Polanyi's term ([1957] 2009): the emphasis placed on the market alone in mainstream thinking means that it is a society that ends up becoming embedded in the economy. This is the project pursued by economic hegemony. On the contrary, the criminal issue shows that the economy is only one dimension – albeit a fundamental one, but not the only one – of criminal systems. Criminal organizations, and particularly their extreme form, the mafias, re-embed the economy in broader dimensions such as the social, political, cultural, psychological, anthropological, and geopolitical.

Integrating the psychological dimension of human behavior and the interrelationships between people seems essential, given the historical propensity of human beings to live in groups rather than as isolated atoms. Human attitudes then also reflect positions in relation to the group, the collective. Veblen identifies two categories of human propensity: one destructive and the other constructive. The first concerns human predatory and parasitic tendencies: the instinct for rivalry, the propensity to fight, the tendency to hierarchize beings by means of disparaging comparisons, and egoism are all human inclinations likely to be harmful to the group. The second category includes inclinations that are favorable to the group: the workmanlike or artisanal instinct for a job well done, parental concern for humankind, a sense of community, and idle curiosity. These different propensities are hereditarily transmitted without being immutable, as they are the fruit of long-term selection in the course of man's biological and social history. The two types of propensity coexist, but the destructive type is likely to endanger man's long-term survival if it becomes too preponderant. These predatory and parasitic tendencies must therefore be kept under control to guarantee the group's safety and survival. This is why we need to create institutions, both informal and formal, to regulate and supervise these harmful instincts. So there is a fundamental connection between human nature and institutions. Taking an interest in human actions – including those that defy such institutions by not respecting their prohibitions – cannot be done without an analysis of these institutions, even if this means integrating work from outside the field of economics. Kapp has thus linked the contributions of various disciplines on the specificity of the human with the institutionalization of behavior. These contributions can be summarized as follows (Kapp, 2011, pp. 51–55). Because he is characterized by a high degree of "unreadiness" at birth (in the sense that he is unable to fend for himself during his first years of existence), man compensates for this handicap by developing specific potentialities and capacities to ensure his survival. Man's malleability enables him to achieve results that are specifically human (differentiating him from animals) and cultural, compensating for his relative biological weakness. But man must also find ways of transmitting these capacities to the group and to his descendants and thus, through enculturation, orienting human behavior by formulating prescriptions and proscriptions aimed at the survival of the human species. This presupposes the development of a capacity for abstraction, enabling man to learn, select, and stabilize his behavior. These lessons from anthropology and biology help us to better understand the centrality of institutions both to the functioning of societies and, from an evolutionary perspective, to the preservation of the species. The institutionalization of human behavior thus appears, to use Kapp's (2011, p. 53) expression, "an adaptive tool, a learning system intimately connected to man's biological structure" and, from this perspective, institutions "can provide man with the modicum of fitness for existence and survival that animals already possess by virtue of their fixed instinctual endowment" (ibid.). Despite the forbidding dimension that accompanies the formulation of proscriptions, in this description, institutions appear less as constraints on human freedoms than as guarantees for the survival of the species. This positive dimension of institutions, which was widely taken up by Commons in particular, contrasts with an ultraliberal vision for which the only valid institution would be the market, with any other element tending to hinder its efficient operation. By restoring the protective value of institutions, original institutionalism restores the meaning of lawlessness to that of undermining the social pact and the good life together and even to its lethal dimension for the human species.

The transmission of prescriptions and proscriptions vital to the human species takes place through a crucial process of enculturation. Enculturation

> is indeed a necessity . . . . It is nothing less than a prerequisite of human life, a stabilization of behavior patterns which in the light of past experience have proven safe and useful. It enables each new member of society to cope with the problems of living by applying the accepted collective wisdom of past generations.
>
> *(Kapp, 2011, p. 53)*

This acquisition is a profoundly cultural process. As such, it is rooted in an era and a territory. This means that, over time, these habits of doing and thinking evolve to incorporate new solutions that render others obsolete, as well as to integrate new challenges posed to the human species. So, once again, the analysis of institutions is dynamic. It is also possible for acquired behavioral patterns to become unsuitable without being immediately changed. Change does not prevent inertia phenomena, which can be found in the definition at a given moment in a society of what is legal and what is not (both in the sense of legalizing an activity that was previously forbidden and in the sense of forbidding an activity that was previously legal because it was wrongly considered to be non-detrimental, or because it was new and its negative consequences were not yet visible). Naturally, recognizing the importance of culture and enculturation in human behavior, including that expressed in the economic sphere, implies rejecting methodological individualism and considering that utility maximization is only one of the determinants of individual choices. From the point of view of criminal behavior, this means that the choice to commit an offense is not the result of a hypothetical cost–benefit calculation (even if a form of rationalization of the act can be claimed by the agent). The choice of illegality also marks a positioning – the motives for which will have to be explored – against the society in which the individual acts: does the person who commits an offense do so because the enculturation process is incomplete? Or does he not recognize the proscriptions as legitimate? Does he belong to other groups whose informal norms contradict those established by the law? It is even possible to reintegrate the dimension of the utilitarian postulate by showing how it has itself become a habit of thought, thus fostering the development of an economic criminality arguing for the efficiency of the offense in the absence of a sufficiently dissuasive sanction to reverse the cost–benefit calculation (see Chapter 7).

The method inherent in original institutionalism provides a better understanding of the criminal economy. Considering man in both his individual and collective dimensions opens the way to an analysis of both individual delinquency and membership of a criminal organization. Historicism makes it possible to study criminal dynamics on a global level (appearance of new activities, disappearance, or, on the contrary, resurgence of old illegal activities), as well as on the level of the actors (trajectories of criminal organizations, possible diversification of activities, upstream strategies, etc.) or of States (internationalization or not, criminal establishment according to the relative characteristics of territories, notably from a legislative point of view). These are all elements that traditional crime economics is unable to address. Beyond the method, original institutionalism also provides a number of concepts – ignored by mainstream economics – that are particularly fruitful for renewing the economic analysis of crime.

Relevant concepts

The aim here is not to set out all the key concepts developed by original institutionalism: there are too many of them, and the catalog would be tedious. The principle is to highlight a few of the most essential ones, without precluding the mobilization of others as a complement in subsequent chapters. The ones presented here are those that will form the framework on which to build a renewed crime economics. Representative of the original institutionalism, they underline the break with the dominant approach: it is they who carry the originality of the applications that will be presented in the second part of this book.

Naturally, it is impossible not to mention the concept of institutions, as it lies at the heart of the critique of methodological individualism. An attempt has indeed been made by mainstream economics to reincorporate the institutional dimension into economics. This branch, generally referred to as neo-institutionalism, is not, however, the one to which I shall refer. It has certainly brought the beginnings of regeneration to the economics of crime. Some economists have focused on the impact of the institutional framework and law enforcement on organized crime. In particular, work has focused on the effect of the institutional framework on the birth and development of mafia-type organizations and their place in the economic and political system. As examples, Bandiera (2003), Konrad and Skaperdas (2012), and Buonanno, Durante, Prarolo, and Vanin (2015) illustrate the link between the need for protection and the emergence of criminal groups privately offering a public good that is insufficiently offered, particularly with regard to the enforcement of property rights. Pinotti (2015) points out that the emergence of organized crime coincides with a sudden slowdown in economic development measured as a loss in GDP per capita. More marginally, neo-institutional work has focused on the impact of organized crime on politics, more specifically on the quality of electoral competition (see, e.g., Acemoglu, de Feo, and De Luca, 2019) or on the quality of elected politicians (Daniele and Geys, 2015). These works, among others, reinsert the criminal economy in its interrelations with the political context and pave the way for assessments of legal instruments to combat corruption and the conditioning of economic life by organized crime.

However, although these works have the merit of recognizing the importance of the institutional framework, they do not exploit the richness of the original institutionalism. To take up Dugger's (1990) criticism: the approach remains strongly neo-(classical) and too little institutionalist. Institutions are still too often evaluated in terms of transaction costs, the level of which, more or less high, may – or may not – enable efficiency to be achieved. Original institutionalism, as its name implies, places institutions at the heart of the debate, without however operating a dichotomy between the individual and the collective. As we have seen, individuals are recognized as pursuing their own interests, but they do so in an "institutionalized" way, as they are embedded in collective structures that structure and influence their choices and preferences. Methodological individualism is irrelevant insofar as man owes his survival solely to his identification with a group, a tribe. Since prehistoric times, man has lived, fed, proliferated, and died within a community. There is no such thing as a sudden, exogenous "social contract", uniting individuals who had previously lived well in isolation. Human beings are by nature social animals. The study of economic behavior cannot therefore be based on analysis of the individual behavior of an agent isolated from any social framework. Nor is the institution an exogenous datum, still less a disruptive element hindering the freedom of action of rational, maximizing individuals. The notion of institution is linked to that of culture and takes many forms and registers. There are thus a variety of institutions that shape individual behavior and that are articulated, including in hierarchical logics. The result is a broad vision of what institutions are. For Veblen, institutions are defined as "prevalent habits of thought with respect to particular relations and particular functions of the individual and of the community" (1899, p. 118). This gives rise to a "cultural scheme", which is made of the result of the "complex of the habits of life and of thought prevalent among the members of the community" (Veblen, 1919, p. 39). Every society has its own institutions, which evolve over time, are interwoven, and coexist. These different institutions pursue specific general functions and can thus be grouped into clusters. Following in Veblen's footsteps, Dugger (1980, p. 898) thus describes the American society as composed of six clusters of institutions, each pursuing its own objectives:

- Economic institutions related to the production and distribution of commodities,
- Educational institutions in charge of the production and distribution of knowledge,
- Military institutions that prepare and wage wars,
- Kinship institutions in relation to child production,

- Political institutions that enact laws and enforce them with the possibility of using violence,
- Religious institutions which "instill faith in a system of supernatural doctrines".

All these institutions are present in society and each member of society is a participant in several of them. However, these different clusters are not on an equal footing and are not autonomous. In 1919, Veblen already noted that the values carried by economic institutions had largely shaped the cultural scheme of what he called the "pecuniary civilization". The dominance of economic institutions has only increased since then. This means that non-economic clusters tend to attach themselves to the values carried by economic institutions. An institutional articulation of a hierarchical order takes shape. This hierarchical order makes the question of power central. The preponderance of values stemming from the economic sphere (rationality reduced to cost–benefit analysis, maximization of utility and profit, individualism, etc.) is a reality that provides keys to understanding at least two criminal issues, namely, the choice of entry into a criminal career, on the one hand, and the trivialization of crime and white-collar delinquency, on the other.

The focus on institutions also calls for a broader reflection on the State, as well as on the organizations of all kinds to which individuals belong and participate. Commons uses the term going concerns[3] to refer to the whole range of organizations or institutions. Every economy and society corresponds to a complex set of such organizations (economic, political, and cultural), ranging from the family to the State. Once again, there is a hierarchy of these different organizations. Some correspond to small collectives (families, neighborhood associations, sports clubs, etc.); others take on a much broader dimension (notably the State). But all refer to a community of individuals. Each institution is characterized by its own working rules: here too, the articulation of the different institutions is based on a hierarchical structure. In theory, State rules prevail over those of subordinate institutions. Criminal organizations that do not respect legislative prohibitions are therefore an interesting subject for study. It is even possible that certain criminal organizations, by taking on functions traditionally devolved to the State, are following a logic of stateness, to use the term coined by Dugger (1992).[4] In addition to defining working rules, going concerns are characterized by their durability: they pre-exist individuals and can endure after their departure. They exercise forms of autonomous power commensurate with their position in the institutional hierarchy and are perceived as legitimate. Their long-term functioning is guaranteed by the existence of a credible system of sanctions in the event of non-compliance with the rules. The rules shared by members of going concerns do not reflect a natural harmony of individual interests. On the contrary, they are set during conflicts and result from an artificial selection of unorganized rules that become organized rules. Nor is there any guarantee that the most economically efficient rules will be selected. For Commons, the aim is to ensure "practicable mutuality" for all and relative security for individuals' anticipations.

In a synthesis article on the subject of institutions, Hodgson (2006) defines them as "systems of established and dominant social rules that structure social interactions". For him, too, there is a wide variety of institutions that go far beyond the State, insofar as these rules can be rules of law as well as norms of behavior and social conventions. Language, money, law, the system of weights and measures, companies, and organizations are all institutions. They are characterized by durability (which does not exclude mutability, evolution, and even, in some cases, disappearance). This durability is useful because it creates stable expectations among participants as to the behavior of others. The recognized legitimacy of institutions means that we can expect a majority to respect the rules. Once again, a contrario, the analysis of criminals' non-compliance with common rules fits perfectly into original institutional reasoning. To evade the rule is to reject institutional constraint (libertarian argument), but it is also to deny oneself choices and actions, and even guarantees and protections which, without institutions, would not exist. The choice of illegality is therefore not neutral, nor can it be equated with the choice of respecting legality. It is also a choice that has both an individual and a collective dimension. To take a trivial example, far removed from the problems of organized crime, the highway code is an institution. It imposes rules (respecting traffic signs, priority rules, speed limits, etc.) that can appear to restrict individual freedoms and infringe on the right to use a vehicle. This is to forget that, as the number of cars on the road begins to increase, the introduction of a highway code is the sine qua non for making traffic flow more smoothly and safely. Breaking these rules means taking risks not only for oneself but also for the community as a whole (harming the physical integrity of others and damaging the overall functioning of road traffic). The elaboration of rules, and the resulting institutionalization of individuals, opens the field to many questions that are particularly relevant to crime economics: there's the question already addressed in Chapter 2 of the elaboration of prohibition measures, but it goes beyond that. The codification of rules makes it possible to explicitly identify transgressors, and this justifies the adoption of sanctions. The ensuing reflection goes beyond the framework of cost–benefit analysis to assess the relevance of a crime-deterrence policy. It raises questions about more complex issues, such as how to deal with the potential conflict between rules for different groups. For example, the debate on the implementation of international environmental legislation to protect endangered species of flora and fauna can be reconsidered when such legislation is considered illegitimate by a population that traditionally uses and consumes these species. The choice of non-compliance with rules – whether tacit or explicit – can make it possible to draw the de facto boundaries of a community: in criminal matters, this means that we can reason in terms of establishing a criminal order over territories. The introduction of a state of emergency in Ecuador in January 2024, following a full-scale insurrection by drug traffickers, illustrates an extreme case. This reminds us that an institution only exists if individuals adopt certain beliefs and mental attitudes. Obedience to the law is based not only on the dissuasive nature of punishment but also, above all, on the existence of legal systems that have the force of moral legitimacy and therefore win the support of the majority. It is clear, then, that the issue of drug trafficking is not limited to the market and illegal profits, but also touches on deeper questions relating to the rule of law and democracy.

If the concept of institution is the key concept on which to base a new approach to the economic analysis of crime, other related terms also seem to me of particular relevance. In particular, the notions of power and coercion, in conjunction with the term sovereignty, are crucial to a better understanding of the reality of criminal behavior and its possible consequences for the behavior of law-abiding individuals, society, the economy, and politics.

The notion of property has been studied many times in economics, mainly in connection with the legal market economy. The illegal sphere has also been linked to property rights theory via the notion of "aleatory property rights" (Demsetz, 1967) specific to illegal activities in the absence of an authority guaranteeing the enforcement of such rights. The illegal sphere is characterized by economic insecurity, as the criminal or criminal organization can lose its assets (confiscated by the State or by other criminals) with no possibility of recourse, unless a criminal authority is set up to provide services in the illegal sphere equivalent to those provided by the State in the legal sphere. In original institutionalism – and more specifically in Commons – the concept of property is fundamental and not purely corporeal. Property is not limited to the material thing held; it also has an intangible dimension. Intangible property includes the right to the future income derived from a particular source or opportunity. Commons' "futurity" influences the nature of economic transactions. These are not just totally freely-agreed transactions, as in the pacified world idealized by mainstream economics. Commons introduces the possibility that transactions are the fruit of persuasion or, more interestingly in criminal matters, coercion. Yet persuasion and coercion are linked to the problem of power, a category – as we saw in Chapter 1 – rejected by mainstream economists. Commons (1924) develops the idea that there are now two distinct forms of power: the "economic power of property" and the "physical power of sovereignty". Economic power stems from the transformation that took place in the United States at the end of the 19th century. Capitalist industrialization transformed the nature of property, in particular with the emergence of corporations. Until then, ownership could be defined as a principle of exclusive holding of physical objects for the owner's private use. With corporations came the power to withhold from others what they need but do not own. In Commons' description (1924, pp. 6–7), there was a shift from "producing power" to "bargaining power". This allows Commons to put the issue of power relationships between owners and non-owners back at the heart of economic theory. He does this for the legal sphere of the economy, even if certain forms of persuasion or coercion may be the subject of legal debate about their acceptability, and may therefore be condemned and prohibited by case law. Chapter 5, in particular, will exploit this notion of power to withhold to explain the various aspects of criminal infiltration of the legal economy. It is also a concept that can be used to relativize the association between organized crime and conspicuous violence. Coercion does not necessarily require the use of force and can be achieved through a capacity for conditioning. Once again, this shows that criminals are not necessarily driven exclusively by the quest for profit but also by the quest for power (profit can be a lever in the acquisition and deployment of this power).

The identification of this economic power embodied in property forces us to reconsider the hypothesis of free and equal agents in markets. Individuals are not on an equal footing in markets, except in the unrealistic ideal of pure and perfect competition. The State therefore has a role to play. It can indeed choose to take account of the asymmetry of power and decide to create legal devices aimed at curbing the bargaining power of property where it seems excessive (Commons, 1934b, p. 29). Usury laws can be interpreted in this way: interest-bearing loans are authorized, but only insofar as the interest rate is not exaggeratedly high. The State is under no obligation to intervene, but in a Commonsian perspective, where the State is not a neutral umpire, the State can and indeed must identify and restrict economic power through the physical power of sovereignty (Dawson, 1998). The fundamental reason is that this asymmetry of power has an impact on the opportunities available to individuals and on their ability to express their will. Commons (1924, p. 69) rejects the notion of free will as evoked in mainstream economics. For him, it is an empty term, a "will-in vacuo" reduced to a "mere faculty of acting and not acting". Each individual would then exercise the same right to choose between doing and not doing (to work or not to work, to consume or not to consume, to obey the law or not to obey the law, etc.). For the original institutionalists, the actual content of the free will of individuals is formed in interaction with the free wills expressed by other members of the community (Commons, 1924, p. 65). What counts is "will in action", that is, will "continually overcoming resistance and choosing between different degrees of resistance, in actual space and time" (69). This is where the question of wills meets that of property and economic power:

> For the will is not an empty choosing between doing and not doing, but between different degrees of power in doing one thing instead of another. The will cannot choose nothing – it must choose something in this world of scarcity – and it chooses the next best alternative. If this alternative is a good one, then the will is free and can be induced only by persuasion. If the alternative is a poor one, or if there is no alternative, then the will is coerced. The will chooses between opportunities, and these opportunities are limited by principles of scarcity (Commons, 1924, pp. 303–304).

Giving actual content to the notion of free will – rather than abstracting from it – enables us to understand criminal actions and their capacity to condition other actors in both the illegal and legal spheres. It also allows us to consider the market's inability to prevent criminal expansion, even when criminal organizations are less efficient than legal enterprises in the use of resources and the production of goods and services. Finally, the question of the pattern of relative withholding capacity (and thus the pattern of liberty and exposure) of individuals, because it is linked to the question of the relative bargaining power of individuals, must be taken into account before establishing any public policy whatsoever, particularly in the fight against crime.

A dual purpose: to understand and act in the name of economic security

The concepts specific to original institutionalism enable us to move away from an all too often naïve, sometimes cynical, vision of the reality of the criminal economy. The analysis is rooted in reality, as it does not seek to present an idealized, artificially harmonious vision of how the economy works. It aims to understand the mechanisms actually at work, from a problem-solving perspective based on collective action. The criminal economy goes far beyond the issue of illegal markets. The original institutional approach also goes beyond this fragmented vision, dynamically reconnecting activities and organizations with the institutional framework.

As a result, this approach is also transforming the way we approach crime control. The traditional approach to the economics of crime assesses its desirability through cost–benefit analysis. As we have seen, this may remove all ethical and moral considerations from the equation. It also means that the effectiveness of the fight against crime depends on the possibility of modifying the opportunity calculations of individual actors, without taking an interest in their relationship with the rule itself, without taking an interest in the perception of the offense in the society in which the individual evolves, and without taking an interest in the consequences of committing offenses on the ways of thinking and acting of non-criminals. A change of perspective means taking on board the fact that illegal enrichment is not the only problem posed by criminal activity. Original institutionalism does not reject the question of profit, but it is also able to add to it the dimension of power: the power that is sought by certain criminal organizations; the symbolic power that the State can lose if it tolerates certain offenses without bringing the weight of punishment to bear.

As soon as we take into account the dimension of power that accompanies economic activity, the stakes involved in fighting crime, and more specifically fighting organized crime, become more global, temporally more extensive, and more interwoven with dimensions that go beyond the economic framework alone. The fight against the criminal economy then goes beyond preventing illegal enrichment[5] and reducing unproductive expenditure linked to an economically excessive level of crime (corruptive expenditure and investment in security devices first and foremost). The fight against the criminal economy (i.e., illegal markets, but also criminal infiltration of the legal economy) is becoming a necessity, as it is a question of power, security, and social cohesion, not to say democracy. An original institutional crime economics cannot ignore the political dimension of the subject and therefore the impact of the criminal economy on the exercise of power by the State. Nor can it ignore the fact that the State's response to the problems associated with the criminal economy will have an influence on the present and future behavior of individuals, as well as on the sense of security they develop.

As we have seen, one of Commons' major concerns is to help establish a "reasonable capitalism". This is in line with a vision in which the institutionalization of the individual – his active participation in organizations and institutions that go beyond his singular existence – corresponds to a survival issue. The group and the establishment of common rules of conduct are the guarantees of this survival. Institutions play a role in securing expectations because they provide a framework that makes "futurity" possible. An effective institution is one that offers "the security of present expectations of future profits, investments, jobs and contracts" (Commons, 1950, p. 104). The institution makes it possible to project into the future on the basis of expectations formulated in the present. This is in contrast to mainstream logic, which works backward, aiming for a predetermined target (utility maximization) in an individual, isolated, and supposedly rational way.

For Commons, the emphasis is on the search for economic security for workers. Reasonable capitalism requires the State to legislate in order to correct the fundamental asymmetry – particularly in times of unemployment – between employers (especially corporations) and job seekers. In the absence of protection for workers' rights, the employer who has a choice from a pool of applicants can make demands that go beyond the scope of the required professional skills. The job-seeker, for whom the position may be the only way of obtaining resources, is forced to accept conditions that he or she would not accept in any other context. Commons thus considers that the US Supreme Court plays a positive role in terms of access to economic opportunities for all when it condemns employers who insert clauses prohibiting union membership in employment contracts. More generally, in our so-called market economies, the quest for "economic security" must be conceived as a collective process: economic security must be thought of "as the result of ongoing social/cultural processes, not as a consequence of individual efficacy" (Waller, 1992, p. 156). The lack of economic security experienced by some individuals does not reflect individual failures or moral weaknesses; it is the result of the way the economy works. As economic insecurity is intrinsic to the system, it is the role of institutions to make adjustments. Waller (1992, pp. 156–157) lists three areas in particular to which the State must pay particular attention in order to counteract the spread of economic insecurity and its deleterious effects on the effective participation of all members of society in the economic sphere:

- Alleviation of poverty to prevent some real incomes from being at inadequate levels
- Counter-cyclical policies to cushion the effects of economic downturns
- Provision of "opportunities for individuals to participate more fully in the economic activity of society in a meaningful and rewarding way".

(157)

These concerns may seem far removed from the question of crime. In fact, as with Commons, they are formulated within a framework disconnected from crime economics. However, it is possible to broaden the reasoning by making criminal economic activities factors in the growth of economic insecurity. In particular, crime feeds in part on major disparities in the distribution of wealth (much more than on poverty per se, it is the juxtaposition of pockets of wealth and poverty that will encourage the crime of envy: theft, occasional racketeering, black-marketing, vandalism, etc.). Organized crime participates in economic crises: it exploits them; it is sometimes the architect, as was the case with the so-called "yakuza recession" in Japan in the 80s.[6] We might add that the 2008 financial crisis was also caused by the widespread fraudulent marketing of junk bonds.[7] Not only the violence but also the ability to condition (without ostensible violence) to which crime can resort also represent as many attacks on the exercise of the free will of non-criminals in the economic sphere. Furthermore, failure to respect the common rules and prohibitions set by the community concerned contributes to social and economic instability: at the very least, these infringements call into question the expectations that each individual may have of the behavior of others; at worst, repeated and widespread infringements in the social fabric undermine the legitimacy of the rules. At best, this can lead to a reassessment of the relevance of the rule (provided this assessment is not purely economic). In the worst case, it can lead to an underground process of spreading illegality (the norm ceases to be perceived as legitimate and is no longer respected, thus annihilating legitimate authority and deconstructing the community) or to a violent process of openly questioning the system.

State action against crime helps maintain the legitimacy of the institution. This is true from a political and social point of view, but also from an economic one. When it fights crime, the State reaffirms that it is not the market's adversary (according to the logic of the antagonistic State versus market duality typical of mainstream economics), nor is it a stranger to it. The State constructs the market; the State and the economy are inseparable (Dugger, 1992, p. 100). By guaranteeing punishment for those who break the rules (by marketing illegal goods and services, but also by resorting to fraud, intimidation, or swindling in the legal sphere, by improperly appropriating the wealth of others, etc.), the State reaffirms its sovereignty and legitimacy. What is more, it builds economic security by defending it: economic security guaranteed in this way is an incentive for everyone to participate in economic progress and development. This regular and ongoing attention to crime control is a guarantee of social stability and a precondition for effective democracy, as the participation of law-abiding people is made possible, effective, and fruitful.

Notes

1 The illusion of knowing refers to the cognitive bias whereby we rely on false beliefs to apprehend a reality without seeking to gather other information.

2 Anchoring bias is a cognitive bias in which a piece of information is used as a reference, often because it is the first piece of information acquired on an issue.

3 According to Commons, "the principle of going concerns is concerted action for ends foreseen in the future. . . . the principle of . . . Going Concerns is Willingness" (1934a, pp. 619–620).
4 I will come back to this question in greater depth in Chapter 5.
5 It should be noted that even this issue can end up disappearing from economic discourse as soon as the dominant economy develops a discourse advocating independence from moral considerations and as soon as certain illegal activities (drug trafficking, prostitution, and alcohol and tobacco smuggling) are officially included in the calculation of GDP (see, in particular, the instructions given by Eurostat to members of the European Union since 2014). It should also be remembered that the criminalization of dirty money is very recent: the first anti-money laundering legislation dates back to the United States in 1986; it will spread internationally via the United Nations Vienna Convention in 1988. Until then, the circulation of dirty money did not seem to be a major concern. This legislation also arose from the failure of the war on drugs waged by the US administration: while actions penalizing demand and attempting to reduce supply by destroying the raw material (coca plantations in particular) did not produce the expected results, attempts were made to attack the profits made in order to make the market less attractive (much more so than because the money made in this way would be amoral).
6 The financial bubble born in 1986 in Japan around real estate speculation was largely fuelled by the dirty money of the yakuza, hence the name "yakuza recession" when the bubble burst.
7 The financial crisis of 2008 was partly due to the deliberately outrageous granting of high-interest mortgages to low-income populations. The risk of default was high, and the bursting of the financial bubble ruined first-time buyers while devaluing mortgages. Banks involved in the distribution of these loans then tried to conceal their holdings of so-called junk bonds.

References

Acemoglu, Daron, Giuseppe De Feo, and Giacomo De Luca, "Weak States: Causes and Consequences of the Sicilian Mafia", *The Review of Economic Studies*, 87(2), 2019, 537–581.

Bandiera, Oriana, "Land Reform, the Market for Protection, and the Origins of the Sicilian Mafia: Theory and Evidence", *Journal of Law, Economics and Organizations*, 19(1), 2003, 218–244.

Becker, Gary, "Crime and Punishment: An Economic Approach", *Journal of Political Economy*, 76(2), 1968, 169–217.

Buonanno, Paolo, Ruben Durante, Giovanni Prarolo, and Paolo Vanin, "Poor Institutions, Rich Mines: Resource Curse in the Origins of the Sicilian Mafia", *Economic Journal*, 125, 2015, F175–F202.

Commons, John R., *Legal Foundations of Capitalism*, New York: Macmillan, 1924.

Commons, John R., *Myself*, New York: MacMillan, 1934a.

Commons, John R., *Institutional Economics*, New York: MacMillan, 1934b.

Commons, John R., *The Economics of Collective Action*, New York: MacMillan, 1950.

Daniele, Gianmarco, and B. Geys, "Organized Crime, Institutions and Political Quality: Empirical Evidence from Italian Municipalities", *Economic Journal*, 125(586), 2015, 233–255.

Dawson, Richard, "Sovereignty and Withholding in John Commons's Political Economy", in W. Samuels (ed.), *The Founding of Institutional Economics: The Leisure Class and Sovereignty*, London: Routledge, 1998, 47–75.

Demsetz, Harold, "Towards a Theory of Property Rights", *American Economic Review*, 57, 1967, 347–359.

Dewey, John, *Human Nature and Conduct: An Introduction to Social Psychology*, New York: Henry Holt and Company, 1922.

Dugger, William M., "Power: An Institutional Framework of Analysis", *Journal of Economic Issues*, 14(4), 1980, 897–907.

Dugger, William M., "The New Institutionalism: New But Not Institutionalist", *Journal of Economic Issues*, 24(2), 1990, 423–431.

Dugger, William M., "An Evolutionary Theory of the State and the Market", in William M. Dugger and William T. Waller, Jr. (eds.), *The Stratified State. Radical Institutionalist Theories of Participation and Duality*, New York and London: M. E. Sharpe, 1992, 87–115.

Hodgson, Geoff M., "What Are Institutions?", *Journal of Economic Issues*, XL(1), 2006.

Kapp, William K., *The Foundations of Institutional Economics*, London and New York: Routledge, 2011.

Konrad, Kai A., and Stergios Skaperdas, "The Market for Protection and the Origin of the State", *Economic Theory*, 50(2), 2012, 417–443.

Pinotti, Paolo, "The Economic Costs of Organised Crime: Evidence from Southern Italy", *Economic Journal*, 125(586), 2015, 203–232.

Polanyi, Karl, *La grande transformation*, Paris: Gallimard, 1957 (2009).

Schelling, Thomas C., "Economics and Criminal Enterprise", *The Public Interest*, 7, 1967, 61–78.

Sutherland, Edwin, "White-Collar Criminality", *American Sociological Review*, 5, 1939, 1–12.

Veblen, Thorstein, *Theory of the Leisure Class: An Economic Study of Institutions*, New York: MacMillan, 1899.

Veblen, Thorstein, *The Place of Science in Modern Civilization and Other Essays*, New York: B. W. Huebsch, 1919.

Waller, William T., "Economic Security and the State", in William M. Dugger and William T. Waller, Jr. (eds.), *The Stratified State. Radical Institutionalist Theories of Participation and Duality*, New York and London: M. E. Sharpe, 1992, 153–171.

PART 2

Original institutional economic variations around criminal realities

4

CHOOSING CRIME

Beyond rational calculation

The Beckerian model of criminal behavior is merely an extension of the theory of rational choice to the law-breaking/law-abiding alternative and makes the criminal a rational being who chooses the option that maximizes his gains. The purpose of the chapter is to show that this traditional economic view is doubly reductive:

- It is limited to individual rational choice and seems irrelevant for a clear understanding of criminal organizations.
- It limits the criminal logic to that of profit maximization or, at least, to monetary gains.

Thanks to notions such as "values", "emulation" and "going concerns", which are typical of original institutionalism, I will focus on criminal motivations that go beyond mere rational calculation. For instance, the concept of "going concerns" (Commons) allows us to understand criminal organizations much better than methodological individualism does. It highlights the working rules that the members obey. Loyalty to these rules calls into question reasoning in terms of rationality and maximization of individual utility. These notions also allow us to understand the variety of criminalities: from the isolated delinquent to the most structured organizational forms. Furthermore, the original institutional approach reintroduces the issue of power instead of limiting crime to merely a quest for profit. Thus, the economic analysis of criminal behavior will not be limited to the so-called productive forms of crime but can include other economically less "rational" forms (theft, vandalism, etc.). Furthermore, the focus on equal access to economic opportunities opens the way to taking into account the interaction between the individual and the economic and social context in which he acts. At an individual level, emulation plays a role in entry into a criminal career. The same applies to the socio-cultural

DOI: 10.4324/9781003350958-7

context in which the individual evolves. Finally, the stable criminal organization institutionalizes crime and provides its members with benefits that make it attractive for both financial and status reasons.

Money as a goal: crime for greed

The original institutional approach does not exclude the attraction of financial gain as a criminal motive, but it reintegrates it into a broader reflection in the sense that, on the one hand, there are crimes without financial gain (notably crimes against public order) and, on the other hand, motives can be plural. What is more, the quest for profit may not be the ultimate goal, but the means to achieve something else, such as the assertion of status, or even power. The analysis of criminal behavior cannot therefore be reduced to a single explanatory factor.

Criminologist Albanese (2000) refers to economic rationality when studying the "causes of organized crime". This being the case, two remarks are in order. The first is that he does not adopt a strong Becker-style rationality, but uses the notion of "criminal opportunity" combined with other factors. The second is that his definition of organized crime (discussed on the basis of a literature review in the first part of the article) includes "rational profit through crime" as a second major characteristic after continuity over time. This raises the question – a very Veblenian question, after all – of whether the economic influence exerted on the definition of organized crime introduces a rhetorical loop and predetermines the outcome of the reflection. Are we not in fact forced to identify a profit-maximizing motive once we have, by hypothesis, described the actors as driven by a logic of economic rationality?

Furthermore, the type of economic rationality described is more a profit-oriented view than a perfect profit-maximizing behavior. Indeed, criminal opportunities are pictured as follows:

> Criminal opportunities are of two types: those that provide easy access to illicit funds without incurring high risk and those that are created by motivated offenders. The easy-access type includes the traditional provision of illicit goods and services that are in high public demand: gambling, pornography, and narcotics. Added to these are new criminal opportunities that are made possible by social or technological change. These would include misuse of the Internet, cell phones, and companies or banks for money-laundering, among others. The precise type of crime or product is not as important as the use of illegal means for its use, acquisition, or exploitation.
>
> Those criminal opportunities that are created by offenders often involve bribery or extortion. Examples would include protection rackets and schemes to defraud that involve the manufacture of a criminal opportunity in an otherwise legitimate enterprise.
>
> *(Albanese, 2000, p. 414)*

Alongside these opportunity factors (namely, economic conditions, government regulation, enforcement effectiveness, demand for a product or service, new product or service opportunities created by social or technological changes or by criminals), Albanese (2000, p. 415) integrates the criminal environment ("assessed by the extent to which individual offenders and pre-existing crime groups are available to exploit such opportunities") as well as "the skills or access required to carry out the criminal activity" (including connections with other criminal groups). The issue of economic rationality as the driving force behind the choice of illegality is thus reinserted into a broader framework. This reminds us that, for criminologists, the analysis of crime is largely multi-factorial: a single motive cannot explain the totality of behavior. Similarly, Waller stresses that the human valutational process is not univocal, and that human choices, including in economics, can be reconciled with several motivations:

> Individuals may value something for its utility, meaning the satisfaction derived from its consumption, or for the labor it took to produce it, or because it is instrumentally useful, or because they have always liked it (tradition), or because they want it.
>
> *(Waller, 1992, p. 164)*

By recognizing these different elements, original institutionalism makes it possible to apprehend criminal choices in all their diversity. In particular, it restores a place for culture, habits of thought, and the context in which the offender (whether already established or in the making) evolves. As a consequence, it becomes possible to include criminal behavior that is *a priori* "economically irrational" in our thinking: What is the justification for offenses against public order? Why do criminal organizations involved in highly lucrative trades (notably narcotics) simultaneously practice extortion, which, when regular and systematic, is logistically costly for sometimes modest sums?[1] Two notions typical of the original institutional approach provide relevant reading grids: the principle of emulation (Veblen) and going concern (Commons).

Criminal emulation as a behavior

Crime is not a central theme in Veblen's work, although in *The Theory of the Leisure Class* (1899), he makes occasional references to criminals. The exposition of human instincts in which he indulges gives full scope to illegal behavior. Where prevailing theory, as we saw in Chapter 1, too often presents a pacified version of the economic world, Veblen observes contradictory but coexisting inclinations in the human species. As a reminder, there are two instincts:

- The instinct of workmanship values efficiency and well-done works. It includes group spirit, a sense of community, selfless curiosity, and care for the species. In this sense, this instinct is beneficial to the group as a whole.

- The predatory instinct, on the contrary, is harmful to the group. It is based on rivalry, egoism, violence, hierarchical disparagement, and "the habit of invidious comparison".

(Veblen, 1899, p. 227)

Both types of instincts are naturally present in human beings and play a part in the formation of preferences.[2] The prevalence of one type of instinct over the other will evolve over time and space, as they clash within constituted societies. There are therefore temporal dynamics and spatial specificities that differentiate societies and explain the historical stages of human evolution. There is no need here to go back over the historical phases identified by Veblen.[3] The point is simply to explain the difference in the relationship to crime across time and space. The predatory instinct does indeed potentially refer to the criminal dimension, notably through predation and violence. Nor does the predatory instinct exclude the productive dimension, but production follows in this case a logic that Veblen describes as business-oriented rather than industry-oriented.[4] Here again, the productive dimension of some criminal activities enters the field with a logic in which business aims to direct consumption toward products not necessary to man (which is typically the case with narcotics and the continual invention of new drugs). We can postulate that societies which value the predatory instinct more than the instinct of workmanship, or which fail to channel the predatory instinct toward a dynamic quest for the common good, will be more prone to the spread of criminal behavior. The real economy is clearly not that of a world naturally pacified by the market. It includes patterns of force involving recourse to coercion, violence, and conditioning; it is crisscrossed by conflicts (including those linked to lawlessness) and animated by the logics of power materialized by rules (formal or informal). This leads Veblen to a rather pessimistic view of economic actors, the upper class in his terms being more inclined to ruthless predation than to a sense of the common good.

Among the characteristics of the predatory instinct, Veblen identifies invidious comparison, which he links to "honorific waste" (1899, p. 226). This behavior is guided by emulation, a notion fundamental to the understanding of human choices, which enables both to understand criminal behavior and to show how it can also – and paradoxically – pass for the expression of strict economic rationality. The notion of emulation is more specifically developed in Chapter II of *The Theory of the Leisure Class*. Emulation is described as "the stimulus of an invidious comparison which prompts us to outdo those with whom we are in the habit of classing ourselves" (74). Emulation is part of human behavior and not necessarily a problem in itself. It becomes questionable when it is diverted toward pecuniary goals. Such is the case in modern society, where "the possession of wealth confers honour; it is an invidious distinction" (22). This is not neutral when we consider that "With the exception of the instinct of self-preservation, the propensity for emulation is probably the strongest and most alert and persistent of the economic motives proper" (75).

Emulation, in basic terms, consists in aligning oneself with the behavior of a category of people embodying a form of economic and social domination. The aim, here, is to exploit this essential motive to analyze criminal behavior. I develop it on two levels. The first level concerns emulation within the criminal world, and relates to the individual's entry into illegality, as well as the emulation that characterizes criminal organizations among themselves. A second level focuses more specifically on the goals pursued and is based on the emulation that materializes in the ostentation of wealth by criminals and in the conviction that crime enables quick and easy enrichment. The scope is to show that the pursuit of profit is not necessarily sought after *in primis*, but rather as a means because it enables the display of honorific status through conspicuous consumption. This is in line with Veblen's observation that delinquents and leisure class have much in common.

The processes identified by Veblen of emulation, status-seeking and the desire for recognition by peers, which define the beliefs and habits of "use and wont" (Miller, 1998, p. 16), can be applied to the illegal world. The importance of encounters in criminal careers can be seen in the autobiographies of delinquents or in the descriptions of their backgrounds by legal authorities. Economic rationality is not the recurrent element in these accounts. More frequent motives are associative opportunities and the desire to be recognized by the group. This is in line with the theory of differential association in criminology (Sutherland, 1939), which emphasizes the social learning of crime: criminal behavior is learned through interpersonal exchanges (family, friends, and peers). Akers (1973, 1994) developed this theory further. In particular, he emphasizes two points. "Definitions" favorable to deviance and carried by relationships are important in criminal learning: they can be positive (the criminal act is presented as morally desirable) or, more often, neutralizing (the criminal act is excused, justified, or rationalized). In both cases, the barrier to the act is lowered. The second element concerns imitation (and ties in with earlier work by Gabriel Tarde, 1890). The example set by peers is particularly influential when it is backed by the prestige of the model and the observation of some form of success. It is important to note that these elements have been empirically verified and validated. Veblen's notion of emulation is in line with this criminological approach. The speeches of the Sicilian mafia's collaborators in justice, for example, are full of references to justifications revolving around the notion of the "honorability of crime". In Marseille, for example, the DZ Mafia is a small criminal organization involved in the retail sale of narcotics, but lacking the range of activities and potential of mafias in the strict sense.[5] In the same way, gangs originally from the Moroccan community and involved in drug trafficking in the Netherlands and Belgium adopt – surely with pride – the name "mocro-mafia" given to them by journalists. Criminal hierarchies exist just as much as social hierarchies. Criminal emulation translates into a desire to resemble – in action and thinking – what is considered the "criminal elite".[6]

Emulation at the individual criminal level is based on discourses valorizing aspects associated with success. Interestingly, these aspects are broadly the same in both the legal and illegal spheres: ostensibly displayed wealth (or power) and a form of freedom from the constraints of work. As Veblen notes, "In order to gain and to hold the esteem of men it is not sufficient merely to possess wealth or power. The wealth or power must be put in evidence, for esteem is awarded only on evidence" (1899, p. 29) – hence, the use of conspicuous leisure and conspicuous consumption. Many criminals flaunt their success through conspicuous consumption,[7] even if it means attracting the attention of law enforcement agencies, as the wealth they display is incompatible with their declared (legal) income. As Antonino Calderone, a justice collaborator from Cosa nostra, explains:

> When the young people in a neighborhood see the respect, the deference, the attentions with which the man of honor is surrounded, they end up falling in love with the mafia. They see the uncle who walks into a bar and everyone rushes to meet him to pay their respects, vying with each other to serve him to the best of their ability . . . . They begin to think of the mafia as something great that allows them to surpass others, to rise above the masses. These young people would do anything to get into the family.
>
> *(Arlacchi, 1992, pp. 148–149)*

The words of Italian Luciano Violante, president of the Parliamentary Anti-Mafia Commission from 1992 to 1994, are along the same lines:

> The Mafia's presence in a town or neighborhood can be seen more in the small details than in the big words. The boss who enters a bar is greeted with special respect and served as soon as he arrives, even if it's not his turn. He usually doesn't pay because there's someone else who's honored to pay for him, or it's the owner himself who does the favor. The car or motorcycle is parked anywhere, but no one will notice the infraction.
>
> *(2002, pp. 153–154)*

In parallel,

> Conspicuous abstention from labour therefore becomes the conventional mark of superior pecuniary achievement and the conventional index of reputability; and conversely, since application to productive labour is a mark of poverty and subjection, it becomes inconsistent with a reputable standing in the community.
>
> *(Veblen, 1899, p. 30)*

Many criminals also express contempt for legal work as demeaning. The idea is not only to "make a quick buck" in the illegal sphere, it is also fed by the – often illusory – idea of not having a boss or of being able to quickly prove oneself and move up the ranks. The alternative between legal and illegal activity is, then, no longer even really taken into account, and the final choice ignores or misunderstands the risk: the gains are generally overestimated and the risks underestimated. In this sense, we can better understand Veblen's observation that "the temperament of the delinquent has more in common with the pecuniary and leisure classes than with the industrial man or with the class of shiftless dependents" (1899, p. 136).

Insofar as criminal behavior is also shaped by "acquired tastes and . . . canons of usage and conventional decency" (Veblen, 1899, p. 69), there are historical and institutional contexts that are more conducive than others to the development of predatory behavior and therefore also to criminal behavior. For example, historically, Veblen associates post-war periods with periods favorable to the rise of predatory and fraudulent activities. He describes the years following the Civil War in the United States as follows: "Habituation to war entails a body of predatory habits of thought, whereby clannishness in some measure replaces the sense of solidarity, and a sense of invidious distinction supplants the impulse to equitable, everyday serviceability" (1899, p. 242). In such a context

> there was perceptible a gradually advancing wave of sentiment favoring quasi-predatory business habits, insistence on status, anthropomorphism, and conservatism generally. . . . recrudescence of outlawry and the spectacular quasi-predatory careers of fraud run by certain "captains of industry".
>
> *(1899, p. 242)*

Once again, we see a convergence between illegalities in the underworld and fraud perpetrated by people in the upper world. This is reminiscent of the debates over the true nature of the great figures of American industrialization, such as the Rockefellers, Carnegies, Vanderbilts, etc.: were they "robber barons" (Josephson, 1940) or valiant captains of industry? We could go further back in time, recalling that the immense fortunes of great merchant bankers of the late Italian Middle Ages, such as the Medici, were due as much to large-scale commercial transactions as to a very distant relationship to the law (such as that prohibiting, in theory, usury) (Champeyrache, 2019, pp. 102–108).

More generally, according to Veblen, the competitive system as a whole is not conducive to honest behavior, as it inherently favors those least endowed with virtues such as good nature, equity, and indiscriminate sympathy. On the contrary,

> Freedom from scruple, from sympathy, honesty and regard for life, may, within fairly wide limits, be said to further the success of the individual in the pecuniary culture. The highly successful men of all times have commonly been of this type; except those whose success has not been scored in terms of either wealth or power.
>
> *(1899, p. 147)*

This concern is not unlike that expressed by the liberal economist Frank Knight. In 1935, in *The Ethics of Competition*, Knight worries about the advent of a capitalist system that leaves honest economic agents little chance of surviving the competitive process.

Far from the virtuous vision of the market propagated by mainstream economic thinking, these considerations also call for a reconsideration of the notion of economic rationality. In the end, economic rationality is not clearly defined, except as being characterized by a utility-maximizing approach. But, as preferences are exogenously fixed, utility is not subject to evaluation. Especially if, in the tradition of Smith's "invisible hand", we assume – but fail to demonstrate – that individual and collective utilities converge. The contribution of original institutional thinking lies in not rejecting the notion of utility and rationality out of hand. When individuals act, they do so according to their preferences and the utility they derive from them, but – beyond the fact that they are partly constrained in the materialization of their choices, if only by their consumption budget – there is no guarantee that the utility perceived individually is also a utility from the point of view of humanity as a whole, and passes what Veblen calls the "test of impersonal usefulness" (1899, p. 68). This test consists in verifying that the good consumed is useful for enhancing human life as a whole. However, it is quite possible that "the interest of the community no longer coincides with the emulative interests of the individual" (Veblen, 1899, p. 149). Indeed, proclivity to emulation favors conspicuous consumption, even to the detriment of consumption of goods considered essential (e.g., the use of certain narcotics in some recreational or professional circles, while essential food needs are not necessarily satisfied).

The connection between individual trajectories and the socio-economic and cultural context

The "Free to choose" (*Liberi di scegliere*) experiment conducted by Judge Roberto Di Bella from 2012 onward, when he was President of the Juvenile Court of Reggio Calabria, an Italian province affected since the 19th century by the criminal clutches of the 'ndrangheta, is highly instructive. It provides elements for questioning the Beckerian logic of criminal behavior on two levels in particular: the issue of the determinants of the choice of a criminal career and the relativity of cost–benefit arbitration in crime deterrence. In parallel, the experience provides arguments in favor of a Veblenian, or more generally original institutional, version of crime economics.

Admittedly, this experience concerns a very specific and particularly long-lasting and all-encompassing form of criminal organization, the Calabrian mafia. But it shows that economic rationality, far from being the exclusive motivation for crime, is even surpassed in certain configurations. From the outset, the program was aimed at minors and young adults from mafia families. It has now been extended to mothers wishing to embark on a return to legality, without having to become collaborators or witnesses in court. The aim is to remove children from Calabria and their mafia families, within a strictly defined legal framework and after assessing each individual situation. This removal is not intended to be permanent. It is not punitive for the parents, but preventive for the children.

The figures are clear: in around 25 years, the Juvenile Court of Reggio Calabria has had to deal with over one hundred cases of mafia association (as defined in article 416 bis of the Italian Penal Code) trials involving teenagers, more than half of them for homicide or attempted homicide. This is part of a criminal context in which 'ndrangheta families do not hesitate to use their children to associate them with their trafficking activities (drugs, extortion, homicide, etc.). Observing these facts, Judge Di Bella considers that there is a real "criminal education" within mafia families, which conditions the trajectories of children. They often find themselves serving prison sentences at an early age. This first conviction becomes the gateway to a criminal career that is largely inherited rather than chosen, in the absence of any real arbitration between legality and illegality. Recidivism rates for these minors are extremely high. The judge also observes that criminal sanctions and periods of incarceration have no deterrent effect on these young people. In a book about his experience, the judge describes

> emotionally lonely young people, without parents to understand them or share their daily lives with, either because they are absorbed by the suffocating mafia mentality or because they are incarcerated. Their culture – inspired by archaic, tribal rules – does not allow for the formation of an individual conscience, and compresses the demands for freedom and intellectual curiosity typical of young people in training.
>
> *(Di Bella and Zapelli, 2019, pp. 193–194)*

Birth into certain mafia families very often translates into a destiny already written, without free will, and conditioned by illegality. This observation clearly shows that Beckerian rational free choice is ill-suited to understanding this type of criminality. The individual is constrained by the "will-in-action" described by Commons: his freedom clashes with the exercise of the freedoms of others, in this case, his criminal family and his living environment. Economic opportunities are not evaluated according to a cost–benefit logic, but with reference to a very specific socio-economic and cultural framework: that of the mafia subculture and its own values. The transmission of 'ndrangheta mafia codes and behaviors from one generation to the next explains the durability of these criminal structures. It shows that we cannot validly reason in terms of the individual in isolation from his/her context. Moreover, the fact that individuals are involved in criminal dynamics from an early age also calls into question a theoretical model based on free will (the choice to participate in trafficking is "transmitted" or even imposed by relatives) and isolated choice (recidivism does not reflect the repetition of a calculation in favor of the criminal option, but the difficulty of getting out of a criminal trajectory and even of contemplating another path of life).

Initially criticized by many as a "confiscation of children", the program has proved a great success: to date, at least 80 minors have benefited from these measures and have not re-offended. In seven cases, the removal measure has led to a parent's cooperation with the justice system. Calabrian mafiosi incarcerated under the "hard prison regime"[8] wrote to Judge Di Bella to thank him for offering their child a future other than that of criminal predestination: abandoning the option of a way out of illegality for themselves, these convicts wish to reintroduce the possibility of a choice for their descendants and admit that choice is only possible through distancing. This success enabled the program to be transformed into a full-fledged regional law in June 2023. The aim of the law is to guarantee equal opportunities for minors from mafia families,[9] a project that recalls the importance of the legal-economic nexus in original institutional thinking, and the usefulness of the legal framework for resolving conflicts of interest and guaranteeing greater equality in access to economic opportunities.

It should be noted that this capacity for criminal conditioning of minors has been recognized outside Calabria, and juvenile courts in areas with a high mafia density are now being asked to pay close attention to this issue. For instance, in Milan, the capital of Lombardy in northern Italy, a minor was removed from her father's care. The man, convicted of involvement in Calabrian mafia criminal circles, was deemed likely to expose his child to criminal activities and a highly criminogenic environment.[10] More than the territory, it is a form of "familism" of 'ndranghetist essence that is singled out: it would constitute the crucial criminal instrument of the mafia organization.

Of course, this experiment concerns a very specific form of organized crime, the 'ndrangheta. That said, it is also one of the most powerful and dangerous forms of crime today. It is therefore not irrelevant that it falls outside the scope of the Beckerian logic. We might add that many criminals commit their first offense at a young age, an age when peer influence and scrutiny play a non-negligible role. The influence of context, family, and friends cannot be erased by economic rationality alone. It would be interesting to put on the agenda for an original institutional approach to crime economics studies on the narratives of recidivist offenders and "career" criminals in order to examine their backgrounds and the justifications they provide for their offenses. It is a safe bet that the economic motivation will not be the only explanation given.

The importance of the institutional context – or habits of thought, to use Veblenian terminology – is not limited to the behavior of offenders alone. Crime can also develop because certain practices are regarded as traditions justifying their acceptance, even by those who may in the end suffer the negative consequences. The institution of custom then comes into conflict with the official institution of law. Two examples will illustrate this point.

In his 1996 article, Chin, a criminologist, focuses on the racketeering activities carried out by Chinese gangs against Chinese-owned businesses in New York

City's Chinatown. The practice is widespread: around 70% of businessmen are approached for money or forced to buy goods and services (40), and these requests are repeated three to four times a year. However, the findings are clear: "most Chinese business owners comply with gang extortion demands because such practices are considered consistent with Chinese customs and not worth resisting. Businesspeople are generally willing to pay the gangs some money to avoid further, more significant problems" (Chin, 1996, p. 97). The institutional dimension of the sustainability of this criminal activity can be seen in the ethnic dimension (Chinese gangs extort Chinese entrepreneurs) and, even more fascinatingly, in the fact that extortion is linked to a custom, known as "lucky money", which encourages the circulation of envelopes of cash on festive occasions. There is thus a ceremonial dimension that justifies the victim's acceptance of the racket. To explain the acceptance of racketeering by economic operators, Becker's followers would develop a market model in which extortion is transformed into an offer of protection (see, e.g., Gambetta, 1993), to which corresponds a demand for protection when the State fails to provide a satisfactory service. This commodification of extortion facilitates the advance of economic hegemony but betrays the reality of extortion. Catanzaro (1988) points out, for example, that the demand for protection is artificially created by mafiosi, who sabotage the establishment of trust between individuals and fuel insecurity. As for the reality of the protection actually offered once the racket has been paid, this remains questionable in many areas. The violence that can accompany these undue levies also shows that the demand for protection is largely constrained.

The second example concerns the discrepancy that can exist between local traditions and international legislation, which is often perceived as being imposed from above by people or institutions unfamiliar with these customs. The field of environmental crime is very much part of this problem. Shelley (2018) explains that, in the case of rhino horn trafficking in particular, the actors in charge of applying and enforcing the ban do not perceive these rules for protecting endangered species as legitimate. Some then choose rules of conduct – such as authorization to poach – which become tacit criminal rules. The institutional dimension of resorting to illegality is twofold. On the one hand, poachers go beyond the law because they consider it to be contrary to their habitual way of doing things. On the other hand, some game reserve wardens ostensibly turn a blind eye to these practices because they consider them legitimate. The problem is the same with the ban on bush-meat consumption, even when the reasons for the ban are twofold (protection of the species and prevention of zoonotic risks). The traditional and ceremonial dimension takes precedence over the evaluation of the possible cost of the sanction and/or the health risk.

Society's perception of these offenses also varies according to their nature. The greater or lesser degree of disapproval of a given illegal act is also the result of a culture rather than a cost–benefit calculation. This has repercussions on penal sanctions, which may well not reflect the cost of the offense to society, as well as on representations of crime, and thus on the phenomena of emulation and enculturation identified by Veblen. As he points out,

> The thief or swindler who has gained great wealth by his delinquency has a better chance than the small thief of escaping the rigorous penalty of the law; and some good repute accrues to him from his increased wealth and from his spending the irregularly acquired possessions in a seemly manner. A well-bred expenditure of his booty especially appeals with great effect to persons of a cultivated sense of the proprieties, and goes far to mitigate the sense of moral turpitude with which his dereliction is viewed by them.
>
> *(1899, p. 79)*

We can note a convergence with what criminologist Sutherland wrote when he developed the notion of white-collar crime: "The financial cost of white collar crime is probably several times as great as the financial cost of all the crimes which are customarily regarded as the 'crime problem'" (1940, pp. 4–5). Committed by people with established reputations, these crimes, he notes, are less singled out and less punished, whereas economic rationality would dictate that they should be the object of greater penal and moral sanction.

Finally, there are phenomena of diffuse illegality that can be analyzed in terms of institutional isomorphism. When the level of crime becomes very high in an area, and there is a feeling of impunity, a reversal in the population's relationship with the law can occur. Even people who have not broken the law and are not members of any criminal organization end up adopting illegal or borderline illegal behavior. This contributes to establishing a gray zone that blurs the contours of illegality. This deconstructs the relationship with the legal rule. We find ourselves in the case identified by Medema where "the institutions of norms/customs and law come into conflict and in which custom supersedes, in a *de facto* sense, the law" (1998, p. 111). It stresses that the discourse of economic actors is important in terms of the values it expresses. Two territories among others illustrate these institutional configurations, where habits of thought (in this case, sayings as an expression of popular wisdom or tradition) are at odds with the law and contribute to the spread of illegality independently of any rational economic calculation. The first example is Sicily. Numerous dialect expressions testify to a distrust of the law and a logic of justification for its non-observance. Here are just a few of them: "Cui inventa liggi, inventa frodi" (Who invents a law, invents a fraud), "Nova liggi, nova malizia" (New law, new mischief), "Megghiu amicu cu lu latru ca cu lu sbirru" (It's better to be friends with the thief than with the policeman), "La leggi è fatta per li minchiuni" (The law is made for fools), and "Cui havi dinari 'nun po' esseri 'mpsisu" (Whoever has money cannot be hanged). Sayings from the island of Haiti, plagued by crime and corruption, reveal the same distended relationship with the law. Tolerance of illegality is reflected in popular expressions such as "Degaje pa peche" (Scavenging is not a sin) and "Se pa mwen kap vin ranje peyi a" (I am not the one who will change the country). The expression "Bien l'État se chwal papa" (State property belongs to everyone, it has no master) signifies contempt for public property, which can be appropriated and misappropriated by anyone.

Organized crime as a quasi-State

Generally speaking, criminals do not act alone. Entry into crime may be an isolated act, but the maintenance of criminal behavior is based on extremely varied organizational forms. Becker's model (1968) does not capture this associative reality, and even less does it take into account the extreme variety of criminal organizations. In contrast, an analysis inspired by original institutionalism cannot abstract from a reflection on the reasons behind the organization of crime. The articulation and different combinations of these reasons also make it possible to identify the various possible forms of organization.

Broadly speaking, there are two main explanations for the organization of crime (Champeyrache, 2009). If we attempt to draw up a typology of criminal organizations, these explanations constitute the two poles between which a continuum of structures unfolds. The first explanation is basic: certain illegal activities require crime to organize itself. This is typically the case for productive activities, which require a minimum of productive and logistical cooperation. But appropriative activities such as burglary, for example, or destructive ones such as vandalism, can also rely on group work. However, when activity dictates organization, the result – at least initially, since organizations are also dynamic and evolving – is a weak form of organization. This weakness can be seen in the low durability of the association, or in the rather loose nature of the associative links (the group may be formed on an *ad hoc* basis for specific operations, with each member pursuing other activities, including criminal ones, in the meantime). Another explanation is that criminals exploit the organizational advantages of membership. This leads to strong forms of criminal organization, the stronger the organizational advantages. As Commons points out, the organization is not – unlike its treatment from the perspective of methodological individualism – equivalent to the sum of its members. On the contrary, "in this process of organization the whole is greater than the sum of its parts, and the *personality* of each organized individual is greater and more capable than the personality of the unorganized individuals" (Commons, 1950, p. 132). With specific regard to criminal organizations, the affiliated individual can benefit from three effects in particular that give him an advantage over unorganized criminal individuals: these are the effects of reputation, corruption-conditioning, and belonging. The more the organization is able to deploy these effects, the more the action of each of its members is potentiated, inside and outside the economic field. Structuring is indeed a source of power.

The reputation surrounding a criminal organization is a progressive construction that, to be understood, must integrate the dynamic dimension of the economy and society. Temporal evolution is at the root of a reputation effect that has an impact on criminals' relationship to the use of violence and on their connection to other actors. The more established a criminal group's reputation, the longer it can establish itself in a given territory without having to resort to actual violence. And vice versa: a long-lasting presence in a territory encourages learning about the nature of the criminal presence (type of activities, capacity for violent and non-violent coercion, reliability of its members, etc.). The violence indicator thus loses its relevance for assessing the criminal permeation of a society and its economy. Paradoxically, the most powerful criminal organizations – such as mafias in the strict sense of the term – are also those that least need to use violence to impose their conditions, on both illegal and legal markets. The name of the criminal organization that knows how to exploit this reputational effect then becomes like a brand to which its affiliates can lay claim. The reputation effect also facilitates the practice of certain criminal activities: criminal intermediation, which I will discuss in the next chapter, but also racketeering practiced on a regular and sustained basis without necessarily involving, on the one hand, intimidation and violence (glue in locks, arson and destruction of equipment, even physical harm to individuals) on the part of criminals and, on the other hand, denunciation to the judicial authorities on the part of victims.

The corruption-conditioning effect reinforces and follows on from the reputation effect. Again, the more established a criminal organization is in time and space, the more its corrupt practices can change in nature, both quantitatively and, above all, qualitatively. Quantitatively, the criminal organization's financial cover can enable it to corrupt at more or less high levels, sometimes reaching the very top of the State, as in the case of so-called "narco-States", that is with States aiming for a drip-feed of dirty money. From a qualitative point of view, the effect is just as important, and often overlooked in an approach based on methodological individualism. Yet it also generates systemic, regular, and, precisely, organizational corruption. Corruption ceases to be an interpersonal relationship between corruptor and corrupted, that is a relationship subject to renegotiation on a case-by-case basis. It becomes the relationship between a criminal organization – backed by the reputation effect – and society. Each affiliated member can then become the bearer of the corruption link on behalf of his organization. Regular conditioning relationships then develop which, for the strongest forms of criminal organization, can lead to reciprocal exchange relationships, notably with the political sphere but also with the legal private sphere. In such extreme cases, it is hard to tell who is asking, as the corrupt pact is so beneficial to both parties. The Italians use the term "bargaining vote" (*voto di scambio*)[11] to refer to this situation, where mafiosi who are in a position to control bundles of votes offer them to the politician who, once elected, returns the favor by awarding public contracts or, more trivially, places in crèches or retirement homes, changing town-planning schemes to make areas suitable for building, granting permission for the construction of shopping centers, and so on.

Criminal organizations can also leverage their economic power by developing a sense of belonging. This ability to create associative links varies according to the type of organization involved: bands are rather loose (Reuter (1983) even speaks of disorganized crime), gangs tend to be more structured in terms of affiliation, and the strongest criminal organizations develop initiation rites prefiguring "life and death" affiliations. At the very least, the effect of membership makes it possible to delimit who is and who is not a member. It ensures a certain visibility for members internally, and sometimes externally too, in cases where members use conspicuous distinctive signs such as tattoos. The larger the group, the greater the risk of defection or betrayal. The belonging effect aims to counteract the risks associated with numbers. It seeks to create a common feeling in order to ensure the loyalty of members. As with any organization, or going concern, this loyalty is acquired through the existence of working rules guiding the behavior of members, compliance with which is guaranteed by a system of sanctions deemed credible. For instance, the tradition of cutting off the little finger *(yubitsume)* among Japanese yakuza refers not to criminal affiliation, but to a punishment for disobedience and an acknowledgment by the person thus mutilated of his error. The "repressive" aspect can be complemented by more "incentive" measures. Some organizations offer protection schemes for criminals, in particular by guaranteeing an income for the family in the event of imprisonment.

Depending on their ability to develop one or more of the three effects described earlier, criminal organizations will be situated closer or further away from the strongest form of criminal organization on the organizational continuum. This idea of continuum reflects the diversity of the actors involved. It fits in with the study of organizations as developed by original institutionalism. In particular, it ties in with Dugger's (1992) reflections on the notion of "stateness". Just as the State is a strong form of organization, criminal organizations develop more or less assertive forms of stateness. As long as these organizations are characterized by the "existence of some kind of permanent governing apparatus that serves as an arbiter for a wide group, controls the use of violence for that group, and establishes and maintains social provisioning processes sufficient to sustain the group materially" (Dugger, 1992, p. 88), they partake of stateness. The more a criminal organization succeeds in offering these State-like services, the more it is able to exercise power, including economic power. This is not least because, as Dugger points out, the market and the State are not separate or antagonistic entities. If we allow criminal organizations to develop their stateness (including by focusing on their illegal economic activities without taking into account the interweaving with the legal and political sphere), then we accept to give them a power that is problematic for democracy and for common trust in institutions. Dugger's lines in the following are fundamental to understanding the extent to which original institutionalism can transform crime economics, both in terms of understanding organizations and their impact and thus in adapting the fight to the real issues at stake:

> controlling violence is not the real issue. Establishing the economy is. The legitimacy of a state is intimately connected to how well it establishes and maintains

> the social provisioning processes that sustain its population. State use and control of violence may be necessary but they are not sufficient. State power and state legitimacy are tied to the security, the sufficiency, and the perceived equity of the social provisioning processes promoted and stabilized by the state. . . . the street gang's power and legitimacy extends only so far as it provides security, sufficiency, and equity to its members. That is, its power and legitimacy extend only so far as it can stabilize and protect a sufficient economic foundation for its membership. And its sovereignty – its ability to settle disputes – does not depend ultimately on its control of violence, but on its ability to establish a secure, sufficient, and equitable economy for its membership.
>
> *(Dugger, 1992, p. 100)*

This quotation reminds us that the question of security is crucial in Commons' thinking. If the individual finds this security through membership of a criminal organization, then it is to the latter that he will give his allegiance, to the detriment of State institutions. The choice of criminal behavior goes beyond a simple *hic et nunc* cost–benefit calculation. Even if the expected economic gain from affiliation is a factor, it is not the only motivation. What is more, affiliation in turn influences people's habits of thought, shaping future behavior. Affiliation also transforms members' will-in-action: it provides members alone with access to certain economic opportunities and resources, which are all the more important when the effects of reputation, corruption – conditioning, and belonging are strong. What affiliates gain is not only financial but also expressed in terms of power. Power, which can be based on wealth, shapes the economy and influences the way it operates. This can be seen not only in the illegal sphere (Chapter 5) but also in the legal sphere (Chapters 6 and 7).

Notes

1. Judge Falcone reported in Falcone and Padovani (1992) his astonishment at the chance discovery of the Madonia family's account book, which listed all the sums periodically deducted by the clan from various local entrepreneurs and traders. In the end, the sums were very modest, sometimes around 200 euros a month, even though Cosa nostra was at the same time at the heart of the drug trade.
2. Whereas preferences are exogenous data in rational choice theory and thus in Becker (1968).
3. For Veblen, the history of Western societies can be divided into four phases: the savage age, the barbaric age, the artisan age, and the machine age.
4. Veblen links industry to the instinct of workmanship: the aim is to provide material services capable of satisfying man's primordial needs. Business, on the contrary, develops a pecuniary logic of predatory inspiration: the aim is to make money by arousing envy, even if this means encouraging the production and consumption of non-essential goods of an ostentatious nature.
5. By mafia *stricto sensu,* I mean certain particularly powerful criminal organizations as defined in article 416 bis of the Italian Penal Code. An extract from this article is particularly revealing of the singularity of these criminal organizations: "An association

is mafia-like when those who belong to it use the intimidating *force of the associative bond* and the condition of *subjection* and *omerta* that derives from it to commit crimes, to *acquire directly or indirectly the management or at least the control over economic activities*, concessions, authorizations, tenders and public services, or to make unfair profits or advantages for oneself or others, or to *prevent or hinder the free exercise of the vote* or to procure votes for oneself or others in electoral consultations" (my emphasis).

6 The words of Sicilian justice collaborator Antonino Calderone are, in this respect, edifying: "You'll forgive me for making this distinction between the mafia and common delinquency, but I insist on it. All Mafiosi insist on it. It's important: we're mafiosi, the others are just ordinary men. We are men of honor. And not so much because we've taken an oath, but because we're the criminal elite. We are quite superior to common delinquents. We are the worst of them all" (in Arlacchi, 1992, p. 5). For more on justifying myths in mafias, see Champeyrache (2007, pp. 35–68).

7 As an example, in his autobiography, Michel Lepage, a member of the Banlieue Sud gang in the Paris region, recounts: "Our gang works hard, especially as we have to face multiple expenses related to the run, but not only: with my friends, we develop a taste for clothes, cars, good restaurants, and our outings become more and more expensive" (2011, p. 109). This remark is more akin to the conspicuous consumption described by Veblen than to the capital-accumulating behavior characteristic of the capitalist logic put forward by the classics and Marxists.

8 Particularly harsh prison regime (article 41 bis of the Italian Penitentiary Code) for mafia bosses who refuse to cooperate with justice.

9 See, in particular, the memorandum of understanding signed in November 2019 between the parties involved in the initiative: protocollo_dintesa_liberi_di_scegliere_5_nov_2019.pdf (minori.gov.it) (accessed 01/22/2024).

10 Milan Juvenile Court, decree November 15, 2018.

11 This offence of "politico-mafia electoral exchange" is defined in article 416 ter of the Italian Penal Code.

References

Akers, Ronald L., *Deviant Behavior; a Social Learning Approach*, Belmont: Wadsworth Pub. Co, 1973.

Akers, Ronald L., *Criminological Theories: Introduction and Evaluation*, Los Angeles: Roxbury Publishing, 1994.

Albanese, Jay, "The Causes of Organized Crime", *Journal of Contemporary Criminal Justice*, 16, 2000, 409–423.

Arlacchi, Pino, *Gli uomini del disonore*, Milan: Mondadori, 1992.

Becker, Gary, "Crime and Punishment: An Economic Approach", *Journal of Political Economy*, 76(2), 1968, 169–217.

Catanzaro, Raimondo, *Il delitto come impresa. Storia sociale della mafia*, Padoue: Liviana, 1988.

Champeyrache, Clotilde, *Sociétés du crime. Un tour du monde des mafias*, Paris: Cnrs Editions, 2007.

Champeyrache, Clotilde, "Gangs, cartels, mafias . . .: la grande famille de la criminalité organisée", *Cahiers de la Sécurité*, 8, 2009, 7–11.

Champeyrache, Clotilde, *La face cachée de l'économie. Néolibéralisme et criminalités*, Paris: Presses Universitaires de France, 2019.

Chin, Ko-lin, *Chinatown Gangs: Extortion, Enterprise, and Ethnicity*, New York: Oxford University Press, 1996.

Commons, John R., *The Economics of Collective Action*, New York: MacMillan, 1950.

Di Bella, Roberto, and Monica Zapelli, *Liberi di scegliere. La battaglia di un giudice minorile per liberare i ragazzi della 'ndrangheta*, Milan: Rizzoli, 2019.

Dugger, William M., "An Evolutionary Theory of the State and the Market", in William M. Dugger and William T. Waller, Jr. (eds.), *The Stratified State. Radical Institutionalist Theories of Participation and Duality*, New York and London: M. E. Sharpe, 1992, 87–115.
Gambetta, Diego, *The Sicilian Mafia: The Business of Private Protection*, Cambridge, MA: Harvard University Press, 1993.
Josephson, Matthew, *The Robber Barons. The Great American Capitalists*, New York: Amereon Ltd, 1940.
Knight, Franck, *The Ethics of Competition*, New York: Harper Brothers, 1935.
Lepage, Michel, *Banlieue Sud. Ma vie de Gangster*, Paris: J'ai Lu, 2011.
Medema, Steven G., "Commons, Sovereignty, and the Legal Basis of the Economic System", in Warren J. Samuels (ed.), *The Founding of Institutional Economics. The Leisure Class and Sovereignty*, London and New York: Routledge, 1998, 97–114.
Miller, Edythe S., "Veblen and Commons and the Concept of Community", in Warren J. Samuels (ed.), *The Founding of Institutional Economics. The Leisure Class and Sovereignty*, London and New York: Routledge, 1998, 14–29.
Reuter, Peter, *Disorganized Crime: The Economics of the Visible Hand*, Cambridge, MA: MIT Press, 1983.
Shelley, Louise, *Dark Commerce. How a New Illicit Economy is Threatening Our Future*, Oxford: Princeton University Press, 2018.
Sutherland, Edwin H., "White-Collar Criminality", *American Sociological Review*, 5, 1939, 1–12.
Tarde, Gabriel, *Les lois de l'imitation: étude sociologique*, Paris: Félix Alcan, 1890.
Veblen, Thorstein, *Theory of the Leisure Class: An Economic Study of Institutions*, New York: MacMillan, 1899.
Violante, Luciano, *Il ciclo mafioso*, Rome and Bari: Laterza, 2002.
Waller, William T., "Economic Security and the State", in William M. Dugger and William T. Waller, Jr. (eds.), *The Stratified State. Radical Institutionalist Theories of Participation and Duality*, New York and London: M. E. Sharpe, 1992, 153–171.

5

ILLEGAL MARKETS

An evolutionary and cooperative view

When we think of the criminal economy, we think first and foremost of illegal markets and trafficking. It is therefore only logical that a chapter should be devoted to these issues. The contribution of the original institutional approach is to deconstruct the conventional stereotypes stemming from traditional crime economics. In this respect, Schelling's 1967 article structured the dominant thinking by associating – often more peremptorily than Schelling states – illegal markets with monopoly and violence. Drawing in particular on the concepts of legal-economic nexus and power, I shall emphasize that the empirical reality of the criminal economy points instead to a strong capacity for internal cooperation and external conditioning. This translates into less recourse to overt violence, both to manage trafficking and to impose certain activities on the non-criminal population. However, not all criminal organizations have the same capacity to do without violence. Understanding the strategies behind the greater or lesser use of violence thus becomes a source of information on the nature of the criminal organizations observed. Paradoxically, it is not the use of violence that determines power. This has implications for the way we approach the fight against organized crime. Moreover, the issue of violence connects directly with another contribution of original institutionalism: the emphasis on evolutionary aspects restores the temporal dynamics of organized crime and its various activities. The criminal economy evolves in line with the legal, economic, and technological context. Criminal organizations themselves evolve and adapt, including in response to criminal sanctions: the quantitative approach of cost–benefit analysis, which associates greater dissuasion in choosing law infringement as the probability and/or cost of punishment increases, is replaced by a qualitative approach in which it is the structuring of agents and organizations that is transformed in response to greater repression. What emerges is an evolutionary and largely cooperative illegal economy, far removed from the

DOI: 10.4324/9781003350958-8

clichés of crime. This new picture needs to be understood in order to adapt public policy instruments.

A pacified economic illegal world?

The association between organized crime and violence is widespread, and not just among economists. The problem arises when the use of violence becomes the characteristic systematically regarded as inseparable from organized crime. By its very nature, violence is more readily used when agents are operating in a lawless world. This being said, many illegal activities do not require the use of violence, or even need to avoid it in order to run smoothly. Thus, Gassin (2003) defines crime – whether committed individually or in groups – fundamentally as a disturbance of the social order; he associates this disturbance with the use of various means, including violence but also guile. This relativization of violence and emphasis on guile is important insofar as it allows us to reintegrate into our thinking aspects of the criminal economy that are too often neglected as being difficult to analyze in market terms. These include frauds (welfare fraud, subsidy fraud, tax fraud, insurance fraud, health fraud, excise fraud, etc.), swindling, and some thefts. In view of this dimension of the criminal economy, it is important not to make violence the benchmark indicator of criminal activity. Even activities such as racketeering cannot sustainably and systematically be associated with the deployment of violence, as I will come back to below. This observation is reinforced from an evolutionary perspective. Thus, when Volkov (2002) describes the emergence of a "class of violent entrepreneurs"[1] to explain how criminal activities plagued the Russian economy, his analysis is valid for a specific moment in Russian history and economy, that of the savage transition from the Soviet system to the market economy. The criminal is not systematically an entrepreneur of violence. Indeed, the second-half 2022 report by the DIA, Direzione Investigativa Antimafia (Anti-Mafia Investigation Department), underlines the continuing tendency of Italian mafias to resort less to violence:

> The investigative evidence gathered so far confirms that mafia-type criminal organizations, in their relentless process of adaptation to the changing contexts, have implemented relational capabilities by replacing the increasingly residual use of violence with strategies of silent infiltration and with corrupt and intimidating actions.
>
> *(DIA, 2022–2, p. 8)*

Redimensioning the place of violence is fundamental to understanding the illegal economy. But this does not mean denying it. On the contrary, the question of violence makes it possible to mobilize the original institutional approach in order to understand how criminal organizations are articulated, how they hierarchize, and how they position themselves economically and politically. By political positioning, we do not mean the adoption of this or that ideology, but the development of a specific relationship with politics, or even the development of forms of criminal "stateness" (Dugger, 1992).

The violence of criminal organizations can be directed against affiliates or members of other criminal organizations or against the rest of the population. The stakes are not the same, nor are the consequences. While settling scores between criminals can be tolerated on the principle of "let them kill each other", violence against non-affiliates is likely to provoke a reaction from the population and law enforcement agencies and thus ultimately be detrimental to trafficking. Criminal organizations, especially the most powerful, understand this challenge. As the DIA report points out: "the modus operandi of the Australian 'ndrangheta, which has assumed a leading role in cannabis cultivation and the importation of other drugs, is characterized by a limited use of violence in order to avoid attracting the attention of the Authorities" (DIA, 2022–2, p. 349). However, this rationalization of the use of violence cannot be deployed so easily by all criminal organizations. This is where the logic of rational calculation (whether or not it is opportune to employ violent methods) is only relevant in reconnection with the original institutional logic.

Indeed, the use of violence to carry out illegal activities reveals the criminal organization's position in the criminal hierarchy, the durability of its establishment, and ultimately its degree of institutionalization. Thus, the longer a criminal association is established, the greater its level of stateness. We might even consider that mafias are very similar to States in their relationship to the use of violence. A parallel can indeed be drawn insofar as a State holds the "monopoly of violence": yet the legitimacy that normally surrounds the State means that the actual exercise of violence becomes the exception rather than the rule. The recognized right to resort to violence, and the credibility of such recourse, render State violence useless in most cases. The same applies to mafias. Thanks to the reputation and conditioning they have established as a strong form of criminal organization (see Chapter 4), the threat of violence is sufficient to dissuade many from questioning the mafia order. This contributes to the institutionalization of mafias both in the illegal world and in the territories they control. It explains why an illegal activity traditionally associated with violence, such as racketeering – as emphasized not only by Schelling (1967) but also by Volkov (2002) and others – can also be carried out without violence or even denunciation. A map drawn up on the basis of – admittedly patchy – data on forms of racketeering in Sicily shows a wide diversity of situations depending on the different families at work and therefore the territories (Champeyrache, 2013). In addition to showing that there is no unitary Cosa nostra structure that dictates how families should behave in their respective territories, this mapping indicates that there are areas where racketeering is practiced systematically (virtually all shops and businesses are racketeered on a regular basis) with an extremely low level of violence (attacks on people and/or property). For instance, the provinces of Palermo and Catania, where Cosa nostra has traditionally operated, can generally do without violence.

On the contrary, in the province of Messina, where the mafia's presence is more recent and its territorial sovereignty is contested by other organized criminal groups (including the 'ndrangheta, whose territory borders Messina via the Strait of Messina), it is still necessary to use sporadically violence to obtain payment of the racket. The level of denunciations recorded by law enforcement agencies and associations also reveals the degree of power wielded by the criminal organization. The acceptance of racketeering proves that criminal power is *de facto* accepted in some territories.

In short, there is a dimension of temporality and sovereignty that conditions the relevance of resorting to violence. The way in which a territory is racketeered cannot really be explained by a cost–benefit calculation made by the racketeer, but it does provide crucial information for a better understanding of the nature of the criminal organizations operating there. If the racketeering is accompanied by violence, this may betray a criminal organization that is emerging or, on the contrary, declining, or even being challenged by a competitor. In contrast, a non-violent racket indicates a criminal organization with established power. At the same time, the denunciations made by the victim are evidence of a still healthy economy or, in some cases, of a territorial recomposition of crime, resulting in double racketeering phenomena (the same person is ordered to pay by two rival organizations with territorial pretensions), driving victims to exasperation.

Paradoxically, the ability to gain acceptance for racketeering can also be a major step in the conquest of new territory and the expansion of criminal power. The configuration is extreme, but there is at least one case in which a criminal organization has succeeded in its strategy of infiltrating the legal economic sphere through racketeering. It is the case of the Calabrian 'ndrangheta in Emilia-Romagna in northern Italy. The mechanisms described by Dalla Chiesa and Cabras (2019) are explicit in demonstrating how an illegal economic activity served to enclose part of the legal economy in the nets of crime. The 'ndranghetists proposed a formula in which the sums paid for racketeering were the subject of false invoices (thanks to legal companies owned by the mafiosi), which enabled the victims of racketeering to partially offset their costs but also prevented them from denouncing the facts, as they themselves were guilty of tax fraud.

Schelling (1967) associated violence with obtaining monopolistic situations. While this may well apply to the first attempts at racketeering a territory, as we have just seen, it does not necessarily apply over time. Above all, it does not apply to all illegal activities. On the contrary, empirical observation of the main illegal markets shows a proliferation of players. This is borne out by various reports published by the UNODC.[2] Different empirical evidence shows that the criminal world is characterized by increased cooperation between criminal organizations, by delegation phenomena, and by tacit recognition of hierarchies between criminal groups. It would be totally naive and wrong to say that criminal organizations have totally renounced violence. But it would be equally misleading to consider that violence to eliminate competition is the only way to manage relations between these groups. Understanding the cooperative dimension of today's criminal organizations is essential to understanding the workings of the illegal economy, and therefore to adapting the means of combating it. Three examples illustrate this multi-player cooperation in illegal markets: human trafficking, with its exploitation of illegal migration, narcotics, and cybercrime.

When it comes to transnational illegal migration orchestrated by criminal organizations, a 2020 UNODC report established a typology of the various players involved and highlighted their multiplicity. Three categories were identified:

- Small-scale service providers: on the bangs of organized crime because they are often isolated individuals who operate on an *ad hoc* basis, these agents generally earn only small profits and exploit – as a means of subsistence and/or as a complement to a legal activity – momentary opportunities linked to their positioning in border or transit zones.
- Loose networks with no strict hierarchy: they are able to intervene in parts of the human exploitation process (e.g., to ensure part of the journey, such as crossing the Mediterranean or the Sahara) and maintain business relations with non-exclusive smugglers, with a significant intermediation dimension.
- Large-scale criminal operators with a clear hierarchy: they are able to organize sophisticated, transnational operations, including complete packages from the point of departure to the point of arrival (transport and accommodation logistics along the entire route, provision of false papers and documents, corruption of the authorities, care on arrival, possibly including the management of forced-crime-type jobs where the migrant is forced into prostitution, drug dealing, or other criminal activities).

These different players depict a market that is anything but monopolistic. The UNODC report also highlights the fact that, far from fighting each other for exclusive market share, the players are developing strategies of cooperation and interdependence. The first two categories position themselves as service providers or subcontractors for other, more seasoned criminal groups. Less developed criminal groups may therefore only be active locally while participating in international trafficking.

These criminal cooperative links are even more obvious in the case of narcotics, even though there is still a strong illusion that this is typically a monopoly market. This preconception is largely conveyed by the misleading term "drug cartels", which is no longer appropriate to describe the current configuration in South America. In the booklet devoted to "Special points of interest" for the UNODC's World Drug Report 2023,[3] the issue of the fragmented structure of the narcotics market features prominently. It states:

> Fragmenting supply chains and loosely connected criminal groups are driving the expansion of drug supply, notably cocaine, with new hubs and markets, as

> well as increasing use in traditional markets. Trafficking groups are less rigid and hierarchical, and more innovative and adaptable.
>
> *(UNODC, 2024, p. 12)*

As a result, the global supply organization is extremely resilient, with the possibility of replacing supply chains without major difficulty. The report also mentions that "drug trafficking groups are increasingly fragmented, managing only parts of the drug supply chain" (UNODC, 2024, p. 13). Concentration in illegal markets seems the exception rather than the rule.

In the field of cybercrime, "ransomware as a service" also seems to be based on a logic of cooperation rather than monopolistic concentration. Indeed, ransomware designers allow external players to use these tools without mastering the technical skills required to design them. This is achieved through subscriptions (often a monthly payment for a flat fee or with a percent of the profits given to the ransomware creator) or rental systems (such as a one-time license fee). This creates an ecosystem with a wide range of players of different kinds and skills.

What is even more interesting is that this fragmentation goes hand in hand with a logic of market and sector sharing. This makes once again the illegal economy far less conflictual than economists often tend to think. This is a new element in favor of a crime economics based on the notion of organizations and their working rules. It also strengthens the case for thinking in terms of institutional hierarchy and emulation. In these strategies of sharing and cooperation, not all criminal organizations have the same bargaining power, and some are in a position to condition others, define the boundaries of their activity, or even instrumentalize them. For example, the Ironside operation carried out in 2021 by Australian law enforcement agencies uncovered criminal cooperation between 'ndrangheta families based in Australia and local criminal groups, in a pattern that highlighted the domination of the Calabrian mafia. This information is echoed by the Italian DIA's report for the second half of 2022, which states that in Australia the 'ndrangheta is in the habit of "resorting to the actions of other criminal gangs, such as motorcycle gangs, for marginal illicit activities" (DIA, 2022–2, p. 329). In particular, motorcycle gangs work on behalf of Calabrian crime in the distribution of narcotics to end consumers. This is clearly a subordinate position, and it demonstrates the criminal organization's ability to manage lucrative economic activities while developing a logic of power. The press release published by AFP, Australian Federal Police,[4] is very clear in this respect. It states:

> 'Ndrangheta members regularly collaborate with other organised crime groups, such as outlaw motorcycle gangs, Asian organised crime groups and Middle Eastern organised crime groups to assist with the facilitation of criminal activity, including drug importations, money laundering, tobacco distribution and acts of violence,

but also

> The 'Ndrangheta are flooding Australia with illicit drugs and are pulling the strings of Australian outlaw motorcycle gangs, who are behind some of the most significant violence in our communities. They have become so powerful in Australia that they almost own some OMCG's (Outlaw MotorCycle Gangs), who will move drugs around for their 'Ndrangheta financiers, or carry out acts of violence on behalf of the 'Ndrangheta.

I will come back to the evolutionary dimension of these strategies of cooperation/subordination later on, as they reveal an institutional logic of differentiation between strata, with phenomena of recognition of the superiority of certain actors, but also, through cooperation, learning effects that promote both the criminal values and the methods carried by the dominant criminal organizations.

If the Australian police have been able to partly trace these interrelationships in the world of illegality, it is thanks, in particular, to the decryption of messages exchanged by criminals via AN0M as they did not know it was a Trojan horse built by the FBI and AFP. The decryption of messages sent by criminals via EncroChat and Sky ECC also reveals a world of cooperation between criminals from different organizations. Millions of messages (120 million for EncroChat, several hundred million for Sky ECC) still have to be analyzed, revealing not only subcontracting relationships for certain services (notably the execution of murders) but also portage operations for drug deliveries so as to obtain better prices by ordering larger quantities.

Cooperation as an alternative to violent confrontation can be found in extremely diverse geographical areas, indicating a general trend rather than a singular configuration. For example, Rome's Chief Public Prosecutor, Francesco Lo Voi, interviewed by the Parliamentary Anti-Mafia Commission in July 2023, describes drug trafficking in the Italian capital as follows:

> In Rome we have a number of mafia-type criminal organizations some of which are linked with traditional mafias, operating throughout the region. These are joined by structured groups of another nature and origin. We have a robust presence of organized crime of Albanian origin that interfaces with local organized crime. We have a presence of Nigerian organized crime. So we have a co-presence of different kinds of organizations on a territory that is, yes, vast but has limits and then this territory has to be occupied, and therefore there is an alliance or some form of conflict opens up.[5]

The observation is not new. In 2018, the DIA's Report (DIA, 2018–1) also focused on Rome's criminal landscape. The general picture is also one of criminal profusion, with criminal organizations extremely diverse in their structures, origins, and activities. Broadly speaking, there are three main categories of players:

- Local criminal groups such as the Magliana gang, the Casamonica family (particularly involved in car fencing, drug trafficking, usury, extortion, fraud, real estate and business investments), and the Ostia families (extortion, usury, and drug trafficking);
- Mafia crime in the strict sense of the term, with a proven presence of Cosa nostra, camorra, and 'ndrangheta, particularly in connection with recycling, corruption, and investment in the legal economy;
- Finally, non-Italian criminal organizations are also widely represented: Chinese organized crime (multiplying front companies for tax evasion and money transfers to China), Albanian (rather specialized in robberies and hold-ups), Nigerian (for human trafficking), South American (active mainly in prostitution and the exploitation of Colombian and Brazilian transsexuals), North African (involved in illegal immigration networks), and criminal groups from the former USSR and Romania (notably involved in female prostitution and illegal or black market male labor in the construction industry).

Yet the density of crime in Rome goes hand in hand with a relatively low level of conflict, proof that these groups have been able to develop a widely accepted modus vivendi. Moreover, the DIA reports several cases of investigations highlighting alliances and cooperation between criminal organizations. For example, it is noted that the rise of the Casamonica family results not from the violent elimination of competition, but from a strategy of cooperation:

> Over the years, demonstrating a marked "relational" ability, the clan has managed to create important connections of mutual interest and support with other criminal organizations such as the mafia, camorra, and 'ndrangheta, as well as with other indigenous gangs.
>
> *(DIA, 2018–1, p. 429)*

Similarly, according to criminologist Valentin Pereda,

> The Sinaloa cartel maintains relations with criminal networks in several Canadian provinces. This alliance is often mediated by Mexican brokers, who reside temporarily or permanently in Canada, or even Canadian nationals establishing connections in Mexico with the cartel.[6]

In France, at the end of 2023, Customs investigators identified a money-laundering system in Aubervilliers, in the Paris suburbs, made available by Chinese organized crime to criminal networks holding cash of illicit origin.[7] Among the "clients" of this system are even Calabrian mafiosi. Operations take place behind a legal façade, Aubervilliers having developed a platform of Chinese wholesalers specializing in prêt-à-porter clothing. The situation in Ecuador also shows a country gangrenous with multiple criminal actors coexisting with episodes of violence but also with flexible cooperation. The survey published by Insight Crime in March 2024 describes a country that has become a major player in cocaine trafficking but is far from being characterized by the establishment of a violent monopoly:

> Sandwiched between the world's top cocaine producers, Colombia and Peru, Ecuador has become a hub and base for several transnational criminal networks. Its long coastline and large container ports make it a perfect launch pad for drug shipments heading to the United States and Europe. Colombian, Mexican, and Balkan drug trafficking organizations (DTOs) all have an established presence in the country.[8]

Violence is directed against the State when it tries to regain control of the territory, much less between criminal organizations. This process of building relatively peaceful cooperative relationships shows that ostensible violence is not a reliable indicator of the criminal threat, but also that it is the result of a criminal dynamic built up over time. There is therefore an evolutionary dimension to the illegal economy, with evolving trajectories that escape static accounting analysis.

An evolutionary illegal economy

Integrating the dynamic nature of the illegal economy into the analysis is essential to a comprehensive understanding of the phenomenon. Criminal organizations have a history that shapes and differentiates them from one another. They also adapt more or less well to the context in which they evolve. They reorganize to face new challenges; they also learn from their experiences and criminal partnerships; they also experience inertia, like all institutions in Veblen's sense, with sometimes archaic responses to new configurations. But, being less formally codified than official institutions, they are also undoubtedly more malleable, which does not prevent them from combining modern dimensions (where the emphasis is placed on what original institutionalism calls instrumental values) and traditional dimensions (based more on ceremonial dimensions). The study of the illegal economy must take this evolutionary capacity into account, so as not to remain anchored in old schemas that are ill-suited to the reality on the ground.

One of the main reasons why the illegal economy is evolutionary is the simple fact that laws, and therefore prohibitions, also fluctuate in time and space. What falls within the scope of the illegal economy evolves and must take into account the trajectories of legalization or liberalization of certain illegal markets, as well as the criminalization of activities initially considered legal. These evolutions create or destroy criminal opportunities; they not only make some organizations prosper but can also cause the loss of others. Such was the case with Prohibition in the

United States in the 1920s, which led to the rise to power of Al Capone and his bootlegging activities. But while the figure was legendary, the gangster's career lasted only about four years, with no organizational legacy (Reppetto, 2004). On the contrary, the ability of criminal organizations to adapt or not to a change in prohibition measures is an important indicator of the type of actors involved: a mafia-type organization is able to survive the loss of a trade (this also applies to the rise of a rival criminal organization capable of taking over a market), even if it is particularly lucrative, because it is never a single-activity organization.

As criminal organizations are human constructions, they evolve by combining the characteristics of institutions, namely, adaptation and inertia. Inertia relates to the deep-seated characteristics that have conditioned the emergence of the criminal organization in question. Thus, the initial positioning, even if it can be transformed, partly conditions the structure that the organization will assume, but also its way of managing its traffic. A mafia-type positioning implies a presence in both the legal and illegal spheres from the outset; the quest for power and the use of ceremonial values – such as, for example, the persistence of highly ritualized initiation ceremonies for members – will constitute benchmarks for the deployment of mafia activities. A young, single-activity criminal organization will be more likely to develop a profit-driven rationale, with behaviors and activities more strongly marked by short-termism on the one hand and opportunism, predation, and rejection of legality on the other, resulting in an investment in the legal sphere linked to the logic of money-laundering rather than territorial control (see Chapter 6 on the motivations of criminal investment in the legal productive economy). The ceremonial dimension of these criminal organizations is therefore less pronounced, which is also often reflected in the fact that they are less firmly rooted in the long term.

Alongside these factors of inertia, criminal organizations are resilient and integrate – successfully or not – new criminal opportunities, changes in the socio-economic and legal context, and new possibilities offered by technological advances. On this last point, we need only look at the impact of the Internet on organized crime, with Interpol rightly distinguishing between two main effects: on the one hand, the increased potential of existing criminal activities via "cyber-enabled crime", and on the other, the emergence of new illegal activities specific to the network and computers in the form of "cybercrime" or "high-tech crime". Many illegal activities have become internationalized as a result of globalization, with trafficking routes following trade routes. This globalization is evident in production, marketing, and even the composition of certain criminal organizations. Here again, however, not all criminal organizations exploit globalization in the same way, and there is no generalized pattern to the internationalization of crime. Moreover, organized crime is not systematically transnational: many criminal organizations operate on a national or even regional territory, possibly interacting with actors whose activities are geographically more extensive. The acceleration of economic liberalization in the 1990s enabled criminal organizations to potentially expand the markets they supply. This triggered industrialization dynamics in certain sectors, moving from small-scale production in clandestine workshops to mass production for export. The counterfeiting sector is the most emblematic of this transformation. The same applies to the growth of drug trafficking[9] with, for example, the saturation of the North American cocaine market offset by growth in European[10] consumption and, eventually, the capture of the African market. The internationalization of production goes hand in hand with the internationalization of consumption insofar as criminal organizations implement global value chains by breaking down the production process. The DEA clearly describes this internationalization of production in the case of fentanyl:

> While the cartels' operations are based in Mexico, DEA has identified more than 50 additional countries where these criminal networks operate. DEA has also traced the cartels' global supply chain around the world. The cartels purchase chemicals from companies in China, mass produce the fentanyl in Mexico, and then traffic and distribute finished fentanyl widely throughout the United States.[11]

The process is also marked in the case of cocaine, as we have moved from a situation where Latin American drug traffickers shipped a finished product to a production chain where refining laboratories can be relocated: the EMCDDA's European Drug Report 2023 mentions that, by 2021, Spain had dismantled 16 cocaine laboratories, Belgium 11 sites related to cocaine processing, and the Netherlands seven cocaine secondary extraction laboratories; to this can be added, still in the Netherlands, 14 cutting or packaging sites and major seizures (over 1,000 kilos) of precursor chemical potassium permanganate useful for refining happened in Belgium and the Netherlands.[12] This dynamic is sometimes accompanied by the globalization of criminal teams: mastery of techniques can be achieved through the migration of drug chemistry experts to conquer new markets, where they will work on behalf of criminal organizations operating in new territories. This logic can be seen, for example, in the transformation of the origins of the members of the so-called[13] "mocro-maffia" in the Netherlands: initially made up of people of Moroccan origin involved in cannabis trafficking, the criminal organization diversified into cocaine and other narcotics, and now includes Dutch and Surinamese nationals.

Globalization has indeed brought with it an increase in the number of criminal actors and a reorganization of trafficking. The use of global value chains, for example, also means the end of South American drug traffickers' stranglehold on cocaine trafficking. Although the term "cartel" is still used to describe drug trafficking, it implies representations that are disconnected from criminal reality. In November 2022, Europol announced the dismantling of a drug "super-cartel", presented as a network controlling around a third of the cocaine trade in Europe. It has to be said that, although the operation that led to the arrest of 49 people was a fundamental success, particularly from the point of view of international cooperation, consumers did not suffer the slightest shortage, contrary to what the term "super-cartel" should have implied. Here we find a tendency, already mentioned, of cognitive bias to try to fit reality in the field into the reassuring framework of what we think we know about a problem: the notion of cartel refers to what the traditional crime economics has inculcated. The original institutional approach, on the contrary, focuses on what the arrests tell us: the emergence of a system of criminal cooperation focusing on several networks with bridgeheads, specializations, and intermediations, which have the advantage of flexibility and resilience, enabling recompositions and the possibility for traffickers to reorganize very rapidly.

The information gleaned from Europol's operation shows a form of crowdsourcing resulting from the – non-formalized – association of members of different criminal organizations to exploit cocaine trafficking. Those involved[14] include people as varied as an Irish drug kingpin (Daniel Kinahan), an Italian camorrist leader (Raffaele Imperiale), a Moroccan-Dutch trafficker (Ridouan Taghi), and a Bosnian leader of the "Tito and Dino" clan (Mirza Gačanin). The aim of the cooperation was not to unite the criminal networks, but to negotiate jointly with each other's contacts to obtain degressive prices according to quantities. Far from following Schelling's logic of a monopoly favoring high prices, the criminal bosses via portage operations played up competition and seemed to join forces to co-finance shipments of goods. Gačanin had links with independent producers in Peru as well as with the Colombian Norte del Valle cartel; Imperiale benefited from connections not only with the camorra and 'ndrangheta in Italy but also with correspondents in Colombia such as the Urabeños; Taghi had developed commercial relations with Surinam and Colombia; finally, Kinahan had established contacts in Panama and with the Urabeños. The diversification of supplies shows both a varied criminal panorama and the possibility of cashing in on the eventual dismantling of a criminal network, including the supply of the raw material for cocaine.[15] The trials will hopefully reveal more about the workings of these agreements, their recurrence, and even the logic of loss-sharing in the event of seizures.

In a number of internationalized trafficking operations, intermediaries and emissaries are becoming increasingly important. Mandated by the criminal organization to which they belong, they are responsible for contractualizing transactions; they also manage subcontracting operations and coordinate joint portage operations. They therefore interact with criminals from different organizations, and when these relationships are maintained over time, they promote learning effects as well as emulation. In the case of Ecuador, for example, the redeployment of drug trafficking to this territory and the subsequent arrival of these emissaries from drug importers have had an impact on local criminal structuring. An InsightCrime investigation into foreign criminal activity in Ecuador describes a situation where "By paying Ecuadorian transport groups, dispatch networks, chain gangs, hitmen, and corrupt officials, foreign groups have spurred the development of sophisticated and powerful homegrown networks in Ecuador and helped weaken institutions".[16] Colombian, Mexican, and Albanian groups now operate in Ecuador. The Colombians subcontract local criminal networks to store, transport, and load cocaine for shipment to wholesale buyers. The Mexican Sinaloa cartel is present in the form of representatives who, according to the investigation, are dispatched for short, fixed periods to conclude contracts with Colombian suppliers and Ecuadorian transporters, ensure proper execution, and make cash payments. The strategy adopted by the Sinaloa Cartel in Ecuador is indicative of the ability of logistics to adapt and evolve in order to ensure business continuity: previously present in the territory on a permanent basis, the cartel has diversified its commercial partners and rotated its emissaries. This makes it more difficult for law enforcement agencies to identify them and also allows them to use different service providers, diversifying their modes of transport and working methods. Albanian criminal operators have also experienced an evolutionary rise in power. Initially commissioned by the Italian 'ndrangheta to handle cocaine shipments to Europe, they are said to have freed themselves from mafia control in the space of some fifteen years. They, too, have developed inclusive contractual relationships with Ecuadorian criminal networks, competing on price but also, in the field of the illegal economy, on the criminal group's reputation for reliability.

Fentanyl trafficking also relies on this crucial broker figure. Another InsightCrime survey establishes a typology of brokers of the precursor chemicals needed to produce fentanyl[17]:

- Facilitators bring buyers and sellers together.
- The wholesalers buy the precursor chemicals, store them in hidden warehouses, and then distribute them to the various drug production networks.
- Employees at chemical plants use their profession to divert chemicals for criminal networks.
- Custom brokers put their professional position at the service of traffic coverage.

The result is a fragmentation of actors and complex interrelationships; all the more so as some of these brokers (notably employees and customs officers) are not necessarily affiliated to a criminal organization. This means that illegality is spreading beyond organized crime *stricto sensu*, a major institutional issue that will be explored in greater detail in Chapter 7. But these criminal connivances – between criminal organizations and with outside participants – once again encourage the use of cooperative rather than confrontational logics. The fact that Chinese criminal organizations have largely become launderers of the dirty money of numerous non-Chinese criminal organizations, for example, creates convergences of interests between organizations that previously developed business independently of each other. This "crumbling" of crime, far from being a sign of weakness, highlights the issue of institutional hierarchies. Criminal organizations do not cooperate on an equal footing. Activities are delegated for the benefit of the most powerful criminal organizations and may involve a strategy of potential sacrifice on the bangs. The dominant criminal organizations will capture the strategic activities of intermediation and wholesaling, that is, the most profitable but also the least conspicuous. In narcotics trafficking, the most visible link is the one from the distributor to the end consumer, via dealing points: this link runs the greatest risk of arrest and conviction. Drug traffickers have an interest in subcontracting these perilous operations, in order to complicate the task of tracing the networks. Drug-dealer networks have themselves integrated this logic when they call in intermittent drug dealers at deal points and for home deliveries: idle youngsters lured by the promise of easy money, minors, illegal immigrants, and sometimes even victims of forced criminality. In the event of arrest, these people have no relevant information to provide about the agents and structure of the trafficking network.

Hierarchies within the criminal world are not immutable either. We saw this with the independence of the Albanian clans from the 'ndrangheta. Against a backdrop of expanding narcotics markets, this trajectory did not result in the expulsion of the Calabrian mafia, but in a sharing of markets. It is therefore possible for a criminal organization to grow in power, without involving any concentration on a given illegal market. In terms of the evolution of criminal organizations, the development of diversification (within a sector of activity: e.g., South American drug traffickers investing in the field of synthetic drugs, the mocro-maffia expanding from cannabis to hard drugs), or even poly-activity can be observed. The creation of a logistical route (knowledge of the route, provision of warehouses, a corruptive network, etc.) can lead the criminal organization to make it profitable by circulating several different illegal goods. Poly-activity also guarantees greater resilience, as it can result from the reinvestment of illegal profits in new illegal activities. Above all, it forces researchers and analysts to put purely market-based reasoning into perspective. Just as criminal organizations are interwoven, so are illegal markets, far more so than is often thought. The involvement of some criminal organizations in several illegal activities simultaneously is extremely varied in terms of interlocking logic:

- There can be a direct connection: drug trafficking is logically accompanied by arms trafficking.
- There can be new overlaps: drug trafficking develops bridges to human trafficking when it uses forced criminality for the most exposed activities.
- Finally, there can be a complete disconnection (as is the case with mafias) when a criminal organization operates on different illegal markets without any obvious complementarity or synergy: for example, when there is drug trafficking and waste trafficking.

These different configurations – which can also combine – lead us to rethink the illegal economy in a more global way, and to focus more on the actors and less on the markets alone.

Relativizing market-based reasoning also helps to reintroduce dynamics other than the quest for profit. The original institutional approach is indeed capable of highlighting the capacity of criminal organizations to create social consensus and exercise an alternative power, including through practices that Gary Becker would consider economically irrational. The issue of racketeering deserves to be revisited. If we look more specifically at the systematic, capillary type of racketeering, as practiced in certain mafia territories, we may well wonder about its economic opportunity. This type of extortion, which is regularly repeated and affects a very large proportion of a territory's entrepreneurs and shopkeepers, requires the repeated deployment several times a year of heavy human logistics: the manpower and time required to collect the sums demanded, and to resort to intimidation or even violence in the event of resistance, are not negligible. This is sometimes done for relatively small sums – according to the principle of "make them pay little but make them all pay" – which will certainly serve to remunerate the personnel used without necessarily generating any real profits. In fact, Judge Giovanni Falcone was astonished when he discovered a mafia family's account book listing all the sums extorted: in the end, they were very modest and ridiculous compared with the profits that Cosa nostra was making from heroin trafficking at the time (Falcone and Padovani, 1992). The justification for the maintenance of racketeering by a criminal organization that had become extremely wealthy lay not in any supposed economic rationality, but in a quest for territorial power. Giovanni Falcone's colleague, Judge Paolo Borsellino, perfectly sums up the importance of power for mafia organizations when he explains:

> even in those moments [of the 1986 maxi-trial] and even when there were mafia criminal families earning hundreds and hundreds, if not thousands and thousands of billions [of lire] from the trafficking of narcotic substances, these same families did not neglect to continue to carry out what were the essential activities of mafia crime, because drugs were not and never have been. The fundamental characteristic of mafia crime, which some call territoriality, can be summed up in the claim not to have but to be the territory, just as the territory is part of the State, so that the State "is" a territory and does not "have" a territory, given that the territory is an essential component of the State. The mafia family has never forgotten that one of its essential characteristics is to exercise full sovereignty over a given territory.
>
> *(Collettivo, 1992, p. 28)*

As another form of economic irrationality explained by a logic of power, criminal organizations offered genuine social services during the COVID health crisis: food baskets were distributed by the brother of a mafia boss in the sensitive Zen district of Palermo[18]; at the same time, the sister of drug trafficker El Chapo launched a campaign to distribute food and masks marked with the logo of his company El Chapo 701[19]; in Japan too, the yakuzas offered assistance to the population.[20] The list could be even longer. These charitable activities serve to establish criminal power, make it acceptable, and win the population's at least tacit support. Consequently, "coercion is becoming less necessary as the power of the mafia is increasingly secure and unnoticed, relying on voluntary submission by others"

(Champeyrache, 2014, p. 636). Obviously, not all criminal organizations have the capacity to provide these services in part or in full on a non-repayable basis. Only the most powerful can use this power strategy. It is interesting to note that the quest for profit is not necessarily an end in itself, but a means to conquer and/or retain power. This is a complex dimension where the economic meets the political. This means taking into account the worrying fact that the illegal economy is a problem not just of illegal enrichment but also of disruption of the foundations of our societies and democracies. This is all the more true when criminal power is also exercised in the legal sphere, turning mafia organizations into veritable territorial rulers through privatization of the law such that criminals end up defining the working rules of an economy and a society (Champeyrache, 2022).

Public policy implications

The scope of the illegal economy is immense and expands as new regulations open the way to new ways of circumventing them. This chapter does not pretend to describe all the illegal markets, but, in keeping with the original institutional approach to crime economics, it focuses on current dynamics that challenge conventional wisdom on how these markets operate (strict economic rationality, violence, and monopoly). These dynamics call into question the way in which economists can suggest ways of combating organized crime. The aim is to be operational; the proposals are also a function of the dynamics observed at the time of writing. The evolutionary nature of crime means that anti-crime measures need to be rethought on a regular basis. There is no single pattern of deterrence or repression that is valid at all times and in all places. Observing reality calls for modesty, but also vigilance. Only an empirical understanding of the workings of the illegal economy and ongoing monitoring of criminal trends will bear fruit in the development of policies to combat it. It is not a question of claiming to annihilate crime. That would be like claiming to annihilate man's predatory instinct. Rather, the aim is to better define the issues at stake and to exploit what the logics of institutional hierarchy, cooperation, and power can teach us.

The abundant evidence of cooperation between criminal organizations must be understood as a hindrance to the activities of law enforcement and judicial authorities. The UNODC's World Drug Report 2023 underlines this point in the case of drug trafficking: "Transformations in the ways that criminal groups are organized or operate may make them less susceptible to traditional law enforcement interventions, as parts of the supply chain or product can be replaced" (UNODC, 2024, Booklet 1 "Special points of interest", 12).[21] However, taking note of these new configurations is useful. Effectively combating drug trafficking, for example, means targeting the intermediary who carries out the wholesale trade rather than the small retail dealer. Hit-and-run operations against drug dealing centers are part of a short-term policy that is incapable of drying up the markets: dealing points will be recreated, alternative delivery methods (such as the "uberization" of drug trafficking) will develop, quantities seized will be modest, arrests unlikely to feed criminal intelligence and – with limited resources available – law enforcement agencies will be exhausted by an endless battle and the justice system by court congestion without any real disruption to trafficking.

Targeting the major players in drug trafficking, at the very top of the criminal hierarchy, calls for greater international cooperation in terms of information sharing, rapid action, and the harmonization of procedures and evidence. As the UNODC points out:

> Drug trafficking groups are increasingly fragmented, managing only parts of the drug supply chain, and law enforcement operations can be effective only if they target the wider ecosystem of illicit markets rather than single cells or single shipments. This requires sophisticated operational analysis and trust-building within and between national law enforcement agencies in order to share intelligence and ensure smooth and prompt national and international cooperation when required.
>
> *(2024, p. 13)*

This applies much more broadly than just to drug trafficking. This cooperation will be all the more fruitful if it can free itself from reasoning too constrained by the logic of silos. Focusing on the notion of the market is not the most relevant approach; as we have seen, it prevents an overall vision of criminal systems. A closer focus on criminal organizations is required to identify their institutional characteristics, their capacity for coercion and persuasion, their working rules, and their ability to promote criminal values. Analysis of the dynamics of criminal organizations would gain in relevance and the targeting of the fight in finesse. By way of illustration, let us look at an example of a criminal evolution whose misinterpretation could lead to a misdiagnosis. Since around the mid-2010s, in the Ballarò district of Palermo, cradle of the Sicilian Cosa nostra, residents could observe that street prostitution and drug retailing had passed into the hands of Nigerian criminal networks. A market-focused analysis suggested that this signified a loss of power for the Sicilian mafia, replaced by new, younger, and more violent actors. Police investigations contradicted this thesis, identifying the existence of what came to be known as the "Ballarò Pact" (DIA, 2020–2).[22] Actually, the Nigerian networks obtained authorization from the mafia families to operate in a territory that remained under mafia control. This delegation of criminal services is done in return for the payment of a compensatory sum. Cosa nostra thus retains control of the territory and taxes illegal activities, thus exerting a hierarchical ascendancy. Moreover, a dual protection strategy cannot be ruled out. Dealing and street prostitution are visible activities that expose those who practice them to the risk of arrest and conviction. By delegating, Cosa nostra protects itself against this risk. At the same time, these activities are seen as dirty and inconsistent with the myth of the "honorability of crime" developed by Cosa nostra. By not appearing visibly in these trades, the mafia families cultivate the myth of respectability and even instrumentalize racism by diverting any public anger against these trades to easier targets. The practice seems to be confirmed in other regions, leading the DIA to consider that "in the southern regions [of Italy], foreign organizations act in a subordinate manner or with the agreement of national mafia clans, including through the granting of a quantum as recognition of territorial sovereignty" (DIA, 2019–2, p. 611).

The multiplication of layers of actors in the trafficking business allows criminal organizations to activate a strategy that hinders police investigations into the most powerful criminal organizations. This process of fragmentation increasingly involves actors at the end of the chain who are not very well integrated into organized crime, or who are not affiliated with even an extremely loose structure: social networks, the instrumentalization of consumers to turn them into resellers, the use of online services to promote, market and ship goods (drugs, counterfeit goods, etc.) and services (notably prostitution) online, all help to recruit workers to be exploited without transferring any knowledge of how criminal organizations and activities operate. But a market-based reasoning, especially when the market is reduced to its idealized vision of the unmediated encounter between supply and demand, condemns us to see only the latter segment. Breaking out of this vision restores the patterns of interaction between criminal organizations and also enables us to envisage probable future dynamics, notably the rise to power through learning effects of certain criminal groups in direct contact with the top of the criminal hierarchy. With better targeting, the ability to combat trafficking should increase, enabling more disruptive action to be taken against trafficking. This would transform the question of whether or not to legalize. By reaffirming the importance of abiding by the law, an effective anti-crime policy would make it possible to reassess the arguments, including the non-economic ones, which underpinned the introduction of prohibitive measures.

As already said, to be effective, such a policy relies on international cooperation. It still needs to be improved, and may even be difficult to implement between some countries (due to a lack of political will or antagonism, the absence of extradition agreements, etc.). Cooperation must therefore also be complemented by the reintroduction of the notion of frontiers: not only symbolic frontiers between legality and illegality but also physical and logistical frontiers. A great deal of trafficking takes the form of flows of goods crossing territories. Materiality and territoriality are major entry points for effective action. Controlling flows, particularly through customs, remains a major challenge. It is a reminder that our economies, driven by the liberal credo, have all too often sacrificed security in favor of a poorly defined economic efficiency. The operation of major commercial ports is a perfect illustration of this problematic position, as narcotics, counterfeit goods (including potentially dangerous products such as engine parts, medicines, and electrical or electronic devices), smuggled weapons, protected species of fauna and flora, waste disguised as second-hand exports, and so on transit through them without any real risk of seizure (see, e.g., Sergi, 2020). The ports of Antwerp and

Rotterdam control only around 2% of incoming goods, while the figure for French ports is barely 4–5%. This is a general trend, with ports competing fiercely to capture more and more container ships. It results in gigantic infrastructures, massive capacity investments, and a predilection for the fastest possible containership handling methods. In Europe, the port of Rotterdam prides itself on working 24 hours a day, seven days a week, and handling a container every six seconds. These speeds are incompatible with container control. Checking takes time: the goods (which may be perishable, which explains why drug traffickers like to mix cocaine with loads of fresh produce and frozen foods) have to be unpacked or repacked, and specific procedures must be followed, depending on the nature of the products. Controls also mean a potential loss of money as goods are immobilized. The resulting slowdown in business makes the port less attractive, at least that's the argument put forward by ports to keep inspection levels as low as possible. This short-term economic logic, with its emphasis on the smooth flow of goods and profits, fails to take into account the medium- to long-term risks posed by the massive influx of illegal goods.

The importance and urgency of rethinking the trade-off between economic efficiency and security paradoxically leads us to analyze the criminal economy also through the prism of the legal economy.

Notes

1 He describes this emergence as the fact that "seemingly different groups were all engaged in the same activities: they intimidated, protected, gathered information, settled disputes, gave guarantees, enforced contracts, and imposed taxes. Their similarity . . . was derived from the management of the same resource: organized violence. Hence I called them violent entrepreneurs and their activity violent entrepreneurship" (Volkov, 2002, p. 5).
2 See www.unodc.org/unodc/en/index.html.
3 World Drug Report 2023, ONUDC, Booklet 1 "Special points of interest": Special_Points_WDR2023_web_DP.pdf (unodc.org).
4 See www.afp.gov.au/news-centre/media-release/afp-target-italian-organised-crime-and-money-laundering-year-operation.
5 *La Repubblica*, July 12, 2023: Lo Voi: "Droga a Roma fuori controllo, domanda enorme. A Palermo solo Cosa nostra, nella capitale una serie di mafie" – la Repubblica.
6 Quoted in Libre Média, September 18, 2023: https://libre-media.com/articles/reportage-dans-le-sinaloa-au-coeur-de-lempire-du-crime-12.
7 See, for example, *20 Minutes*, September 23, 2023: www.20minutes.fr/paris/4054304–20230923-aubervilliers-entre-reseaux-chinois-blanchiment-argent-grossistes-textile.
8 Unmasking the Foreign Players on Ecuador's Criminal Chessboard (insightcrime.org).
9 In its annual World Drug Reports, the UNODC highlights this observed increase in the use of narcotics worldwide: in 2010, there were an estimated 226 million drug users in the world, a figure that rises to around 284 million by 2020, representing an increase of 26%. Moreover, the UNODC considers that the trend will continue to rise in the future, forecasting +40% by 2030 in Africa and +11% by 2030 worldwide (UNODC, 2021).
10 Always difficult to quantify, the rise in cocaine consumption is reflected in several indicators: the growth in number and value of drug seizures (in 2021, EU Member States reported 68,000 seizures of cocaine amounting to a historically high 303 tons, compared

with 211 tons in 2020), the results of analyses of wastewater and syringes used by drug addicts, and the number of people admitted for treatment (EMCDDA, 2023).

11 Year in Review: DEA Innovates to Fight Fentanyl.

12 www.emcdda.europa.eu/publications/european-drug-report/2023/cocaine_en.

13 A name coined by journalists, the term actually refers to a nebulous group of criminal networks initially of Moroccan origin (hence the prefix mocro), which distinguished itself by violent settlements of accounts in the Netherlands and Belgium from the late 2010s onward.

14 Pending their trial, these people remain presumed innocent.

15 See Was a Super Cartel Really Controlling Europe's Drug Trade? (insightcrime.org).

16 Unmasking the Foreign Players on Ecuador's Criminal Chessboard (insightcrime.org).

17 Brokers: Lynchpins of the Precursor Chemical Flow to Mexico (insightcrime.org).

18 The affair had been reported by a journalist who was subsequently threatened, as reported in the article in La Repubblica, Palermo edition, of April 8, 2020: https://palermo.repubblica.it/cronaca/2020/04/08/news/il_fratello_del_boss_su_fb_orgoglioso_di_essere_mafioso_giornalisti_peggio_del_coronavirus_-253480726/.

19 See https://lanouvelletribune.info/2020/04/el-chapo-la-fille-du-baron-de-la-drogue-fait-un-geste-envers-les-plus-demunis/.

20 www.lefigaro.fr/vox/monde/japon-l-influence-persistante-des-yakuzas-se-verifie-a-l-occasion-de-la-crise-sanitaire-20200520.

21 Special_Points_WDR2023_web_DP.pdf (unodc.org).

22 See also: La Repubblica, Palermo edition, February 8, 2021: https://palermo.repubblica.it/cronaca/2021/02/08/news/ballaro_le_mafie_nigeriane_spadroneggiano_con_la_complicita_della_mafia_locale-286542294/ and the 2020 Showdown survey.

References

Champeyrache, Clotilde, "L'économie mafieuse: entre principe de territorialité et extraterritorialité", *Hérodote*, 151(4), 2013, 83–101.

Champeyrache, Clotilde, "Artificial Scarcity, Power, and the Italian Mafia", *Journal of Economic Issues*, XLVIII(3), 2014, 625–639.

Champeyrache, Clotilde, "Institutional Mistrust, Instrumental Trust and the Privatization of Law: The Mafia as a Territorial Ruler", *Journal of Economic Issues*, 56(4), 2022, 945–958.

Collettivo, *Magistrati in Sicilia. Interventi pubblici di Giovanni Falcone e Paolo Borsellino a Palermo*, Palerme and Sao Paulo: Ila Palma, 1992.

Dalla Chiesa, Nando, and Federica Cabras, *Rosso Mafia. La 'ndrangheta a Reggio Emilia*, Florence and Milan: Bompiani, 2019.

Direzione Investigativa Antimafia, *Relazione Semestrale*, Rome, 2018–1.

Direzione Investigativa Antimafia, *Relazione Semestrale*, Rome, 2019–2.

Direzione Investigativa Antimafia, *Relazione Semestrale*, Rome, 2020–2.

Direzione Investigativa Antimafia, *Relazione Semestrale*, Rome, 2022–2.

Dugger, William M., "An Evolutionary Theory of the State and the Market", in William M. Dugger and William T. Waller, Jr. (eds.), *The Stratified State. Radical Institutionalist Theories of Participation and Duality*, New York and London: M. E. Sharpe, 1992, 87–115.

European Monitoring Centre for Drugs and Drug Addiction, *European Drug Report 2023: Trends and Developments*, 2023. www.emcdda.europa.eu/publications/european-drug-report/2023_en

Falcone, Giovanni, and Michelle Padovani, *Cose di Cosa Nostra*, Milan: Rizzoli, 1992.

Gassin, Raymond, *Criminologie*, Paris: Dalloz, 2003.

Reppetto, Thomas A., *American Mafia: A History of Its Rise to Power*, New York: Henry Holt, 2004.

Schelling, Thomas C., “Economics and Criminal Enterprise”, *The Public Interest*, 7, 1967, 61–78.
Sergi, Anna, *The Port-Crime Interface: A Report on Organised Crime & Corruption in Seaports*, Independently Published, 2020.
UNODC, *Global Report on Trafficking in Persons 2020*, 2020 (United Nations Publication, Sales No. E.20.IV.3). www.unodc.org/documents/data-and-analysis/tip/2021/GLOTiP_2020_15jan_web.pdf
UNODC, *World Drug Report 2020*, 2021. https://wdr.unodc.org/wdr2020/en/index2020.html
UNODC, *World Drug Report 2023*, 2024 (Special_Points_WDR2023_web_DP.pdf (unodc.org)). https://www.unodc.org/unodc/en/data-and-analysis/world-drug-report-2023.html
Volkov, Vadim, *Violent Entrepreneurs. The Use of Force in the Making of Russian Capitalism*, New York: Cornell University Press, 2002.

6

THE INFILTRATION OF LEGITIMATE BUSINESSES

Beyond money laundering, a power issue

The – somewhat reassuring – conviction that the legal and illegal worlds are watertight is widespread among many economists. This leads to a dichotomous reasoning in which the two spheres exist in juxtaposition. When interrelations are nevertheless recognized between the two spheres, they are often underestimated. Thus, the circulation of illegal gains in the legal economy is regularly reduced to a mechanical logic of dirty financial flows. The market is also seen as capable of protecting itself against the criminal threat: its competitive mechanisms should, in theory, enable it either to transform the criminal agent into one who conforms to the "normal" behavior expected in the legal sphere or to expel him. This chapter aims to move away from this irenic vision of the economic world. By reintroducing the question of power in economics, original institutionalism renews the analysis of criminal infiltration of the legal economy. It shows that the criminal presence in legal businesses is not limited to masking the dirty origin of criminal capital, that flows constitute stocks, and that the resulting patrimonial dimension confers a conditioning capacity on the most powerful criminal organizations. Mobilizing the notion of legal-economic nexus is fundamental to understanding the real economic stakes involved in asserting – via the legal economy – criminal orders that undermine State sovereignty. This has an impact on the way investigators view organized crime and on the deployment of anti-crime policies.

Why criminals infiltrate the legal economy

The starting point for thinking about the presence of criminals in the legal economy is to ask why criminals choose to invest in the legal sphere. This is all the more true given that, from a strictly profit-seeking perspective, it is astonishing to consider

DOI: 10.4324/9781003350958-9

that criminals can invest in legal activities with returns that are often far less attractive than those provided by illegal activities.

On the whole, criminal infiltration of legal activities is a marginal topic, even among crime economists. Anderson (1979) is one of the earliest works on the subject, which served as a basis for subsequent analyses. This book deals with a Cosa nostra family in the United States and its illegal and legal activities. The thesis developed is that the criminal dimension is weakening due to the lack of a new generation to take over the illegal business. Anderson thus tends to put forward a trajectory that I call the "redemption of the criminal" through legal activities. If this trajectory is possible – in reality more at the individual than the collective level – its generalization is extremely dubious, as I will come back to, especially when dealing with strong forms of criminal organizations. In any case, Anderson also enumerates the underlying motivations for criminal investment in the legal economy, namely:

- Legal activities generate legitimate income that can be used to cover up genuine illegal activities.
- Legal businesses – particularly small shops, bars, and restaurants – provide a basis for loan-sharking and illegal betting.
- Legal businesses can be a way to integrate outputs and inputs that are needed in both legal and illegal activities; this is the case of transport companies and warehouses.
- They can help internalize the laundering of dirty money.
- They may simply serve a portfolio diversification strategy: legal activities often involve not only lower profits than illegal ones but also less risk.

Although varied, the list drawn up is limited to a purely one-sided relationship between the legal and illegal spheres. In fact, in all these possibilities, legal activity appears to be functional and/or subordinate to an illegal activity (legally qualified as the source activity in the case of money laundering). The infiltration of the legal economy would then be secondary for criminals and criminal organizations. This is misleading on several levels. For example, it leads to believe that all dirty money must be laundered, ignoring the fact that a significant quantity of these illicit gains circulates in the legal economy without the slightest operation to disguise their illegal origin: this is notably the case for salaries paid to criminals, bribes, and recurring small sums spent on day-to-day consumption. This standpoint also makes the flows unidirectional, whereas the interrelations between the legal and illegal economies are multiple and go in both directions. This observation has been made by national statistical systems too, following the inequalities observed at year-end between uses and resources by national statistical institutes around the world. Thus, for example, the 2008 System of National Accounts stresses "The incomes generated by illegal production may be disposed of quite legally, while conversely, expenditures on illegal goods and services may be made out of funds obtained quite legally" (Banque Mondiale et al., 2013, p. 101).[1] We therefore need to reintroduce the capacity of the legal economy to feed the illegal economy, because there are indeed flows of legal income spent on the purchase of illegal goods and services, but we need to go even further by considering legal activities for their own sake while integrating the evolutionary dimension. Over time, flows can constitute stocks. The patrimonial dimension takes us away from the instantaneity of flows and their relative anonymity and brings back to the forefront the construction of power relations through ownership, especially when ownership relates to companies. The original institutional approach thus makes tangible another dimension of criminal investment in the legal economy: presence in the legal economy can be sought for its own sake (and not because it is useful to illegal activities), notably in a quest for power. In this case, the raison d'être of businesses owned by criminals is no longer necessarily profit or may only be profit as a tool for acquiring power. In some cases, the pursuit of profit is no longer the end, but the means, of criminal activity. Original institutionalism is perfectly capable of identifying these logics denied by mainstream crime economics.

To summarize, Champeyrache (2016, p. 75) points to three main motivations for criminal infiltration of the legal economy. These are the functionality of legal versus illegal activity, risk minimization, and territorial control. The first two are (somewhat) addressed by some mainstream economists, and the third – the most problematic – is not.

The functionality of legal activities is in line with the aforementioned logic. Investment in the legal sphere depends directly on illegal activities. One of the motivations is to seek cover by claiming social status, especially in the event of police investigations. Of course, legal activity can also be used to launder dirty money. This so-called "low-intensity" laundering has the advantage of internalizing the operation without having to go through intermediaries or resort to highly technical set-ups. This type of laundering is therefore low-cost but cannot be used to launder very large sums unless an extensive network of businesses is available. The markets targeted will mainly be those where it is easy to declare sums in cash and where it is complex (or time-consuming) to verify the effectiveness of the declared activity. As these businesses are subject to a significant risk of confiscation, it is also preferable that they require only a small initial capital investment. Small shops, bars, restaurants, and nightclubs are ideal targets. Functionality can also have a logistical dimension. Here too, internalizing activities such as transport or storage is a strategic choice aiming at controlling the risks of defection and betrayal.

The strategy of risk minimization amounts to turning the criminal into a sort of "good family man" who carefully diversifies his portfolio of activities in order to secure his earnings and eventually pass them on. From a theoretical point of view, this motivation is based on the aforementioned notion of "aleatory property rights" (Reuter, 1983). It is the same as that invoked in the thesis of the criminal's redemption through legal activities, where the security of the latter would accompany a gradual exit from the criminal career. While such a trajectory does exist – for example, in the case of migrants who are initially forced to live on sometimes illegal expedients but then succeed in becoming legal – it is far from systematic. What is more, it applies poorly to criminals who are part of strong criminal organizations and is strongly undermined by measures to confiscate criminal assets. As a result, it has become less relevant since the introduction of patrimonial investigations. When it does come into play, the target sectors are mainly those protected from competition, as criminal entrepreneurs are not necessarily highly skilled in the legal economy. The ideal situation is to capture public contracts (in the building and civil engineering industry, but also in cleaning and maintenance and other public services) to ensure a guaranteed return with high barriers to entry thanks to corruption.

Last but not least, an option overlooked by economists who deny power issues in economics, investment in the legal economy can serve to consolidate territorial control and build social legitimacy favorable to criminal organizations. This motivation can only be implemented by the most powerful organizations, but it is crucial to understanding the systemic risk that organized crime can represent. Through this type of infiltration, criminal organizations – and especially mafias in the strict sense of the term – seek not so much profit as power. Businesses owned by criminals need to focus on the use of local resources, first and foremost labor, in order to gain a foothold in the territory through job creation and income distribution. Logically, labor-intensive activities are favored, particularly for unskilled or low-skilled jobs, which explains why building and civil engineering and agriculture recur so frequently among the controlled activities. Building and public works also have the specificity of opening a door to political corruption, in order to monopolize public contracts in exchange for the conditioning of elections. The economic processes used to turn criminal infiltration of the legal economy into an instrument of power are clearly identifiable in the case of mafias and are revealed by the tools of original institutionalism.

Control over the territory

Criminal infiltration of legitimate businesses for the purposes of territorial control escapes the logic of both methodological individualism (it is a manifestation of collective action) and economic rationality (profit, while not excluded, is not the primary goal; the quest is immaterial, as it is about power). On the contrary, it fully mobilizes concepts typical of original institutionalism, in particular the artificial scarcity evoked by Veblen and the power to withhold conferred by property dear to Commons. In both cases, the process works because it relies on individuals – in this case, criminals – organized as a collective – the criminal organization – obeying common rules and pursuing interests that are both individual and collective, interests that are opposed to the interests of individuals outside this collective.

Mainstream economics has made scarcity an important reference point. Robbins (1932) even describes economics as "the science which studies human behavior as a relationship between ends and scarce means which have alternative uses". But two points are worth noting. The first is that this scarcity, thanks to the market, does not produce conflict or asymmetry of power. This is the irenic vision of a pacified economic world presented in Chapter 1. The second point concerns the "natural" origin of this scarcity: while human needs are potentially infinite, material resources are available in finite quantities. This scarcity is therefore a quantitative and exogenous constraint; moreover, it is imposed evenly on everyone. Obviously, such a kind of scarcity does exist, but it does not describe the full range of scarcities that constrain economic agents. This is where original institutionalism brings in a new element: artificial scarcity refers to a scarcity socially created by an institution or a group of people. Instrumental, it can serve as a tool for the collective capable of constructing it. We owe Veblen in particular for having identified this issue, even if his contribution is not always fully recognized, as Clark points out when he states that "the social creation of scarcity is one of the most important and least recognized insights of the founder of institutional economics – Thorstein Veblen" (Clark, 2002, p. 418). In Veblen's work, the creation of scarcity is seen in two ways: via 'conspicuous consumption' (Veblen, 1899, chapter IV) and via 'industrial sabotage' (Veblen, 1921). Conspicuous consumption – as we saw in Chapter 4 – refers to the consumption of goods that confer social status, rather than those designed to satisfy essential needs. It is the rarity of these goods that confers social distinction on those who can afford them. Galbraith (1967) takes up this idea when he develops the concept of the "revised sequence", by which the modern corporation contributes to feeding a socially created scarcity to the benefit of the leisure class. To this, we can add "industrial sabotage", that is, monopolistic industrial concentration, which uses voluntary limitation of production to raise prices and thus increase profits. At the macroeconomic level, these two phenomena lead to a collectively unsatisfactory situation, as essential needs are not being met as a matter of priority.

Recognition of artificial scarcity implies moving away from the view of the market as a natural order and admitting that the market as a human construct is political in nature. Indeed, artificial scarcity does not uniformly constrain all agents. It is created to strike at those outside the group and to favor the interests of the group creating it and its members. It is therefore a source of conflicts of interest. The emergence of new forms of conflict calls for the development of new working rules, which can lead to the establishment of a new order. But to understand this dynamic, we need to look at the power stakes associated with the ability of certain individuals to form a group and carry weight in the face of others who are themselves disorganized. Yet the market, far from being a meeting place for free and equal agents, lends itself particularly well to such opposition between collectives and isolated individuals. Dugger (1989) explains that markets are fundamentally two-sided: one side is collectivized, and the other is decollectivized, because at least one market participant is an organization rather than an individual. Logically, even if mainstream economics does not admit it, "the collective participant is far more powerful than the individual participant, which is why collectivization takes place" (Dugger, 1989, p. 610). Without rebalancing, an asymmetry of power is established in favor of the collectivized part of the market.

Artificial scarcity can serve to reinforce this asymmetry by accentuating the segmentation of the various market actors. The impact on the bargaining power of the various participants is then differentiated and instrumentalized for the purposes of exercising economic power. As a result, competition will be based on personal characteristics, as *de facto* the collectivized part of the market that implements a strategy of artificial scarcity obtains the power to discriminate between participants in market transactions. The beneficiaries of artificial scarcity can, if they wish, monopolize resources and reap surpluses. Other participants – unless they adopt compromising attitudes – suffer scarcity and shortages. This affects the range of opportunities to which they have effective access, as well as the expression of their will-in-action. Without even resorting to physical violence, a space of coercion is created for agents capable of structuring and implementing artificial scarcity. The conquest of this economic power has every chance of going unnoticed, and the free market is totally incapable of defending itself alone against such phenomena.

In a previous paper (Champeyrache, 2014), I explain how the mafias specifically use artificial scarcity when infiltrating legal businesses. This mode of operation not only governs relations between members of the criminal organization but also regulates relations with non-affiliates.

Internally, legal mafia-owned companies – particularly those in the number-one target sector, the civil engineering sector – succeed in driving out non-mafia building contractors by capturing public contracts through bribery (in the Italian case, through the "vote of exchange" (*voto di scambio*) already mentioned). They, then, divide the "loot" among themselves. Existing data on businesses confiscated from organized crime (see, in particular, for Italy, a pioneering country in the seizure of criminal assets, the Transcrime report, 2013) show that the criminal organizations concerned favor the multiplicity of small businesses. This contradicts the view of organized crime as a monopolistic structure. On the contrary, it reinforces the thesis of the importance of controlling a territory in infiltrating the legal economy. The multiplicity of small businesses likely to work in a network actually reflects the workings and organizational structure of the criminal organization (see Catino, 2019). Mafias are not unitary, pyramidal structures; the Italian justice system has defined the 'ndrangheta, the Calabrian mafia, as a "horizontal-vertical structure". In concrete terms, this means that the criminal organization relies on a group of autonomous, sovereign families, each with its own territory, which is controlled in a capillary fashion. The criminal organization has also set up a number of consultative and supervisory bodies to deal with issues that go beyond the territory of a single family or that are on a large scale, and also in order to be able to settle internally any disputes that, if resolved by violence, would attract the attention of law enforcement agencies and harm mafia activities. However, the role of these umbrella structures should not be overestimated; they do not establish a top-down, pyramid-like relationship.

Mafia-owned companies are a reflection of the families that own them. The internal workings of the organization involve the establishment of a "waiting line" system (Gambetta, 1993, pp. 201–202, 214–217) and common working rules for managing subcontractors according to territorial distribution criteria. As a result, mafia firms in the construction industry take their place in line to win contracts in turn. The company that wins the public contract may also use subcontractors to pool profits, but also to respect the territorial sovereignty of each clan. This territorial sharing of work was particularly highlighted following the construction of the A3 Reggio di Calabria – Salerno freeway: each section of the freeway had been built by a company controlled by the mafia family concerned by the territory crossed (see Champeyrache, 2014, pp. 632–633).

The markets that criminals manage to capture are at the expense of non-criminal entrepreneurs. Artificial scarcity therefore also works against the unorganized part of the market. It even goes beyond the logic of capture to establish a logic of conditioning. In this way, criminal entrepreneurs are able to exert economic power over other economic agents. In this case, the rules specific to the criminal organization are not only imposed on its members but are also at least partially imposed on non-members. This process is more clearly visible when the criminal infiltration of a sector is partial and targeted at key activities in the production chain. In the case of the construction industry – even outside the public sector – two activities are strategic in terms of conditioning the industry: the marketing of concrete and earthmoving equipment. It is on these strategic investments that we can graft what Commons has called (again in a context unrelated to the criminal issue) the exercise of the "power to withhold from others what they need but do not own".

Let us take the example of investment in the field of production and commercialization of concrete. Failing to deliver goods to a construction site, failing to deliver on time, or even simply threatening not to deliver illustrates how criminals can impose their conditions in the legal sphere on non-criminals. Control over the delivery of a product essential to the continuation of work becomes the power to impose the award of subcontracts, to place labor or suppliers, and to impose transactions and economic relationships which, without this economic power, would not have been chosen. Without directly controlling the companies in the entire supply chain, the criminal organization can condition them. In this way, it effectively controls the supply chain, without this being clearly detected. All the more so since, from a formal point of view, delivery delays can be officially justified by supposed technical problems. Police investigations have shown that this conditioning capacity can even be deployed in non-original territories. The conditioning is then exerted on the diaspora. By way of example, Operation Stige (2018) against the Calabrian mafia families of Cirò uncovered ramifications in Germany: Calabrian restaurateurs based in the Baden-Württemberg and Hesse regions were forced to source their wine from a company controlled by the 'ndrangheta, the Cav Malena Pasquale Srl (DIA, 2018–1, 2018–2, p. 429).

Holding property rights to specific resources enables mafia members to exercise monopolistic control over these resources, while markets appear to be atomistic, with a large number of small businesses operating in them. Artificial scarcity consists in making resources scarce for non-mafia members. This process combines with what Commons calls "the power to withhold" allowing Mafiosi to deny non-mafiosi access to certain economic opportunities. Conversely, for non-affiliates of the criminal organization who choose to enter into a relationship of complicity, access to economic opportunities can be – at least partially – restored. Artificial scarcity in action leads to a whole range of behaviors for the population: subjugation is just one variant, and active complicity is another. This makes it extremely complex to establish the exact nature of the relationship between criminals and non-criminals in the legal economic sphere. This complexity is directly linked to the difficulty of apprehending the manifestations of power relations in the dominant economic reasoning.

Another example of the conditioning power exerted by the most powerful criminal organizations comes from the Italian mafias (in particular the Neapolitan camorra and the Calabrian 'ndrangheta) in a very specific economic field, as it interferes directly with the public sphere and, once again, involves the creation of scarcity and its instrumentalization. It is the case of the mafia's *de facto* takeover of the management of low-income housing in areas controlled by the mafia.[2] In theory, the mafia has nothing to do with the management of the market for the allocation of low-income housing, but empirically it is able to exploit the inefficiency of public services (fueled by a demand for social housing that outstrips the supply, and by excessively slow allocation procedures) to graft itself onto the system and select who will or will not have access to this housing. In order to artificially speed up the procedure, the population is then forced to turn to the mafia families. In the case of Calabria, the payment of 5,000–8,000 euros to the clan enabled them to occupy an apartment, an occupation that was then quickly regularized by the corrupt administration. Mafiosi also used the system to their advantage, taking over apartments that were sometimes left empty but made available in case they went on the run. The mechanisms of artificial scarcity, grafted onto an initial objective scarcity (the lack of social housing in deprived areas) and networks of corruption, clearly operate and enable mafia families to discriminate between those who do and those who do not have access to resources, by favoring affiliated members and that part of the population willing to compromise. The particularity of this situation lies in the fact that the mafia is able to condition access to a service over which it has no property rights. This gives them power over the population and over politics, since the objective pursued – and emphasized by one repentant member – is not so much enrichment as control over votes. Indeed, the "beneficiaries" of the system will also receive voting instructions in addition to the apartment.

Infiltration of the legal economy as an exercise of criminal power

Presence in the legal economy in the form of intermediation (as in the case of control over the allocation of social housing) or in the form of enterprises specifically aimed at territorial control does not mark a split between two types of activity – legal on the one hand and illegal on the other – as in the reasoning inspired by time allocation models (see Chapter 1). Such a presence stems from a process of exploitation of the "economic power of property" (Commons, 1924), a power that Commons distinguishes from the "physical power of sovereignty". This economic power stems from a change in the nature of property in our economies and transforms the relationship between State and company while impacting the expression of individual wills in the economic sphere.

In broad strokes, Commons (1924, pp. 6–7) describes the transformation of the nature of property as the shift from a simple principle of exclusive holding of physical objects for the owner's private use to a genuine power to withhold from others what they need but do not own. This transformation creates an asymmetry between owners and non-owners. The economy is no longer, or no longer only, characterized by "producing power", but by "bargaining power". Incidentally, this is reminiscent of Veblen's distinction between industry and business. Producing power aims to increase use-values, while bargaining power seeks to increase exchange-values (Commons, 1924, p. 21). The asymmetry of power induced by the new nature of property means that, contrary to the mainstream model, individuals are not on an equal footing in markets. In concrete terms, unequal economic power translates into differentiated capacities "to hold back until the opposite party consents to the bargain" (Commons, 1924, p. 54). Consequently, the actual content of individual free will will vary according to the relative bargaining power of each party.

In Chapter 3, I introduced the notion developed by Commons of "will-in-action", that is, will "continually overcoming resistance and choosing between different degrees of resistance, in actual time and space" (Commons, 1924, p. 69). The confrontation of different wills in action delineates the pattern of relative withholding capacity and thus the pattern of liberty and exposure (that is to say limit of a right) for participants in the market. In Commons' thinking, the asymmetry of power is linked to the advent of large corporations in the face of disorganized individuals (Commons, 1950, p. 269). More specifically, he illustrates it in terms of the employment relationship and the employer's ability to impose conditions on job seekers who have no real bargaining power, unless the State corrects the asymmetry by making certain clauses unfair. Commons does not deal with criminal issues. That said, the concepts and reasoning used provide relevant and innovative keys to understanding not only the full range of criminal motivations for infiltrating the legal economy and holding legitimate businesses but also how, in the most advanced circumstances of territorial control achieved thanks to the infiltration of the legal productive economy, this can contribute to the construction of an established criminal order. In this case, the criminal economy in the broadest sense (including the legal-criminal economy, that is to say, an economy where activities are legal, but ownership criminal) is not just a collection of illegal markets. It has a structural impact on the functioning of society, the economy, and politics, effectively changing the rules of the game. The impact is all the greater if the criminal organization has been able to develop its organizational advantages (reputation, corruption-conditioning, and membership effects), while the non-affiliated population remains unstructured, with no appropriate response from legitimate institutions, and no collective or association structures to become organized and resist.

The discrepancy between the will-in-vacuo of the dominant theory and the will-in-action actually resulting from the presence of businesses in criminal hands for the purposes of territorial control is not neutral for the local economy and development. In particular, two main forms of "deterrence effect" created by criminal organizations, especially mafia ones, following their presence in the legal productive sphere (Champeyrache, 2014), can be identified, namely:

- A sterilization of entrepreneurial potential in the areas concerned. The economic activity of non-criminals is hampered, and entrepreneurs may choose to forego growth in their business, or even reduce or abandon it. This forced choice is designed to avoid attracting the attention of criminals, so as not to be subject to excessive racketeering or even lose control over the business.
- A migration of talents (also evoked by Arlacchi (1983) in his seminal work on mafia enterprise) to territories uncontrolled by crime, so as to be able to exercise their skills in a less constrained way.

The collective action of criminals and the mobilization of the economic power conferred by the ownership of legitimate businesses enable the criminal organization to distort wills-in-action. This ability does not exist in mainstream models of crime economics. As a result, the impact of organized crime on the legal economy is totally underestimated, and the fragility of the latter in the face of criminal pressure is ignored. The strongest criminal organizations, especially mafias, are able to play on the fragile boundary between freedom and power. This echoes Knight's concern that "freedom to perform an act is meaningless unless the subject is in possession of the requisite means of action . . . the practical question is one of power rather than of formal freedom" (1929, p. 133). By mobilizing its power to withhold, the criminal organization shapes the exercise of other people's freedom and shapes effective access to economic opportunities to its own advantage. As long as the emphasis is placed on the market's capacity to be a vector of harmony and a meeting place for free wills, it is virtually impossible to detect the criminal conditioning capacity over the legal sector. The absence of violence made possible by the exercise of economic power makes the problem almost invisible. If nothing is done to protect individuals from the capacity for criminal conditioning, the State's "physical power of sovereignty" will be undermined by *a de facto* allegiance to the rules set by organized crime, rather than to the law.

The case of mafias is specific insofar as these are the criminal organizations that have best been able to deploy their power thanks to an evolution in their use of violence. The latter has been rationalized and largely replaced by artificial scarcity and conditioning induced by the power to withhold.[3] In this sense, it is even possible to consider that the part of article 416 bis of the Italian Penal Code which associates the strength of the associative bond in mafia-type associations with a capacity for subjugation is now partially obsolete. Mafia power is now more secure and unnoticed, increasingly based on voluntary submission. This makes mafias truly unofficial institutions capable of competing with the State. It is an evolution that is noticed by judges specialized in mafia-trials (see, e.g., Ardita, 2020).

The establishment of this quasi-State power is based on Veblenian principles of emulation and mystification. The ability to condition individuals within a territory is a source of status. Yet this status is not associated with the individual *per se*; it is a status genuinely associated with affiliation to the criminal organization. As described by Champeyrache (2021), the resulting process of legitimization becomes one of substitution, as the mafia *de facto* assumes certain prerogatives of the State. Gradually, this calls into question the hierarchy of going concerns, even though the State should be at the top of such a hierarchy:

> The general status law, the common law, the decisions of courts, in short, the working rules of the general government, are read into the articles of incorporation and into the transactions of principal and agent, employer and employee, stockholders, bondholders, patrons, clients, customers, so that the will of the state, or rather its working rules, perpetuate the rights, duties, liberties and exposures, within which the working rules of a subordinate concern are made up and its collective behavior goes along.
>
> *(Commons, 1924, p. 147)*

The use of economic power by mafias in the legal sphere alters the pattern of opportunities, rights, and exposures normally constructed by the State via the law. Continuing to believe that markets constitute natural orders contributes – paradoxically and, all too often, naively, if not cynically – to making this power exercised by criminals a power that is passively accepted, and sometimes even justified. Mafiosi use their legal businesses to build a form of social legitimacy that goes beyond the quest for profit. By creating jobs and distributing income, the criminal organization, perceived as legitimate, spreads its working rules outside the organization: non-affiliates tend to conform to the mafia's rules of the game too. This works all the more so when the criminal organization succeeds in exploiting State loopholes. This leads to the process of "mystification", which consists in distorting symbols. Negative values are transformed into positive ones, and adherence to mafia working rules (regardless of criminal affiliation) becomes a source of access to economic opportunities. Hodgson reminds us that respect for the law involves not only fear of punishment but also acceptance of its legitimacy when he writes "people

. . . obey laws not simply because of the sanctions involved but also because legal system can acquire the force of moral legitimacy and the moral support of others" (2006, p. 5). This observation can be applied to the configuration of territories under criminal control, with a transfer of legitimacy to illegal actors. In contrast to a discredited State, the mafia can succeed in overturning the hierarchy of going concerns and working rules. This can lead to the point where, *de facto,* criminal rules prevail over those of the State. We then enter a highly complex process of "privatization of the law" (Champeyrache, 2022), where the criminal organization (generally mafia) assumes the effective role of territorial ruler. In short,

> If the economic power of the Mafia remains unconstrained by the physical power of the State, the Mafia will stand as a competing sovereignty because it tends *de facto* to define rules and duties and, through artificial scarcity and the capacity to withhold, to determine who is to be excluded from what, a prerogative usually in the hands of the State. It is also a sovereignty intertwined with the political sovereignty of the State because the Mafia needs a weak State in order to offer supposedly alternative services in terms of protection, intermediation, and justice that are at the basis of the social legitimacy of Mafias.
>
> *(Champeyrache, 2022, p. 424)*

A reaction from the State is therefore essential. Otherwise, the economic power to withhold can undermine the physical power of sovereignty. The State's reaction must not be seen as a disruptive intrusion into the heart of a "naturally" well-functioning legal economy but, on the contrary, as protection for an extremely fragile legal economy that is disarmed in the face of the criminal threat. This means rethinking the fight against organized crime by taking full account of the power dimension.

Implications for the fight against organized crime: from flows to stocks

In order to fight organized crime and the criminal economy more effectively, it is important, on the one hand, to understand the threat in its globality and diversity and, on the other, to recognize that the State has a positive role to play. By positive, I mean a role that is not limited by a short-term accounting logic such as that imposed by cost–benefit analysis, and a role that is emancipatory in the sense that action goes beyond the mere repression of crime to restore opportunities to non-criminal economic agents and legitimacy to institutions.

The original institutional approach integrates the question of power into the analysis of crime. This has an impact on the underlying motivations for fighting crime. It is no longer a question of balancing costs and benefits, but of sovereignty, because the economy and the State are mutually constructed. The inequalities in economic power that criminal organizations sometimes methodically build up over the long term undermine the freedoms of disorganized individuals and the sovereignty of States. It is up to the State to make laws to limit the bargaining power of property where it seems excessive (Commons, 1924, p. 29). This is true, as Commons proved by his thought and deed, in the field of labor law; it is also true in the field of crime control, especially when we take into account criminal infiltration of the legal economy. The State may choose not to do so, either because it believes in the market's ability to get rid of or to discipline criminals on its own, or because, blinded by mainstream thinking, it underestimates the expansion of rival criminal sovereignty through enrichment in the illegal economy and conditioning in the legal economy. In this case, the State gives up investigating the ability of criminal organizations to withhold and allows the economic power of property to spread without restriction. The risk is that withholding becomes a "customary, legal, quiet way" to take something away from someone "under the institution of private property" (Commons, 1934, pp. 58–59). It is up to the State to identify and restrain economic power by exercising the physical power of sovereignty (Dawson, 1998). The State can do this because it is part of its prerogative; it must do so because the expansion of criminal economic power implies a transfer of sovereignty to criminal organizations.

In this context, the two main tools in the fight against organized crime, namely, the monitoring of financial flows and the seizure of criminal assets, can be reread and evaluated in very different ways from the traditional one. Despite some minor changes, the emphasis has largely been placed on monitoring financial flows in the fight against money laundering[4] rather than on seizure. Broadly speaking, the focus is on financial flows, and the effort is mainly directed at professions subject to suspicious transaction reporting obligations (generally financial institutions, the legal and accounting professions, traders in high-value goods, art and antiques dealers, voluntary public auction houses, dealers in precious metals and stones). A non-negligible proportion of the duty is therefore placed on people who, from the point of view of strict economic rationality, have no real interest in exercising extreme diligence, unless they fear the cost of punishment. This comment on the motivation of actors will be developed in greater detail in Chapter 7.

Conversely, the seizure of criminal assets is a mechanism that exists in most countries but is less widely publicized and applied. Its implementation relies on asset investigations requiring considerable human resources and time, which may explain why it is not sufficiently implemented. On the contrary, the actors involved in these investigations (law enforcement, customs, justice, etc.) are much more motivated by the success of their work. Above all, the seizure of criminal assets has the advantage of taking into account the lessons learned from crime economics inspired by original institutionalism. Indeed, by taking into consideration the stocks built up, rather than just the flows, it is possible to tackle the structural effect potentially created by criminal organizations. More simply, the confiscation of assets makes it possible to strike at all the dimensions of crime: both the accumulation of profit and the quest for power. With regard to the more specific issue of criminal infiltration of the legal economy, confiscation tackles the three motivations mentioned above. Money laundering and the fruits of money laundering are naturally targeted. The strategy of risk minimization loses its meaning when the seizure of assets makes property rights aleatory and uncertain for criminals in both the legal and the illegal spheres. Finally, confiscation, when it includes legal businesses, undermines the foundations of territorial control and the construction of a criminal social legitimacy.

If we take the example of the Italian law of 1982,[5] which is the most advanced patrimonial law in the world, the aim is not to attack isolated individuals, but to target criminal organizations through their members. The law strikes at the assets of individuals but does so because of their affiliation to a mafia-type organization (or terrorist organization, to be precise). The extension of measures to close relations (spouses, family members, close friends, etc.) also reflects the desire to take account of associative links. Moreover, the Italian law in fact reopens Posner's question[6] on the harm that criminals could do by investing in the legal economy, and answers that the investment itself is not reprehensible – which opens the way to the problem of reusing confiscated assets – but that it is the origin of the capital and the characteristics of the investors that are. The fact that all legal businesses in mafia hands, even those not involved in illegal activities, can be confiscated is revealing. What the Rognoni-La Torre law means is that there is no redemption for criminals through legal activities and that it is important to draw a clear line between the legal and illegal spheres. Giovanni Falcone, the anti-mafia judge, puts it bluntly:

> No, the illegally enriched Mafioso – and his descendants more than him – who has entered the legal economic world, is not an example of the mafia being absorbed and neutralized in society. Neither today, nor tomorrow. For one never ceases to be a mafioso. And as such, to refer to the laws and to use the violence typical of Cosa nostra, to retain a caste mentality, a feeling of belonging to a privileged stratum . . . . God knows, in my career I've seen some starving people become rich and successful entrepreneurs. But none of them ever gave up their affiliation or their mafia methods. Nor have their children. If it were just a question of banditry or urban gangsterism, it would be so much simpler.
>
> *(Falcone and Padovani, 1991, pp. 135–137)*

Fighting the mafias and strong criminal organizations aims at reducing or even breaking the power wielded by crime in the territory, preventing it from consolidating gains and legitimacy in the legal sphere.

Moreover, contrary to the Beckerian logic and the reductionist vision of the immediacy of financial flows, laws aiming at seizing criminal assets reintroduce the dynamic and temporal dimension of stock accumulation. In contrast to the model of individual, isolated arbitration, with penalties assessed in terms of their immediacy and proportionality to the offense committed, the 1982 Italian law introduced a form of retroactivity for penal sanctions and the accumulation of penalties. Preventive patrimonial measures, through the transition to confiscation, sterilize illicit gains, even though the illicit activities that gave rise to them had gone unnoticed by law enforcement agencies at the time they occurred. This is a form of retroactive sanction. What's more, the patrimonial dimension of the sanction makes it possible to punish not an isolated act, but a series of offenses, and thus a long-term pattern of criminal behavior (Champeyrache, 2004a, p. 147, 2004b). In this sense, the patrimonial dimension is able to respond to the economic power conferred by ownership.

We can even take this a step further, showing that the relevance of measures aiming at seizing criminal assets reflects the relevance of the legal-economic nexus. This was particularly apparent in the discussion that followed the first confiscations in Italy regarding the use that could be made of these assets afterward. It led jurists to assert a triptych: neutrality of assets – subjectivity of the individual – dangerousness of the network (Collettivo, 1998). For the original institutional economist, this triptych highlights the articulation of individual and collective dimensions. The neutrality of confiscated goods is validated by the objective of their reintegration: goods in themselves are not problematic, as the scope of giving a destination to these goods has become crucial in legitimizing patrimonial prevention measures. This applies not only to luxury goods and real estate but also to companies (whether they have been used for money laundering or territorial control). Wherever possible, business and jobs should be preserved once the criminal owner has been eliminated. The issue of ownership is therefore fundamental because it is the property link that is the vector of subjectivity, as expressed by the jurist Garofoli:

> If, on the one hand, the social dangerousness of the subject who has access, directly or indirectly, to patrimonial values and assets, and their illicit origin constitute . . . the normal presuppositions for applying preventive measures of an ablative nature, on the other hand, they translate into a condition of objective dangerousness which invests these same patrimonial values . . .: dangerousness of the person which is therefore transmitted to the patrimonial values and assets.
>
> *(Garofoli, in Collettivo, 1998, p. 70)*

This also explains why, in Italy, when the patrimonial investigation reveals a discrepancy between the value of the assets held and the income declared, it is up to the mafia member to provide proof of the legitimate acquisition of such assets. Otherwise, sequestration turns to confiscation. It is not up to the courts to directly link the acquisition of property to, for example, profits made from drug trafficking (sentence no. 10549 of 2009). Confiscation can therefore affect the fruit of successive reinvestments in the legal economy if there is a strong presumption that the initial gains that initiated this chain of investments were illicit. In this way, the confiscatory measure takes into account the interaction between the legal and illegal spheres, as well as the temporal dynamics specific to the mafia network. It also refers to the criminal network and its dangerousness. An illustration of this dangerousness can be found in the discussion surrounding collaborators of justice and the advisability of revoking confiscation of assets in their case. Requests to this effect from collaborators of justice were rejected, insofar as "social dangerousness must be considered as distinct from collaboration with the judicial authority".[7]

It is by reconnecting law and economics that the two fields can lend each other a helping hand. The seizure of criminal assets, including legitimate businesses belonging to criminals, enables to combat organized crime on a large scale and in all its diversity:

- Seizure tackles the quest for profit as well as the quest for power.
- It reasserts the immorality of illegal enrichment.
- It provides a guardianship for the economic and commercial activity of non-criminal actors, giving them back access to a range of opportunities no longer constrained by crime.
- Finally, it strikes a broader blow than monitoring flows, by touching on the accumulation over time of gains and not limiting itself to the part of dirty money passing through the financial system to be laundered.

Turning specifically to the issue of confiscated businesses, it is crucial to remember that businesses in criminal hands thrive at the expense of "honest" entrepreneurship. Confiscating does not destroy the industrial and commercial fabric but reconstitutes a space for economic investment by individuals not affiliated to criminal organizations. It contributes to more security for non-criminal economic agents.

In return, the effective implementation of these patrimonial measures in the economic field can only reinforce the legitimacy of official institutions. The fight against illegal enrichment goes hand in hand with the fight against the entrenchment of a criminal power that competes with State sovereignty. By counterbalancing the economic power induced by criminal ownership, institutions reaffirm the importance of law in social cohesion, institutional stability, and the smooth running of the economy. Phenomena of institutional isomorphism, where non-criminals begin to doubt the advisability of complying with the rules and themselves adopt behaviors that are borderline or even illegal, can be countered by the reaffirmation of the legal-economic nexus. The injunctions of mainstream economics must not encourage the development of the gray zone, that zone which blurs the boundary between what is legal and what is illegal. All too often, the extension of the gray zone feeds on economic justifications fueled by a misguided use of the notions of economic efficiency and rationality aimed at freeing the economy from all legal and ethical dimensions.

Notes

1 Available at SNA2008.pdf (un.org).
2 This strategy is identified in the DIA's 2022 report, second semester (Direzione Investigativa Antimafia: DIA_secondo_semestre_2022Rpdf.pdf (interno.gov.it)), p. 123, with regard to the camorra. It was at the heart of the arrests made on February 14, 2024 in

Reggio Calabria (see, e.g., the article in the Italian daily *La Repubblica*: Reggio Calabria: anche sulle case popolari comandano i clan, 9 arresti. L'ex assessore, pentito di 'ndrangheta: "Significano voti" – la Repubblica).

3 Thus, for example, Italian anti-mafia prosecutor Giovanni Melillo says of the Neapolitan camorra: "the major camorrist cartels (which control a large share of the city's illicit and not-illicit activities) today coincide with veritable business constellations" (DIA, 2021–2, p. 112).

4 It should be pointed out in passing that the laundering of illicitly acquired funds was criminalized only very recently. It wasn't until 1986, with the Money Laundering Control Act (Public Law 99–570) adopted by the US Congress, and its generalization following the United Nations Convention against Illicit Traffic in Narcotic Drugs and Psychotropic Substances (Vienna, 1988).

5 Law 646/1982, also known as the Rognoni-La Torre law, on preventive patrimonial provisions. It should be noted that confiscation can be applied without a criminal conviction (hence the term "prevention") in cases of mafia association.

6 As a reminder, Posner (1986, p. 224) asked the question of whether the entry of criminals into legal activities should be encouraged or discouraged, and did not decide.

7 Lecce Court of Cassation, Puglia, Section II, January 12 to June 6, 1995, case of Cosimo Screti.

References

Anderson, Annelise, *The Business of Organized Crime: A Cosa Nostra Family*, Stanford: Hoover Institute Press, Stanford University, 1979.

Ardita, Stefano, *Cosa nostra SpA. Il patto economico tra criminalità organizzata e colletti bianchi*, Rome: Paper First, 2020.

Arlacchi, Pino, *La mafia imprenditrice*, Bologna: Il Mulino, 1983.

Banque Mondiale, Commission Européenne, FMI, OCDE, Nations Unies, *Système de comptabilité nationale 2008*, New York: United Nations, 2013 (SNA2008FR.pdf (un.org)).

Catino, Maurizio, *Mafia Organizations. The Visible Hand of Criminal Enterprise*, New York: Cambridge University Press, 2019.

Champeyrache, Clotilde, *Entreprise légale, propriétaire mafieux.Comment la mafia infiltre l'économie légale*, Paris: CNRS Editions, 2004a.

Champeyrache, Clotilde, "Propriété et accumulation mafieuses: les enjeux théoriques et pratiques de l'infiltration mafieuse dans l'économie légale", *Economie Appliquée*, 2, 2004b, 79–103.

Champeyrache, Clotilde, "Artificial Scarcity, Power, and the Italian Mafia", *Journal of Economic Issues*, XLVIII(3), 2014, 625–639.

Champeyrache, Clotilde, *Quand la mafia se légalise. Pour une approche économique institutionnaliste*, Paris: CNRS Editions, 2016.

Champeyrache, Clotilde, "A Commonsian Approach to Crime: The Mafia and the Economic Power of Withholding", *Cambridge Journal of Economics*, 45(3), 2021, 411–425.

Champeyrache, Clotilde, "Institutional Mistrust, Instrumental Trust and the Privatization of Law: The Mafia as a Territorial Ruler", *Journal of Economic Issues*, 56(4), 2022, 945–958.

Clark, Charles M.A., "Wealth and Poverty: On the Social Creation of Scarcity", *Journal of Economic Issues*, 36(2), 2002, 415–421.

Collettivo, *Le misure di prevenzione patrimoniali. Teoria e prassi applicativa*, Bari: Cacucci, 1998.

Commons, John R., *Legal Foundations of Capitalism*, New York: Macmillan, 1924.

Commons, John R., *Myself*, Madison: University of Wisconsin Press, 1934.

Commons, John R., *The Economics of Collective Action*, New York: MacMillan, 1950.

Dawson, Richard, "Sovereignty and Withholding in John Commons's Political Economy", in W. Samuels (ed.), *The Founding of Institutional Economics: The Leisure Class and Sovereignty*, London: Routledge, 1998, 47–75.
Direzione Investigativa Antimafia, *Relazione Semestrale*, Rome, 2018–1.
Direzione Investigativa Antimafia, *Relazione Semestrale*, Rome, 2018–2.
Direzione Investigativa Antimafia, *Relazione Semestrale*, Rome, 2021–2.
Dugger, William M., "Instituted Process and Enabling Myth: The Two Faces of the Market", *Journal of Economic Issues*, 23(2), 1989, 607–615.
Falcone, Giovanni, and Michelle Padovani, *Cose di Cosa Nostra*, Paris: Numéro 1/Austral, 1991.
Galbraith, John K., *The New Industrial State*, Oxford: Princeton University Press, 1967 (2007).
Gambetta, Diego, *The Sicilian Mafia: The Business of Private Protection*, Cambridge, MA: Harvard University Press, 1993.
Hodgson, Geoffrey M., "What are Institutions?", *Journal of Economic Issues*, XL(1), 2006.
Knight, Frank, "Freedom as Fact and Criterion", *International Journal of Ethics*, 39(2), 1929, 129–147.
Posner, Richard A., *Economic Analysis of Law*, Boston: Brown, 1986.
Reuter, Peter, *Disorganized Crime. The Economics of the Visible Hand*, Cambridge: The MIT Press, 1983.
Robbins, Lionel, *The Nature and Significance of Economic Science*, London: Macmillan, 1932.
Transcrime, *Gli investimenti delle mafie*, Università Cattolica Milano: Transcrime, 2013.
Veblen, Thorstein, *Theory of the Leisure Class: An Economic Study of Institutions*, New York: MacMillan, 1899.
Veblen, Thorstein, *The Engineers and the Price System*, New York: Harbinger, 1921.

7

LEGAL OR ILLEGAL? A FADING FRONTIER

The criminal economy is clearly associated with illegal markets. More rarely, reference is also made to the infiltration of legal activities by criminals. This challenges the myth according to which the frontier between the legal and illegal economies is watertight. It is possible to go even further in exploring the connections between the two worlds. This exploration is based first on empirical findings and then on an analysis of the impact of the dominant economic discourse on the relationship between economic actors and legality. From a purely empirical point of view, one observation is rarely made, even though it could be decisive in the fight against the criminal economy: the expansion of organized crime and its activities relies largely on the tolerance, at best, and complicity, at worst, of the legal economy, because the latter provides tools for crime and thus acts as a "facilitator". The issue of corruption is also crucial in this respect and deserves to be reassessed not in terms of presuppositions about the nature – public or private – of the actors involved, but in terms of the acts committed and the damage done to the common good. In terms of discourse, the aim is to gain a better understanding of white-collar crime, the real blind spot of traditional crime economics. To do this, one needs to move away from a purely market-based vision of rational individual choice and from a static view, in order to understand the extension of the phenomenon and its connection to the spread of a system of thought that allows individuals to disconnect their actual actions from the obligation to comply with formal rules. The cost–benefit calculation does indeed seem to bear the seeds of a trivialization of crime, thanks to a discourse that potentially conveys values – therefore shaping effective behaviors – that are tolerant or even favorable to crime.

Two phenomena that seem to be disconnected from one another because the main actors are in fact different now find a coherent whole. The criminal economy and white-collar crime, criminal organizations, and rogue professions are all part

DOI: 10.4324/9781003350958-10

of the same logic of blurring the frontier between legality and illegality. Between contiguities, ambiguities, and complicities, the frontier becomes a fading frontier, with all that this implies for the weakening of the social pact and the annihilation of political will. Thanks to a crime economics inspired by original institutionalism, crime ceases to be on the margins of economic thought, as if it were a foreign body, an excrescence with little impact on the functioning of the irenic world of the liberal economy; crime becomes again in economic thinking what it is in economic reality: a fundamental and expanding problematic.

Between tolerance and complicity: the legal "facilitators" of the illegal economy

The criminal economy would face many more obstacles if it did not benefit from "facilitators" within the legal economy. Agents in the legal economy lend their support to illegal activities, either by choosing to turn a blind eye to them or by knowingly entering into complicit relationships for the provision of services. There are many examples of these relationships, and it is impossible to be exhaustive. After a few brief illustrations to illustrate the multiplicity of possible configurations, I will focus on the case of the explosion in the consumption of fentanyl and other opioid products in the United States, to provide an overview of the complicity in the legal world supporting this traffic, based on criminal investigations and convictions.

Generally speaking, it should be noted that, empirically, the configuration of market economies bears little resemblance to mainstream theory, in which supply and demand meet directly in a competitive market. What we observe – as in the illegal world (see Chapter 5) – is a growing reliance on intermediation, which is generally unregulated or insufficiently regulated. This intermediation can represent a weakness in the ability of economies to resist criminal influence and an opportunity for a gray market to develop. The term "grey market" refers to a hybrid form in which legal channels are used for illegal purposes by exploiting legal loopholes or circumventing legal obligations, sometimes with the backing of government officials. In this way, the lack of regulation of the weapons broker profession enables arms trafficking to be grafted onto the arms trade. Intermediation opens the way for a transaction that avoids compromising buyer and seller. Financial intermediation also creates at a minimum facilitation spaces for the criminal economy by offering layers of interaction that contribute to the opacification of money circulation circuits. In addition to increasing opaqueness, intermediation also dilutes responsibilities, until the courts can rule on the criminal liability of the various parties involved. The international expansion of banking activities in the context of cost-cutting has encouraged the use of correspondent banks. Rather than maintaining a vast but costly network of subsidiaries and branches around the world, banks can open accounts with banks operating in certain currencies/geographical areas. The correspondent bank and the other bank then enter into a contract, with one bank performing banking services on behalf of a local bank, usually in a foreign country.

The choice of banking partners is therefore crucial, especially when the banking institute is a local bank in a country considered to be at risk (high criminal density and/or poor compliance).[1]

The legal economy also offers tools whose features are clearly appreciated by criminal organizations. Such is the case with offshore locations, where companies such as Limited Liability Companies can be domiciled, with guaranteed anonymity of the beneficial owner thanks to the possibility of registering the company with a nominee director – a person who may well be nothing more than a front man. These services are legal and correspond to recognized legal structures. Equally legal are Trust and Company Service Providers, who can simplify the process of setting up an offshore company. With just a few clicks of the mouse, these online companies can offer you more or less elaborate packages, depending on the price you're prepared to pay, to help you set up a company that may, in fact, be no more than a shell company. Once again, intermediation plays on disempowerment: the service provider provides a legal service (assistance in setting up a legal structure) and can plead good faith if it turns out that the service is being provided for a criminal who will use the said structure to launder money via fictitious financial movements.

On a completely different front, some encrypted telephony operators are lending their support to criminal organizations. The infiltration of the Encrochat and then Sky ECC encrypted communications services, carried out as part of an international collaboration between investigation forces from several countries, has been widely commented on in the news for the abundance of exchanges between criminal organizations it reveals. But beyond this major police success, it should not be forgotten that the encryption applications and other services, such as the remote wiping of all data or the provision of a dual interface to track down investigators, were sold by legitimate telephone companies: the Canadian company Sky Global for Sky ECC and the Dutch company Encrochat. Sky Global's CEO was the subject of an arrest warrant by the US Justice Department in March 2021 for offering services to prevent law enforcement agencies from combating drug trafficking and money laundering. The company defends itself by invoking "the fundamental right to privacy" and arguing that these services were aimed at journalists and activists, not criminals. Encrochat ceased operations in June 2020 following investigations and the compromise of its services.[2] The line of defense is also that of the right to data protection, particularly for sensitive but legal professions. However, the decryption of the messages showed that almost all users were criminals.

We could multiply the number of examples where the line between tolerance and complicity of the legal sphere toward the illegal economy is not always very clear. Chapter 5 showed how the port economy participates in the globalization of certain types of trafficking, not only because of corruption but also because of a problematic trade-off between economic efficiency and security, to the detriment of the latter. Similarly, Maltese legislation on the online gambling and betting industry, in the absence of an active and probative regulatory authority, encourages money laundering on the island (Champeyrache, 2020). However, the case of opioids, and fentanyl in particular, merits special attention, as past and ongoing investigations reveal multiple legal participants in the distribution of these narcotic substances. These participants may act individually or collectively. Their complicity is by no means anecdotal, given that in 2022, almost 11,000 Americans were victims of drug poisonings, and 70% of these cases involved the absorption of fentanyl. Reading through just three months (from December 2023 to February 2024) of the press releases published on the DEA (Drug Enforcement Administration) website in the United States, I can identify different categories of "facilitators".[3]

A category of facilitators acts in an individual or loosely organized way, putting skills acquired in the legal sphere at the service of illegal activities, without necessarily being affiliated to a criminal organization. In the case of opioid trafficking in the United States, doctors in particular are involved. On January 19, 2024, the DEA reported that on January 12, the Miami Federal Court had convicted a doctor of "conspiracy to unlawfully dispense and distribute controlled substances", namely, products such as oxycodone, morphine, and alprazolam. Prescriptions were made in a clinic, at the request of patients, without even a medical examination. Some were even pre-written by the doctor, who sold them for $250 in cash. The office managers of the doctor's clinic also participated in the system, as they were responsible for selling the prescriptions in the doctor's absence.[4]

On January 22, 2024, another doctor was sentenced to up to 15 years in prison for overprescribing opioids, resulting in the deaths of five people. From 2016 to 2018, the doctor prescribed opioid drugs on demand, without any examination or history-taking, to people with obvious signs of addiction. In order to evade controls, the doctor did not use the State's secure electronic prescription system but resorted to paper prescriptions thanks to a waiver granted by the New York State Health Commissioner.[5]

On January 25, 2024, a former doctor was sentenced to 30 months' imprisonment for "conspiring with others to dispense controlled substances without a legitimate medical purpose": the prosecution file identified over 500 prescriptions for more than 40,000 dosage units of controlled substances, mostly opioids. These prescriptions, issued after the expiry of the defendant's medical license, were notably in the name of living or deceased family members and former patients. The doctor did not act alone, as co-conspirators were responsible for collecting the medications and distributing them to people other than those mentioned on the prescriptions.[6]

Among the facilitators of the opioid crisis are also legitimate companies that either passively or actively aid trafficking. In terms of passive complicity, e-commerce is regularly singled out for blame.[7] In particular, it is the online sale of pill presses for transforming fentanyl powder into pills and stamps for printing logos on these pills that is concerned. The Sinaloa and Jalisco cartels and other fentanyl traffickers need these machines to produce pills that resemble their legal counterparts and to sell them via social networks, including by luring buyers about the real composition of the product. As the DEA has observed that presses and stamps are easy to obtain on e-commerce platforms,[8] the latter are subject to compliance with the Controlled Substances Act and must therefore meet the CSA recordkeeping and reporting requirements on distribution, importation, and exportation of pill press machines.[9] Some platforms have chosen to stop offering these products for sale. The requirement to transmit information on pill press machine purchases to the DEA makes the concerned companies criminally liable in the event of non-compliance. For example, eBay had to pay $59 million to settle CSA allegations relating to the online sale of thousands of pill presses and encapsulating machines.[10]

The pharmaceutical industry is no stranger to complicity. On February 7, 2024, the DEA announced a settlement with Morris & Dickson Co, LLC, a pharmaceutical distributor.[11] The charge is "failing to maintain effective controls against diversion of controlled substances, including failure to report to DEA thousands of unusually large orders of oxycodone and hydrocodone". It covers a long period and thousands of orders that were suspicious but not reported as such. Therefore, the company is denounced as having contributed to the opioid crisis in the United States.

Companies such as eBay and Morris & Dickson can partially absolve themselves of responsibility by arguing a lack of vigilance rather than active and voluntary participation in trafficking. This is not an argument that the three chemical manufacturing companies[12] and their five Chinese employees charged in May 2023[13] with "conspiracy to manufacture and distribute fentanyl, manufacture of fentanyl, and illegally concealing their activities, including through customs fraud and introducing misbranded drugs into the United States marketplace"[14] can use. The charge of active participation in fentanyl trafficking concerns the shipment from China to the United States and Mexico of over 200 kg of precursor chemicals for the manufacture of fentanyl or fentanyl derivatives. Complicity is clearly demonstrated by the fact that the companies were aware of the intended use of the precursors and that they used deceptive and fraudulent practices to smuggle the goods (mislabeled packages, falsified customs forms, false declarations at border crossings). Criminal intent also stems from the use of "masking" molecules to change the chemical signature of the product and thus evade detection by testing protocols. These masking molecules could easily be removed on receipt, following deliberate instructions from the accused chemical companies.

These various indictments reveal only part of the gray area that weakens the frontier between the legal and illegal worlds. In any case, they show that dichotomous, even Manichean thinking is not viable and naive. The illegal economy interacts with the legal economy, and these interactions are not limited to violence and subjugation. For the year 2023, the DEA reported that it had served 143 administrative actions against doctors, pharmacies, drug manufacturers, and drug distributors for non-compliance with controlled substances regulations. By acting in this way, the DEA is helping to re-establish the frontier between legality and illegality, condemning both legal actors and criminal organizations, and to reaffirm the legal foundations of our economies.

Corruption: the imperative return to the lost notion of the "common good"

Corruption occupies a major place in the gray zone blurring the frontier between legal and illegal worlds. Yet it is a theme that remains on the bangs of both mainstream and heterodox economic thinking. The neglect of this issue by mainstream economists can be explained by the essence of what corruption is and the incompatibility of this essence with methodological individualism. While corruption can fundamentally be defined as an attack on the common good, mainstream economics, which reduces groups of individuals to an aggregation of agents with no synergies or collective structuring, is ultimately incapable of conceiving this crucial notion of the common good.

Corruption in traditional crime economics is analyzed as unproductive expenditure (notably via bribes) to gain undue advantage or rent. Corruption is reduced to an inefficient allocation of resources and is therefore incompatible, according to liberal economists, with the logic of the market. It can therefore only come from the State and the public sphere. Tanzi states:

> Corruption is generally linked to the activities of the state, and more particularly to its monopolistic and discretionary power. Therefore, as Nobel laureate Gary Becker pointed out in one of his Business Week columns, if we abolish the state, we abolish corruption.
>
> *(1998, pp. 565–566)*

By contrast, the market is virtuous and averse to corruption:

> the increased reliance on the market for economic decisions and the heightened need to be competitive have created an environment in which the search for efficiency has acquired greater importance, and the distortions attributed to corruption attract more attention.
>
> *(Tanzi, 1998, p. 561)*

This biased vision is echoed by international institutions such as the World Bank, which defines corruption as "the abuse of a public function for personal gain".[15] Implicitly, the public administration is both the instigator and the beneficiary of corruption, while any private agents involved are merely victims. The World Bank website also strongly associates corruption with underdevelopment (caused by undemocratic States afflicted by poor governance) and with economic and social misery (the civil servant compensates for his low salary by taking bribes). There may be such links, but they are not the only ones, otherwise how are we to understand the corruption cases that have affected European countries, such as Qatargate in 2023, or the cases of corruption of harbour dockers – salaried employees of the private sector – who nonetheless receive high salaries?

When corruption is seen as potentially involving private agents, it becomes a diffuse practice justified by a quest for competitiveness: the agent is obliged to submit to it in order to participate in the economic game. Once again, the private sector is often presented as a victim. Eventually, corruption is neutralized in its effects and becomes oil in the wheels. Apart from any ethical or moral considerations, corruption is even subject to the inescapable test of efficiency. Leff (1964) paves the way for such work, in which corruption becomes a lesser evil if it nevertheless results in a trajectory of economic development.[16]

The challenge of an original institutional approach is to break out of this partial and one-sided vision in order to understand the different corruptive configurations (public–private, private–public, private–private,[17] and public–public) and the diversity of consequences arising from them. Naturally, the legal-economic nexus is a major key to this process. The notions of power, collective action, and the common good are also typical of the original institutional approach. These concepts allow us to move away from the sole criterion of economic efficiency as the relevant indicator for assessing the impact of corruption. Finally, this approach breaks the deadlock of viewing each agent as an independent atom and places him back into an institutional context. As a result, the starting point for reflection is not the nature of the agent, but rather the act.

Historically, it is interesting to note that the liberal vision of corruption as public and motivated by self-interest has not always been dominant. In many respects, ancient Greek thought may inspire the original institutional approach to corruption. For Socrates, Plato, and Aristotle, corruption refers to the process of abusing positions of power to the detriment of the common good. For the Greek philosophers, corruption is not alien to human nature, but on the contrary, systemic and endogenous to human relations. It stems fundamentally from an antagonism between a private, or personal, interest and the common good. Defined in this way, it refers to an extremely wide range of acts that can be carried out by both private and public agents: embezzlement, fraud, extortion, favoritism, nepotism, and strategies of influence can all be part of it and are not exclusively attributable to one specific type of agents. Above all, ancient Greek thought – even if it did not ignore the problem of good management of household resources, namely, the etymological root of the word *oikonomia* – did not characterize the negative character of these practices in – anachronistic – terms of economic inefficiency, but in terms of corrosion and destruction of the political and moral cement of civil society.

Such a definition puts the legal qualification of the act back at the heart of the reflection and qualifies the act as reprehensible in the name of the common good. This accords well with original institutional thinking and enables us to escape the bias imposed by the over-valuation of the agent and the superiority of the market. In particular, the legal-economic nexus makes it possible to read corruptive phenomena more broadly and to assess their effects differently from the sole yardstick of economic efficiency. Corruption can now also be understood as a system based on collective action and potentially long-lasting power relations, and not just as a momentary interpersonal relationship. This change of point of view transforms the face of corruption and re-maps its perimeter. Corruption thus appears far more diffuse and dangerous than the dominant economic theory would have us believe.

Commons dealt – marginally – with corruption as a result of his experience as a practitioner (Broda, 2016). According to him, any configuration in which the representative of a collective has a disproportionate degree of power over the lives of other economic agents presents a corruptive risk (Commons, 1901). This applies in a variety of cases, from internal factory relations to the spoils system of American politics, where positions are awarded on the basis of political connections rather than merit and competence. Commons regularly denounced this political system. Above all, however, Commons emphasized the extent to which a purely economic logic of efficiency does not allow to properly apprehend the problems raised by corruption. For him, the real question is one of legitimacy, as efficiency can be achieved despite corruption. He illustrates his point with a real-life situation (Commons, 1934). An important businessman had come to him to offer a bribe to the national president of a trade union so that the latter would refrain from taking strike action. This is indeed an offense that would bring undue benefit to the bribe-taker only because he occupies a dominant position in the union collective. However, Commons notes that the aim is to maintain social peace and the company's level of production. From a strictly economic point of view, then, the proposal may seem acceptable because it is efficient. However, Commons considers it unacceptable for ethical reasons, and because in the medium or long term, strategies to exploit the threat of strikes could develop to obtain new bribes. The ultimate risk is that bribery will become so systematized that it becomes *de facto* standard practice. In the name of the legal-economic nexus, Commons refuses to trivialize and accept corruption, even when it might be economically justified. Finally, Commons also insists that civil servants are not the only ones attracted to corruption. Stigmatizing the public sphere is therefore irrelevant. He illustrates this with the question of the provision of public goods and services in the case of a natural monopoly. The traditional debate revolves around the alternative between administrative production and production by a regulated private company. Liberal economists denounce the evils of public management of natural monopolies: rent capture, unproductive expenditure, and wasteful spending are, in their view, the consequences of an activity removed from competition. While Commons did not deny these risks, he also considered that delegating the activity under concession to a private company did not eliminate the risk of corruption: indeed, there was nothing to prevent private entrepreneurs from paying subsidies to political parties, especially when these public service delegations were renewed (Commons, 1907, pp. 93–94).

By re-characterizing what is meant by corrupt behavior in terms specific to original institutionalism, the panorama of corruption changes its face. Widespread associations of ideas on the subject are thus relativized or even invalidated, in particular, that which associates corruption with underdevelopment and economic misery. The scope of corruption is also becoming much broader and more heterogeneous. If corruption is defined as "the promotion of vested interests against the common good in the form of bribery, fraud, embezzlement, state capture, nepotism, extortion, and others" (O'Hara, 2014, p. 279), any manipulation of societal rules for personal gain falls within the scope of corruption.

The informal economy is an illustration of this observation. According to the OECD, the informal economy encompasses legal productive activities that are deliberately concealed from the authorities in order to avoid paying taxes, social security contributions, and standards such as the minimum wage, legal working hours, or health and safety regulations.[18] From a liberal perspective, the informal sector, because it generates wealth, can be seen as economically acceptable. The literature describing the informal sector as a "crisis shock absorber", or even as a healthy and rational entrepreneurial reaction to the constraints imposed on free enterprise by institutions synonymous with obstacles, is in this vein.[19] If the informal economy is harmful, it is only because it distorts competition to the detriment of those who comply with regulations. This vision, in which the institution plays only a negative role in constraining individual freedoms, actually accompanies the disappearance of the notion of general interest, and the disintegration of the very idea of the common good. Conversely, an original institutional reading places institutions and regulation in a potentially positive dimension, allowing the informal economy to be presented as a form of corruption exercised by private agents to the detriment of the common good. Indeed, this common good is guaranteed by rules and standards (in this case, labor law, taxes on production, etc.) formulated not to disrupt the market, but in the name of the general interest (in particular, by protecting workers, financing services via taxation, etc.). From this perspective, the informal sector is not so much a threat to competition as a threat to the common good. Obviously, there are nuances, and it is by studying the empirical reality of different economies that the profound nature of the informal economy must be appreciated. An economy characterized by an overabundance of norms and rules can be effectively hampered by legalism. This underscores the importance of collective action to ensure that these norms and rules are considered legitimate and respectful of the common good. This is a reminder, if any were needed, that there is no natural order in economics, and that it is up to people and the institutions that represent them to shape a reasonable capitalism.

The case of systematic fraud perpetrated by large corporations in the absence of any economic or financial difficulties also illustrates the value of an original institutional approach to the analysis of corruption. This configuration calls into question the all-too-often asserted link between corruption and economic survival. Bribes paid to speed up procedures or obtain contracts, fraud aimed at falsifying data, invoices, and accounts in order to evade taxes, favoritism through the recruitment of people not for their real skills but for their personal connections, the embezzlement of funds from company accounts to private accounts: all these practices constitute attacks on the common good. They harm the interests of the workforce, companies, the State, and society as a whole, to the benefit of a private interest – that of the fraudster and his or her close relations. It should be added that these frauds become institutionalized as soon as an ecosystem develops with service providers who facilitate them. Tax havens play their part in this ecosystem by offering intermediation services literally dedicated to evading common official rules, as we saw earlier with law firms such as Mossack-Fonsecca, made famous by the Panama Papers scandal in 2016, or Trust and Company Service Providers offering the creation of *de facto* shell companies.

By moving away from the traditional vision associating corruption with the public sphere and developing countries, original institutionalism reminds us that corruption is an endogenous and diffuse phenomenon that also affects rich, industrialized countries and that – as Lascoumes (2022) points out in particular – a not inconsiderable proportion of corruption is instigated by private elites in the name of maximizing private enrichment in an assumed logic of subtraction from contribution to the common good. In this way, deviance linked to organized crime and white-collar deviance converge, at the cost of weakening the social bond and the legitimacy of institutions. A return to the centrality of the common good, rather than the centrality of the behavior of the isolated agent, enables a more extensive understanding of the notion of corruption, its multiple forms, and consequences. As a result, a discourse that trivializes, tolerates, or even justifies the use of corruption on the grounds of economic efficiency is problematic. Yet this discourse, driven by the sole criterion of economic efficiency, is far from being in the minority. The economic hegemony claimed by authors such as Becker (see Chapter 2) tends to overturn the institutional hierarchy by instilling the values of rational choice theory and cost–benefit analysis into non-economic spheres and institutions. In so doing, economic hegemony introduces the possibility of a veritable market for transgression, institutionalizing fraud and corruption.

The institutionalization of law infringement

Criminal organizations disrupt people's relationship with the rule of law. Through the sometimes staggering profits made on illegal markets, they promote forms of illicit enrichment. Through the corruption they perpetrate, they contribute to the development of a gray zone of contiguity between the legal and illegal worlds. The previous section's institutional look at corruption also shows that illegality can be driven by non-criminal actors within the legal world. Traditional crime economics has not really taken up this issue, and even less so has the convergence between upper world illegality and underworld illegality. Yet this dual process also contributes to blurring the frontier between legality and illegality. The idea here is to show that the project of economic hegemony claimed by some mainstream economists produces effects on the values upheld by societies with a market economy. Even if this does not necessarily mean that there was intentionality in the approach, the imposition of a supposedly rational economic logic on almost all spheres of human activity induces, among other collateral effects, a commodification of transgression that makes breaking the law a habit of thought, that is, a genuine institution in the Veblenian sense of the term.[20]

Dominant economic thinking is not confined to the theoretical sphere. It has largely permeated teaching and is also found in the business practices of economic agents, which further contributes to the spread of a certain way of thinking. In this sense, the rule of cost–benefit analysis to guide decision-making has gone far beyond the economic sphere and has become a habit of thought. The cost–benefit calculation is asserting itself as an absolute reference, all the more so as it is adorned with the virtue of rationality. Yet this process of widespread adoption of a working rule – which is fundamentally very accounting-based and, as such, very limited in its relevance – actually leads to tacit acceptance of the infringement whenever it is validated by the economic rationality thus described. The "rational offence" – as it might be called – is institutionalized, leading to the emergence of a genuine market for transgression, in a perspective totally different from that of Ehrlich's crime market.

The rise to prominence of utilitarian thinking has been gradual, as is frequently the case with fundamental developments. The tradition dates back to the 18th century, the Age of Enlightenment, and sees in Jeremy Bentham the first true propagator of the comparison between pros and cons, between pleasures and pains, in order to make individual decisions. Bentham connects individual utilitarianism to the well-being of society, as, in his view, it leads to "the greatest happiness for the greatest number". The link between individual and collective dimensions that lies at the heart of Bentham's vision will, however, gradually fade as utilitarian thinking spreads. The notion of collective well-being as an objective to be pursued, which is a constituent part of the Benthamian formulation, faded into the background or even disappeared from the picture. This disappearance accompanies the rise of methodological individualism, which places the agent at the heart of thinking by removing him from his socio-economic and cultural context and de-institutionalizing him. As Wilber points out: "self interest leads to the common good if there is sufficient competition *and if most people in society have internalized a general moral law as a guide for their behavior*" (2004, p. 27, my emphasis). The positive link between the individual and the collective, as defined by utilitarianism, only works if society's members as a whole adhere to common moral rules that determine their decisions. As soon as a significant proportion of society's members detach themselves from this "general moral law" framework, the application of cost–benefit calculation no longer necessarily guarantees that the common good will be achieved. Individual economic rationality, when no longer framed by a common moral framework, may well lead to a degradation of the common good. This is also underlined by Albertson and Fox:

> Rational choice theory allows the social scientist to assess whether an individual has chosen the most rational means of achieving a *given* end. No judgement is

made about whether the individual's preferences are "good" or "bad". Individuals can pursue whichever set of preferences they choose.

(2012, p. 62)

Bentham's utilitarianism is therefore very different from that developed by mainstream economics today. Rational choice theory has become disconnected from notions of good and evil, as we saw in Chapter 2, with Walras' reference to the doctor and the murderer. But this disconnection is by no means neutral; it has implications for the institutional articulation of societies.

Original institutionalism is based on the fact that individuals participate in several institutions at the same time, which can be classified into clusters according to the main functions that characterize them. As mentioned in Chapter 3, Dugger (1980, p. 898) identifies six types of institutions: economic, educational, military, kinship, political, and religious. These different categories are articulated and hierarchical; they do not all have the same weight or autonomy. Depending on the era, certain categories prevail over others. For Veblen (1919), American society – but this applies to many other societies, especially those where the market economy is firmly established – is fundamentally a "pecuniary civilization". This means that the cultural pattern is largely dominated by economic institutions, and thus by the values and habits of thinking and doing that they convey. In a way, Veblen's observation merely anticipates the project of economic hegemony already mentioned. Non-economic institutions adopt, or are pressured to adopt, economic values. The spread of economic values (disconnected from their articulation with common moral rules) throughout all spheres of human activity subsequently reinforces and legitimizes them. The rise in power of economic values transforms the hierarchy of institutions, allowing the erasure of values carried by other categories of institutions. Gradually all types of institutions internalize the values initially specific to the sphere of economic institutions, and we witness the "affirmation of the business ethic as a habit of thought" (Miller, 1998, p. 23). The Veblenian institutionalization of the cost–benefit rule results from the mechanisms of subreption, contamination, emulation, and mystification identified by Veblen (1918).

Subreption refers to the process by which institutional autonomy leads to institutional hegemony. In our case, this is the phase in which even non-economic institutions are put at the service of the objectives of economic institutions. In this way, educational institutions contribute to teaching rational choice theory and thus disseminating it, without really discussing its foundations or limitations. The last chapter of *The Theory of the Leisure Class*, entitled "The higher learning as an expression of the pecuniary culture" (Veblen, 1899, pp. 236–259), perfectly describes the phenomenon of distortion of the values of higher education and the fact that teaching becomes a medium for inculcating habits of thought specific to the upper class in favor of the pecuniary civilization.

Contamination allows "the motives appropriate for the roles of one institution to spread to the roles of others" (Dugger, 1980, p. 902). Very similar to subreption, contamination continues the process of institutional legitimization, whereby certain values specific to one cluster of institutions also become guides tacitly integrated and transmitted by the other clusters. This contamination occurs, for example, when the effects of a law are assessed purely in terms of cost–benefit analysis, without consideration for strictly legal and ethical grounds.

The emulation process completes the sequence at work, insofar as it socially validates dominant values as genuine sources of status. Justifying a decision by using cost–benefit analysis – sometimes real, sometimes purely rhetorical – places economic agents in the camp of economically successful individuals. This recognition encourages other agents to imitate them, in a circular, self-justifying system.

Then comes the mystification that accompanies economic hegemony. In the words of Dugger (1988, p. 99), this involves "confusing those whose values you oppose into supporting your values instead of theirs". Mystification introduces a dose of manipulation. Here, manipulation refers to the discrepancy between Bentham's utilitarianism and that of mainstream economics. While Bentham thinks of utilitarianism in terms of the common good, the reference is lost in today's mainstream economy. Economic hegemony goes even further than the loss of this reference. By asserting that its thinking is disconnected from any legal, ethical, or moral underpinnings, it promotes individual utility-maximizing behavior, even when this runs counter to the common good. The constraint exerted by institutional economic hegemony places cost–benefit analysis at the heart of all decision-making and evaluation procedures for human activities, whatever their nature – economic or otherwise. The result is a discourse and actions in which infringement is accepted in the name of economic rationality.

The strength of this process of institutionalizing economic rationality lies largely in the implementation of a habituation power, that is, the voluntary acceptance of these patterned habits of thought, rather than their coercive imposition. The reduction of economic rationality to the rule of cost–benefit calculation is not questioned.[21] It no longer needs to be justified, since it has been internalized by individuals who adopt its values, thanks to the institutionalization of economic hegemony. The result is that, in the event of conflicts between values held by different clusters of institutions, it is very often the economic values that will prevail. In the previous case, it is the conflict between legal rules and economic values that is relevant and problematic. Indeed, we are faced with a situation where "the institutions of norms/customs and law come into conflict and in which custom supersedes, in a *de facto* sense, the law" (Medema, 1998, p. 111). In concrete terms, cases of law-infringement are the subject of a discourse of economic justification. Because this discourse refers to the supreme value of cost–benefit calculation and economic rationality, it is listened to and perceived as at least partially legitimate. In this way, it further undermines the legal-economic nexus by placing *de facto* legal institutions in a subordinate position. The working rules of business can easily come into conflict with the rule of law. Even agents in the legal economy can perceive breaking the law as rational from a cost–benefit point of view. In the end, the model of rational criminal behavior proposed by Becker (1968) goes beyond proposing an economic explanation of the individual choice of illegal acts and a theory of crime deterrence. From an original institutional viewpoint, this model actually contributes to the trivialization of supposedly economically justified offenses and, while it is dichotomous in its arbitration between breaking and respecting the law, it helps to accept the spread of illegal practices within the legal economy. Bentham's underlying assumption was that the vast majority of society had assimilated common legal and ethical rules. Crime was thus the result of a comparison between pleasure and punishment, but the frontier between the legal and illegal worlds remained clearly defined. The choice of crime had economic underpinnings but also included the social dimension of rule-breaking and its consequences. The barrier of common rules limited the act. In contrast, the economic hegemony that accompanies rational choice theory has led to a world in which corporate and white-collar crime is bound to multiply. The process of trivializing infringements in the exercise of a legal activity is based on a dual process: on the one hand, offenders justify themselves by the rationality of their choice; on the other, this justification is increasingly accepted by other members of society through emulation. The result is a form of tolerance toward white-collar crime and a low effectiveness of existing measures to combat it. The weak deterrent effect of compliance rules, for example, is due not so much to a cost–benefit calculation unfavorable to compliance that is more than just cosmetic, but rather to a crime-tolerant cultural scheme based on economic rationality.[22] The problem is not so much that the potential penalty is not high enough to act as a deterrent. The problem is that compliance with the law is no longer perceived as the frame of reference within which to carry out economic activity, but is downgraded to the level of a potential cost.

The news is full of illustrations where legal agents have committed fraud and the punishment has not been what was expected and/or the fraudsters have adopted a line of defense based on cost–benefit analysis. An interesting aspect of these real-life examples is that configurations where the fraud or offense is committed not by an individual in isolation, but as a result of collective action, are increasing. The involvement of several people, the recurrence of the same types of fraud in several different companies, the offenders' lines of defense based on the excuse that "everyone in the company knew" and "it's the usual practice" – all these elements underline a collective rather than individual dimension in the choice not to comply with the law. We are therefore well within the realm of original institutionalism.

The international banking and financial system represents a major sector where the rules of business conflict with the rules of law and where the low level of global sanction reveals the weakness of non-economic institutions vis-à-vis economic hegemony. The numerous financial crises, most notably that of 2008, have shown how – quietly – political discourse has become subservient to economic values, shifting surreptitiously from "too big to fail" to "too big to jail", to use Garrett's (2014) expression. This shift was not the subject of mass indignation, a further sign of the impregnation of the cultural scheme by dominant economic values. "Too big to fail" could be understood as the impossibility of letting the real economy suffer the heavy consequences of the financial crisis in the event of the failure of major banking institutions. Public bailouts of private banks were intended to safeguard the economic system as a whole, without exonerating the banks from any responsibility. The "too big to jail" approach, on the contrary, exonerates the banks and creates a form of impunity that encourages recidivism. In 2016, Deutsche Bank found itself implicated in over 6,000 lawsuits worldwide, on charges ranging from helping to circumvent embargoes and manipulating exchange and interest rates to money laundering and tax evasion. More recently, the 2020 FinCEN case[23] in the United States has put the spotlight on the difference between façade and real compliance. Leaks concerning 0.02% of Suspicious Activity Reports sent to the Financial Crimes Enforcement Network by professionals subject to reporting obligations (banks, stockbrokers, securities brokers, casinos, financial institutions, etc.) highlight a singular relationship between these professionals (85% of which are very large banks such as Deutsche Bank, Bank of New York Mellon, Standard Chartered Bank, JP Morgan Chase, Barclays, and HSBC) and compliance with the rules. Over the period 1999–2017, more than $2 trillion of financial transactions were first validated by these major banks and only then reported as suspicious. When questioned about this, the banks justified themselves in terms of economic rationality and competition: blocking the transaction by declaring it suspicious would mean a loss of customers and financial gains that could benefit competing banks. The banks thus absolve themselves by complying *de jure with* compliance obligations, but *de facto* emptying them of any usefulness in the fight against financial crime. Once again, this means that economic values dominate over other values. Moreover, this is a very obtuse rationality insofar as, anchored in restrictive immediacy, it is blind to the risks of money laundering for our economies.

However, finance is not the only sector to succumb to the disentanglement of the legal-economic nexus. The Volkswagen engine-rigging affair is an illustration of this in the productive sphere. From 2009 to 2015, the carmaker cheated to pass vehicle pollution tests and obtain its homologation. US authorities sued Volkswagen for violating the Clean Air Act in September 2015; several European countries have also filed lawsuits. The investigation uncovered a collective fraud implemented on a large scale by the firm's executives and based on an economic argument to the detriment of environmental values and the law. The existence of rigged test software materializes "a corporate culture that in conscience endorses the fraud for the sake of profit" (Champeyrache, 2024).

The urgent need to contain the spread and trivialization of crime

In these few examples of white-collar crime, the common goal is corporate enrichment, and the means to achieve it include illegality. In all cases, the freedom of major agents of the legal economy from the law has repercussions on the perception of the legitimacy of the law in all classes of society. It contributes to the spread of illegality. It can also build lasting bridges between the upper and lower worlds. To counter this rising phenomenon of contiguity between mafia organizations and the legal economy (see Sciarrone and Storti, 2019), Italy has created, in addition to the offense of mafia association (art. 416 bis of the Italian Penal Code), an offense of "external conspiracy in mafia association" (*concorso esterno in associazione mafiosa*). This jurisprudential offense is a major step forward in understanding the nature of the links between crime and the legal economy and in combating the gray zone that allows illegal activities to expand while blurring the frontier between legality and illegality. This offense is designed to punish more severely those economic agents who are not affiliated to the criminal organization, but who knowingly provide it with active and voluntary assistance. Specifically targeted are company directors, judges, accountants, notaries, and other professionals who enter into a relationship of complicity with the mafia because the latter enables them to increase their profits and reduce their costs. In fact, the "intimidation" and "subjugation" referred to in the Italian Penal Code are not the only relationships between crime and the legal world. The offense of external conspiracy in mafia association opportunely brings to the fore complicity with the criminal world intended as an economically rational option.

Non-compliance with the law takes on a diffuse dimension when it is perpetrated by very different actors in the economic world (criminals, bankers, company directors, etc.) and when offenses are repeated. This dual aspect reflects the notion of habit of thought. Taken to its extreme, the institutionalization of offending, insofar as it is supposedly economically rational, leads to the establishment of a "market for transgression", the caricatured counterpart of the market of crime modeled by Ehrlich. While Ehrlich and his successors model the supply and demand of crime in order to design and evaluate crime-deterrence policies, the market for transgression that is gradually being established tends to promote a business ethic that makes offending a trivial and justifiable option. From the opportunity to deter inherent in the theoretical model, we have moved on to the promotion of law-infringement in action, as soon as the estimated cost of the offense in the event of punishment is deemed financially acceptable. The offense is commodified in the sense that it is estimated in terms of an acceptable price. This explains why JP Morgan Chase set aside $23 billion in provisions for litigation in 2014, in anticipation of criminal prosecution.

The institutionalization of the offense is justified by the cost–benefit analysis, insofar as agents in the legal economy also knowingly choose to evade the law. But the institutionalization of infringement is also paradoxically reinforced by the attitude of those who should be combating lawlessness. The development of the use of negotiated justice (Garrett, 2014; Lascoumes, 2022) therefore merits further reflection. Inspired by the Anglo-Saxon model, this practice is developing internationally, particularly in Europe. It is generally presented in the positive light of the greater fluidity and lower costs of negotiation compared with litigation; arguments that are, moreover, themselves supported by cost–benefit calculations. However, an original institutional view of the subject calls for a step back in terms of the significance of negotiated justice. Negotiated justice allows the offender (be it a natural or legal person) to avoid trial and negotiate the sentence, that is, the price of the offense. In other words, the offender evades the rules of legal institutions and imposes the logic of the market on the role of justice. Negotiation refers to the pacified world of the mainstream economy: the parties reach a compromise that is supposed to satisfy everyone. In reality, from a social point of view, the notion of negotiation disrupts the way we look at the act of breaking the law. Negotiation presupposes that the parties are on an equal footing. This is reminiscent of how Coase (1960) eliminated the victim-blame relationship in his treatment of negative externalities, including pollution, to affirm the reciprocal nature of the problem. Moreover, the outcome of negotiations should also call for vigilance. On the one hand, negotiating avoids the stigma of litigation. On the other hand, negotiated fines do not correspond to the gains obtained from the infringement and are often lower than they would have been in the event of a trial. Garrett (2014) points out, for example, that for the period 1994–2009 in the United States, of the 3,500 companies prosecuted, 47% had to pay a fine lower than that recommended by the Sentencing Guideline.[24] Taken together, these factors tend to relativize the offense and preserve the offender's reputation, thereby contributing to the emulation process. This guarantees the preservation of the cost–benefit argument as a dominant and structuring way of thinking, both in the economic sphere and in terms of respect for the law. It also feeds the discrepancy between, on the one hand, anti-corruption rhetoric and the deployment of mechanisms and bodies responsible for organizing the fight against fraud and offenses in the legal economy and, on the other, the trivialization and spread of illegalities. This affects not only our economies but also our societies and political systems. Galbraith (2004) denounced the "innocent fraud" of mainstream economics, which overlooks the damaging effects of corporate power:

> the corporate power has shaped the public purpose to its own ability and need. It ordains that social success is more automobiles, more television sets, more diverse apparel, a greater volume of all other consumer goods. Also more lethal weaponry. Here is the measure of human achievement. Negative social effects – pollution, destruction of the landscape, the unprotected health of the citizenry, the threat of military action and death – do not count as such. When measuring achievement, the good and the disastrous can be combined.
>
> *(2004, p. 58)*

In light of this chapter, Galbraith could be criticized for painting an incomplete picture: corporate power also contributes to disconnecting the economy from its legal foundations and promoting *de facto* illegality. In so doing, it weakens the social pact and renders the system inconsistent. What sense can be made of economies in which illegal activities are included in the calculation of GDP and thus contribute to the growth rate, while at the same time money laundering is punishable by law? How can we effectively combat the illegal economy if it finds support, complacency, and even rhetoric in the legal sphere to justify breaking the law? White-collar crime interacts directly or indirectly with organized crime. The two phenomena are two sides of the same coin and must be fought together because they both call into question the social pact, the legitimacy of our institutions, and the legal basis of our economies.

The legal-economic nexus does not lock the real economy into a straitjacket. Laws evolve over time and space. They can be amended and adapted to economic and social developments. Economic agents can participate in these evolutions. But under no circumstances can they allow themselves to ignore the law. The *de facto* de-legitimization of common rules resulting from economic practices that put cost–benefit before the law is undermining the stability of our institutions, quietly and indifferently. Yet the stakes go far beyond maximizing wealth, which is ultimately plentiful but poorly distributed and all too often ill-gotten, since the main aim is to re-establish the link between the economy and its legal foundations, in the name of a reasonable capitalism that guarantees the security of the collective.

Notes

1 The FATF tries to maintain control over these correspondent banking operations as part of the fight against money laundering by publishing guidelines to provide a better framework for the practice. See, for example, www.fatf-gafi.org/en/publications/Fatfrecommendations/Correspondent-banking-services.html.
2 The website can still be viewed at https://encrophone.com/en/. Options such as "messages that self-destruct", "panic wipe", "password wipe", or "secure boot" only hint at the attractiveness of the offer for crime.
3 Press Releases | DEA.gov.
4 https://www.dea.gov/press-releases/2024/01/19/doctor-convicted-trial-unlawfully-dispensing-controlled-substances.
5 https://www.dea.gov/press-releases/2024/01/22/nassau-doctor-sentenced-15-years-prison-overprescription-opioids-led-five.
6 https://www.dea.gov/press-releases/2024/01/25/former-physician-sentenced-30-months-after-conviction-diverting.
7 See, for instance: www.interpol.int/en/Crimes/Illicit-goods/Illicit-goods-the-issues. The EUIPO, European Union Intellectual Property Office, also stressed in 2021 that 56% of custom seizures at EU borders involve e-commerce (eCommerce.docx (europa.eu)).
8 https://www.dea.gov/press-releases/2024/02/26/dea-issues-letter-e-commerce-companies-sale-pill-presses-used-make.
9 eCFR:: 21 CFR 1310.03 – Persons required to keep records and file reports.
10 https://www.dea.gov/press-releases/2024/02/01/ebay-pay-59-million-settle-controlled-substances-act-allegations-related.
11 DEA Announces Settlement with Morris & Dickson Co., LLC: https://www.dea.gov/press-releases/2024/02/07/dea-announces-settlement-morris-dickson-co-llc
12 These are the following three companies presumed innocent until proven guilty: Anhui Rencheng Technology Co., LTD. (Hefei City, Anhui Province), Anhui Moker New Material Technology Co. (Hefei City, Anhui Province), and Hefei GSK Trade Co., Ltd. (Shushan Economic Development Zone, Hefei City, Anhui Province).

13 https://www.dea.gov/press-releases/2023/06/23/three-chinese-chemical-manufacturing-companies-and-five-employees-charged.
14 Southern District of New York | U.S. Attorney Announces Fentanyl Trafficking, Precursor Importation, And Money Laundering Charges Against Chinese Chemical Company And Executives | United States Department of Justice.
15 www.banquemondiale.org/fr/news/factsheet/2020/02/19/anticorruption-fact-sheet.
16 This disconnection of reasoning from law and ethics can be found in other disciplines. For instance, the political scientist Huntington writes: "the only thing worse than a rigid, hyper-centralized, dishonest bureaucracy is a society with a rigid, hyper-centralized, honest bureaucracy" (1996, p. 69).
17 Largely underestimated by economists, private–private corruption is far from marginal, as shown by the seminal book by sociologist Marshall Clinard (1990) with its evocative title: *Corporate Corruption. The Abuse of Power*.
18 For more on the difficulty of defining informality in economics, see: https://read.oecd-ilibrary.org/development/tackling-vulnerability-in-the-informal-economy_103bf23e-en#page1.
19 For an example of a positive vision of the informal sector as a "resource" providing jobs and resources, see this document from the OECD website: 42358563.pdf (oecd.org) (consulted on 25/10/2023).
20 As a reminder, according to Veblen, institutions are "prevalent habits of thought with respect to particular relations and particular functions of the individual and of the community" (1899, p. 118). Societies then obey a "cultural scheme" defined as the "complex of the habits of life and of thought prevalent among the members of the community" (Veblen, 1919, p. 39).
21 In mainstream economics, economic rationality is presented as univocal. Yet economic rationality could be defined in terms other than the utilitarian calculus. For example, it could refer to the capacity of economic agents/the economy to satisfy, first and foremost, essential human needs and ensure the survival of mankind; it could value work well done and therefore the artisan instinct in Veblenian thought.
22 Just look at the reactivity of the media and public opinion when it comes to crimes of blood, passion, madness, or hunger, whereas scandals involving white-collar crime do not last long. To give a concrete example, the bloody settling of scores linked to drug trafficking attracts far more attention than the fact that drug shipments pass through our major seaports with relative ease, thanks to corruption.
23 See, for instance, www.icij.org/investigations/fincen-files/a-roundup-of-fincen-files-reporting-from-europe/.
24 The Sentencing Guideline is a document produced by the United States Sentencing Commission containing sentencing recommendations. These recommendations are non-binding.

References

Albertson, Kevin, and Chris Fox, *Crime and Economics. An Introduction*, London and New York: Routledge, 2012.
Becker, Gary, "Crime and Punishment: An Economic Approach", *Journal of Political Economy*, 76(2), 1968, 169–217.
Broda, Philippe, "Commons, Collective Action, and Corruption", *Journal of Economic Issues*, L(3), 2016, 769–787.
Champeyrache, Clotilde, "Malte, laboratoire de la banalisation du crime", *AOC (Analyse-Opinion-Critique)*, 8 janvier 2020 (Malte, laboratoire de la banalisation économique du crime – AOC media).
Champeyrache, Clotilde, "Economic Hegemony and the Institutionalization of Law-Infringement", *Journal of Economic Issues*, 2024 (to be published).
Clinard, Marshall, *Corporate Corruption: The Abuse of Power*, New York: Praeger Publishers, 1990.

Coase, Ronald H., "The Problem of Social Cost", *Journal of Law and Economics*, 3(4), 1960, 1–44.
Commons, John R., "Special Report on Immigration and Its Economic Effects", in *Reports of the Industrial Commission on Immigration and on Education*, Washington, DC: Government Printing Office, 1901, 293–744.
Commons, John R., "Labor and Politics", in John R. Commons (ed.), *Municipal and Private Operation of Public Utilities: Commission on Public Ownership and Operation*, New York: National Civic Federation, 1907, 88–112.
Commons, John R., *Myself*, Madison: University of Wisconsin Press, 1934.
Dugger, William M., "Power: An Institutional Framework of Analysis", *Journal of Economic Issues*, 14(4), 1980, 897–907.
Dugger, William M., "An Institutional Analysis of Corporate Power", *Journal of Economic Issues*, 22(1), 1988, 79–111.
Galbraith, John K., *The Economics of Innocent Fraud*, Boston, New York: Houghton Mifflin Company, 2004.
Garrett, Brandon L., *Too Big to Jail. How Prosecutors Compromise with Corporations*, Cambridge: Belknap Press, 2014.
Huntington, Samuel, *Political Order in Changing Societies*, New Haven, CT: Yale University Press, 1996.
Lascoumes, Pierre, *L'économie morale des élites dirigeantes*, Paris: Presses de Sciences Po, 2022.
Leff, Nathaniel, "Economic Development through Bureaucratic Corruption", *American Behavioral Scientist*, 8(3), 1964, 8–14.
Medema, Steven G., "Commons, Sovereignty, and the Legal Basis of the Economic System", in Warren J. Samuels (ed.), *The Founding of Institutional Economics. The Leisure Class and Sovereignty*, London and New York: Routledge, 1998, 97–114.
Miller, Edythe S., "Veblen and Commons and the Concept of Community", in Warren J. Samuels (ed.), *The Founding of Institutional Economics. The Leisure Class and Sovereignty*, London and New York: Routledge, 1998, 14–29.
O'Hara, Philip A., "Political Economy of Systemic and Micro Corruption Throughout the World", *Journal of Economic Issues*, XLVIII(2), 2014, 279–307.
Sciarrone, Rocco, and Luca Storti, *Le mafie nell'economia legale. Scambi, collusioni, azioni di contrasto*, Bologna: Il Mulino, 2019.
Tanzi, Vito, "Corruption Around the World: Causes, Consequences, Scopes and Cures", *IMF Staff Papers*, 45(4), 1998, 559–594.
Veblen, Thorstein, *The Theory of the Leisure Class: An Economic Study of Institutions*, reprint, Mineola, New York: Dover Thrift Editions, 1899 (1994).
Veblen, Thorstein, *The Higher Learning in America*, Gloucester: Franklin Classics, 1918 (2018).
Veblen, Thorstein, *The Place of Science in Modern Civilization and Other Essays*, reprint, New Brunswick and London: Transaction, 1919 (1990).
Wilber, Charles, "Ethics, Human Behavior and the Methodology of Social Economics", *Forum for Social Economics*, 33(2), 2004, 19–50.

CONCLUSION

This book has sought to contribute to the construction of a new approach to crime economics. The hope is that economists will become more involved in crime issues and that they will do so on the basis of empirical reality, with the ultimate aim of making the fight against organized crime more effective. To this end, the book began by setting out the theoretical framework – original institutionalism inspired by Veblen and Commons – within which to frame our thinking (Chapters 1–3). This framework was then applied to a number of issues: the determinants of the choice to become involved in crime (Chapter 4), the functioning of illegal markets (Chapter 5), the motivations for criminal infiltration of the legal economy (Chapter 6), the spread of illegal practices, and the difficulty of ensuring a watertight seal between the legal and illegal economies (Chapter 7). However, the conclusion of this book is clearly not an end in itself. The whole book is an opening. So much remains to be done. A number of avenues have been mapped out: these need to be explored in greater depth, and case studies carried out in relation to the various criminal organizations and the different geographical and institutional contexts in which they operate. This work of deepening and appropriating the field of study must also be carried out over time. Crime is constantly evolving, so studying it is an ongoing, humbling task. Today's criminal dynamics are not those of tomorrow. Understanding this means breaking away from the determinism of the supposedly natural laws of economics. It also means giving ourselves the means to act collectively. But before proposing new perspectives, let us take stock of the major contributions of original institutionalism to crime economics.

The contributions of a crime economics inspired by original institutionalism: a new look

Studying the criminal economy and its main players, criminal organizations, through the prism of original institutionalism, enables us to reconnect the individual to the

DOI: 10.4324/9781003350958-11

collective, whether in terms of affiliation to a criminal association or adherence or non-adherence to the rules set by institutions, and to reintroduce the dimension of power into economic relations, both in the illegal sphere and in the relationship of criminal organizations to the legal sphere. The result is a more encompassing vision of organized crime than that of traditional crime economics. As a result, the consequences of the development of the criminal economy also change in nature and scale: beyond a logic of illegal financial flows – sometimes tolerated in the name of the *pecunia non olet* principle – the re-institutionalization of reasoning enables identification of a logic of accumulation, power, and the constitution of alternative or parallel criminal sovereignties. This new look at the criminal economy allows us to treat it as part of broader processes than market exchange and utility maximization. The evolution of organized crime also has repercussions on the functioning of the legal economy, the legitimacy of institutions, the sovereignty of States, and the tolerance toward illegalities in mentalities and habits of thought.

In concrete, empirical terms, the gap between the contribution of traditional crime economics and the new approach proposed in this book can be illustrated using the situation observed since the 2010s in the Netherlands with regard to drug trafficking. In February 2018, the NPB, the Dutch police union, published a pamphlet denouncing the explosion of drug trafficking in the country and the birth of a genuine narco-State accused of complicity.[1] The pamphlet states that the Netherlands leads the world in sales of cannabis and synthetic drugs, and in cocaine imports, particularly via the port of Rotterdam. This publication provoked some debate, not least because of the virulence of the term "narco-State", but it had no real influence on Dutch drug policy. Since the 1970s indeed, the Netherlands has opted for a policy of tolerance toward so-called soft drugs. By authorizing coffee shops, official outlets for the sale of marijuana, the Netherlands was banking on the *de facto* dismantling of clandestine networks and on reduced consumption of so-called hard drugs. At the same time, for law enforcement agencies, priority was given to offenses against persons (homicides, physical assaults, thefts and burglaries, etc.) to the detriment of trafficking in illegal goods. This priority was also reflected in the justice system: sentences handed down for drug trafficking are very low when the lengthy proceedings are completed. Many have seen in this policy the victory of a liberal vision of crime. Merchandise (whether legal or not) is considered from the economic angle of the transaction it entails: the formalization of coffee shops generates tax revenues; the circulation of undesirable products via ports is merely a consequence – possibly regrettable, but accepted – of the dynamics of international trade, a dynamic that would be hampered by more customs controls. Claiming to be a "merchant nation", the Netherlands has promoted entrepreneurship and port, rail, and motorway infrastructures with a view to maximizing the flow of goods. The quest for economic efficiency thus clashes with security objectives, as criminal organizations also use these infrastructures – without any real hindrance. On the contrary, individuals are (theoretically) protected against attacks on their person and property. In reality, the dissociation between individuals (to be protected) and goods (to be allowed to circulate) is debatable. Both arms and drug trafficking directly or indirectly harm the individual. Moreover, the results of these political choices are currently in full view: the Netherlands is the gateway for narcotics into the European Union; criminal networks, including the notorious mocro-mafia, have flourished there in collaboration with foreign criminal organizations; corruption and money laundering have accompanied this expansion. Awareness of the problem was only gradually raised, with the authorities eventually admitting to a certain "naiveté". This awareness was also linked to acts that went beyond the strictly economic sphere and could not go unanswered by the State, namely, violence, particularly against people who were not members of criminal organizations. In a way, the spillover of violence outside the illegal sphere (that is beyond the traditional settling of scores between criminals) has helped to make the criminal economy hidden behind it partially visible. In July 2018, two Dutch media outlets, *Panorama* and *De Telegraaf*, were attacked with rocket launchers and ram cars, respectively, following investigations into drug trafficking; in September 2019, Derk Wiersum, the lawyer of a criminal who had chosen to collaborate with the justice system, was killed; in July 2021, investigative journalist Peter de Vries was murdered; in 2022, Prime Minister Mark Rutte and Crown Princess Amalia were threatened, as was Belgian Justice Minister Vincent Van Quickenborne. This display of violence and intimidation is a stark reminder to the Netherlands and Belgium that the rise of criminal organizations is not just a question of legalizing or prohibiting certain goods. It is not just a question of profit for crime; power is also at the heart of criminal dynamics. The impact of the criminal economy ought to be also measured in terms of reduced security for the population (in terms of both goods in circulation[2] and feelings of insecurity, whether well-founded or not), and the weakening of institutions (through internal corruption and external loss of legitimacy). These effects, while they shake the foundations of our societies, are largely incommensurable. Any attempt at cost–benefit analysis would therefore appear to be largely discredited. On the contrary, the institutional approach enables us to understand the collective logics of power at work. It also offers tools for responding to the threats posed to our societies by the criminal economy.

The original institutional approach is holistic, rejecting the notions of natural order and static equilibrium characteristic of mainstream economics. The major consequence of this position is that it gives the field back to politics, to collective decision-making with an objective that is not purely accounting and financial, but rather the search for the "common good". From the time that individuals can organize themselves to act collectively and define the framework of what is and isn't acceptable in a society, it is possible to move away from the passive acceptance of possible economic excesses induced by reference to the natural order. Economic uncertainty is not just a cyclical uncertainty that can be probabilized, but it is also the mark of human's imprint on the system in which he lives. The real economy is the one created by individuals and by the societies in which they live. This observation underlines the possibility of regaining control (or not), including in criminal matters. The criminalization of the Dutch economy is not the result of uncontrolled and uncontrollable excesses; rather, it is the result of a political choice: that of privileging the market dimension and the illusion of economic efficiency over the protection of the group and the security of exchanges. This second option, protection, remains possible. It even seems desirable in view of the criminal realities discussed in this book. In particular, two lessons from the past and present seem to me to be particularly important for the future:

1 Deterrence policies – as espoused by Becker (1968) – do not work on the whole, not least because they are hampered by an extremely simplistic cost–benefit logic: tackling organized crime more effectively means rethinking the relationship between the economy and the law in terms of prevention, so that a supposedly rational logic does not instill behaviors that discredit respect for the law; moreover, as organized crime is a major trend, repression remains a crucial objective that would benefit from greater emphasis on the study of criminal organizations, rather than proceeding in silos by focusing on this or that illegal market.
2 The massive presence of criminal organizations in the legal economy in the form of legitimate businesses in the hands of criminals[3] is concrete proof that the market cannot defend itself against criminal infiltration and that it cannot expel crime, even when criminal entrepreneurs are poor businessmen. Once again, we need to take into account the fragility of the legal economy (a fragility, it must be stressed, that results not only from intimidation and violence but also from denial and complicity) in order to overcome it. Protecting the legal economy, and consequently honest operators, requires us to reappropriate the Commonsian conviction that the foundations of capitalism are legal.

In the introduction to this book, we deplore the fact that economists have not taken a greater interest in the problem of crime. To be objective, this criticism is also addressed to the original institutional economists. It is up to them to take up the approach taken here, particularly as it is fully in line with the overall project of original institutionalism. We return to the idea (set out in Chapter 3) that institutions, and the resulting institutionalization of the individual as a member of several organizations, are both the product of an imperative to preserve humanity and constituted human collectives and the key to its future preservation. With this in mind, reconciling economics and security, rather than pitting them against each other, becomes both an economic and a democratic imperative. Presenting the real stakes in the fight against the criminal economy as an effort to preserve the collective is more likely to win the support of participants than a cost–benefit calculation that gives the impression of a losing battle. Mobilizing for a reasonable capitalism, to use Commons' (1934) expression, also means taking the criminal issue into account. Prohibiting harmful goods – narcotics, substandard counterfeit products, trafficking in waste and endangered species, and so on – and preserving human dignity by combating the various forms of human trafficking are collective actions that revalorize the notions of the "common good" and the general interest, both of which have been greatly emptied of their content by methodological individualism. This reappraisal of what the economy contributes to the collective rather than to the individual interests of a few offers an opportunity to re-engage all actors in society. Collective action regains its importance in affirming choices with individual and collective repercussions. It potentially gives everyone back the means to express a will-in-action and to fight against the social destructuring in which organized crime plays an active part, reconciling economy and democracy.

An imposing agenda: new perspectives for research and . . . for collective action

Original institutionalism allows us to take a fresh look at the economics of organized crime. In turn, criminal issues can enrich original institutional theory and even give it new relevance at a time when concerns about criminal organizations are increasing worldwide. The agenda for future research is rich and full. It even takes on a strategic dimension if it is put at the service of an agenda for reform in the tradition of Veblen and Commons. A crime economics inspired by original institutionalism is indeed part of a logic of

> recognition both of mutual responsibility among humans, and of a public interest that is more than the arithmetic summation of private interests; that is, the recognition of a common or social good that is part of the achievement of a more efficient – in the sense used by both Veblen and Commons of usefulness and workability – and a more equitable functioning of the economic and social world.
>
> *(Miller, 1998, p. 27)*

Each of the last four chapters of this book deserves to be explored in greater depth, to be supplemented by research into a particular country, region of the world, criminal organization, or cluster of criminal organizations. The principle, in these last lines of this book, is not to close the debate, but to open it up by proposing a few avenues of research among many others. Some seem particularly stimulating. For example, the issue of criminal trajectories seems to me to be particularly rich in lessons. It should provide a better understanding of the motivations behind criminal behavior, without getting locked into the exclusive explanation of rationality. Original institutionalism can also help shed new light on the subject. Indeed, the existence of criminal careers within organized crime places at the heart of the debate the link between the individual (who chooses crime) and the collective (because the individual opts for an organizational form with its own operating rules which, because it is criminal, challenges the institutional hierarchy by breaking the law). This analysis could potentially help us to understand why schemes thought to be incentive-based by rational choice theory (such as the status of collaborator of justice, which offers a reduced sentence and strong guarantees of protection to criminals who agree to reveal well-founded and useful information about the criminal organization of which they are a member) do not systematically function as effectively as expected.[4] A better understanding of the link between individual and collective motivations also opens up new food for reflection on the values conveyed by crime and the way crime is portrayed in the media and in films. The field is vast, as it may involve an interest in the industry (or business, as Veblen would have probably preferred to say) developed around crime (the film and literary industries, e.g., but also the phenomena of recuperating criminal imagery for commercial purposes)[5] or in the effects of mystification and emulation produced by organized crime, especially when it succeeds in combining ceremonial values (initiation rites, social status, etc.) and instrumental values (enrichment through illegal activities using the latest technological advances). The comparison between businessmen and criminals, barely sketched out by Veblen (1899), can even be pursued further: the possible convergence of interests and behaviors between the two categories raises questions about the expansion of illegality beyond the sphere of the strict underworld. Paradoxically, it is even possible to consider the potentially positive role of criminals on the economy, a role to be understood once again in terms of collective action. At the very least, the existence of criminals and criminal organizations is a source of collective action, whether to repress, tolerate, or even absolve. The criminal economy, especially when it is flourishing, reminds us that we are the actors in the economies in which we participate and that markets are fundamentally human and political constructs. The criminal economy is a salutary reminder of what institutions are all about: if they issue prohibitions, they also do so with a view to emancipation. Prohibiting an activity is not simply a reduction of freedom, it is also potentially a guarantee of security for the members of society and even an expansion of economic opportunities in a perspective of the common good. For example, banning trade in certain species of flora and fauna does not mean depriving communities of income, but rather preserving biodiversity – a biodiversity on which the survival of humanity also depends. This is not to say that prohibition is the absolute rule. But the debate about prohibition and legalization cannot be reduced to an (impossible) cost–benefit calculation. Crime must lead us to question our way of thinking about society, which again and again means reconnecting economics and law, re-establishing the legal-economic nexus. A historical perspective on the criminal economy and its players could also offer a much-needed perspective on the relationship between the prohibitions affecting the economic sphere, the players involved in illegality, and the transformation of institutions. In addition to alerting us to the health of our institutions, the positive role played by criminals is that they can lead us to adapt our penal policy and drive sometimes radical political change. The example of Louis Mandrin, chief smuggler in 18th-century France, is a perfect illustration of this, brilliantly analyzed by Michael Kwass (2014). Combining illicit activities and denunciation of royal arbitrariness, Mandrin and his troops, by refusing the royal monopoly on tobacco and salt, the ban on importing calico from India, and the payment of taxes deemed excessive, imposed the idea of a "moral political economy" that would fuel the thinking of Enlightenment philosophers and contribute to the advent of the French Revolution. In the years 1750–1780, the violence of the conflicts between smugglers and the Farm, the institution mandated by the royal power to manage prohibition, led economists to mediate the conflict by proposing reform programs that took into account the question of the parallel economy. Mandrin, on the contrary, instrumentalized the conflict by turning it into a confrontation between an illegitimate royal monopoly and a moral parallel economy, or between a commercial court capitalism with legal but morally illegitimate taxation (because it was arbitrary and too heavy for the people) and an underground commercial capitalism with practices that were certainly illegal but morally legitimate. As Commons pointed out, economics, law, and ethics are interconnected; and as a result, politics takes its place once again where too often in recent decades we have allowed the economy to free itself from the framework that guarantees its reasonableness. Tackling the criminal economy in all its complexity, diversity, and adaptability gives the State and its citizens back the means to think of economic security as a means of consolidating democracy and reforming capitalism in the name of the common good.

Notes

1 In Dutch: Noodkreet-Recherche-DEFINITIEF-20-feb-2018.pdf (politiebond.nl).
2 There are a variety of ways in which the circulation of prohibited goods can jeopardize people's safety: damage to health (drug trafficking, counterfeit medicines), to physical integrity (arms trafficking), to the quality of environment (environmental crime), to product reliability (dangerous counterfeit goods), and so on.
3 See, for example, the Europol report (2024, p. 10): "A key threat vector is criminal networks' strategy to infiltrate the legal business world – as a facilitator to commit their crimes, as a front to disguise their crimes, and as a vehicle for laundering criminal profits. 86% of the most threatening criminal networks make use of legal business structures (LBS)".
4 In Italy, the attractiveness of the status of collaborator of justice has had a highly differentiated impact on the different mafias (as defined in article 416 bis of the Italian Penal Code): with the same system in place, around 600 members of the Neapolitan camorra have accepted to collaborate with the law, while the Calabrian 'ndrangheta is far behind, with fewer than 200 collaborators.
5 Who hasn't seen a restaurant named Corleone? Or gadgets bearing the effigy of Al Capone? There are even tours offered by travel agencies that take you to crime scenes.

References

Becker, Gary, "Crime and Punishment: An Economic Approach", *Journal of Political Economy*, 76(2), 1968, 169–217.
Commons, John R., *Legal Foundations of Capitalism*, New York: Macmillan, 1924.
Commons, John R., *Institutional Economics*, New York: MacMillan, 1934.
Europol, *Decoding the EU's Most Threatening Criminal Networks*, Publications Office of the European Union, Luxembourg, 2024. www.europol.europa.eu/cms/sites/default/

files/documents/Europol%20report%20on%20Decoding%20the%20EU-s%20most%20 threatening%20criminal%20networks.pdf

Kwass, Michael, *Contraband: Louis Mandrin and the Making of a Global Underground*, Cambridge, MA: Harvard University Press, 2014.

Miller, Edythe S., "Veblen and Commons and the Concept of Community", in Warren J. Samuels (ed.), *The Founding of Institutional Economics. The Leisure Class and Sovereignty*, London and New York: Routledge, 1998, 14–29.

Veblen, Thorstein, *Theory of the Leisure Class: An Economic Study of Institutions*, New York: MacMillan, 1899.

Printed in the United States
by Baker & Taylor Publisher Services